report
2003:
a man's guide to women

The Ultimate Source
for Getting the Women,
the Sex,
and the Satisfaction
You Want

edited by Leah Flickinger

RODALE

Sex and Values at Rodale

We believe that an active and healthy sex life, based on mutual consent and respect between partners, is an important component of physical and mental well-being. We also respect that sex is a private matter and that each person has a different opinion of what sexual practices or levels of discourse are appropriate. Rodale is committed to offering responsible, practical advice about sexual matters, supported by accredited professionals and legitimate scientific research. Our goal—for sex and all other topics—is to publish information that empowers people's lives.

Notice

This book is intended as a reference volume only, not as a medical manual. The information given here is designed to help you make informed decisions about your health. It is not intended as a substitute for any treatment that may have been prescribed by your doctor. If you suspect that you have a medical problem, we urge you to seek competent medical help.

Mention of specific companies, organizations, or authorities in this book does not necessarily imply endorsement by the publisher, nor does mention of specific companies, organizations, or authorities in the book imply that they endorse the book.

Internet addresses, telephone numbers, and product information given in this book were accurate at the time this book went to press.

WE **INSPIRE** AND **ENABLE** PEOPLE TO IMPROVE
THEIR LIVES AND THE WORLD AROUND THEM

Report 2003: A Man's Guide to Women Staff

EXECUTIVE EDITOR: Jeremy Katz

SENIOR EDITOR: Leah Flickinger

ASSOCIATE EDITOR: Kathryn C. LeSage

CONTRIBUTING WRITERS: Rick Ansorge; Brett Bara; Nicole Beland; Susan Bremer; Mark Bricklin; Chrissy Brooks; Jeff Csatari; Logan Davis; Shannon Davis; Jennifer Everett; Leah Flickinger; Ron Geraci; Brian Good; Melissa Gotthardt; Greg Gutfeld; Pam Houston; Lauren Janis; Mark Jolly; Lisa Jones; Joe Kita; Larry Keller; Kristen Kemp; Rebecca Kleinwaks; Marshall Lester; Chris McDougall; Michael Mejia, C.S.C.S.; Sarah Miller; Peggy Noonan; Hugh O'Neill; Peter Panepento; Carol Potera; Tracy Quan; Mark Roman; Jen Sacks; Ted Spiker; Bill Stieg; Zachary Veilleux; Angela Walker; Mike Zimmerman; Tom Zoellner

SERIES DESIGNER: Tanja Lipinski Cole

INTERIOR AND COVER DESIGNER: Susan P. Eugster

RESEARCH EDITOR: Deborah Pedron

LAYOUT DESIGNER: Faith Hague

PRODUCT SPECIALIST: Jodi Schaffer

ASSOCIATE CUSTOMER MARKETING MANAGER: Matt Neumaier

CONTENT ASSEMBLY MANAGER: Robert V. Anderson Jr.

OFFICE MANAGER: Alice Debus

ASSISTANT OFFICE MANAGER: Marianne Moor

ADMINISTRATIVE ASSISTANT: Pamela Brinar

contents

3 UNDERSTAND HER

4 EXPLORE EACH OTHER

5 KEEP HER

introduction

When it comes to the mating game, it's great to be human. Let's face it, how many other species have sex just for the sheer pleasure of it? For the rest of the animal kingdom, sex is purely an evolutionary mechanism. Example: When a male honeybee mates with a female, he explodes. Literally. During orgasm, his entire body blows up and he dies. His tiny penis remains inside the female like a plug, rendering her useless to other males and ensuring the legacy of his genes.

Luckily, we humans are more highly evolved. You don't have to blow yourself to bits to hold a woman's interest (although, at times, it may seem as if you do) and pass your pearly whites to the next generation.

So, how *do* you keep her interested?

Easy—just understand her. Now, we realize many of you would rather make like a honeybee than try to decipher women and their complicated psyches. So we did most of the hard work for you. After talking to sex-and-relationship experts, doctors, and, yes, regular women the world over, we proudly offer you the best, most comprehensible and utterly priceless pieces of information you'll need to succeed in the mating game. Like these for example:

● **Her signals unscrambled**
The Hair Toss, the Leg Cross, the Application of Lip Gloss. They all mean something important. See what on page 38.

● **The girlfriend/wife/significant-other test**
Take the quiz on page 57 to learn whether she's even worth the trouble.

● **The top 30 things she wishes you knew**
Photocopy pages 80 and 81, duct tape them to your fridge, make the words your mantra. She'll make it worth your while. We promise.

● **A foolproof formula for getting her pants off**
Try our simple recipe: one part baking soda, one part lemon juice, one part candle wax. Is it as kinky as it sounds? Find out on page 17. Then watch her strip down in a flash.

● **The right ways to reply to such perennial stumpers as "Do I look fat?"**
No more stammering! No more sweating! Respond your way to relationship bliss with the answer key starting on page 93. It's like getting the chemistry test in advance. (And you don't have to memorize the periodic table!)

❶ What you want in bed—and how to get it
Realize your every fantasy. And realize your fantasies aren't all that strange. Find out how to bring them to life on page 168.

❶ The ultimate breast-handling guide
Hone your fondling techniques with the advice on page 144.

❶ Eight reasons to move on
These warning signs of relationship doom will set you free faster than she can say, "It's not you, it's me." Check out page 190 to find out whether it's time to cut her loose.

You'll find all that and more in this edition of *A Man's Guide to Women*. Read it and get your sex life buzzing. In a good way.

—LEAH FLICKINGER
EDITOR

1

IMPRESS HER

A woman will subject you to countless tests that gauge your worthiness as a lover and companion. And, as much as we hate to say it, you'll probably fail a lot of them—you know, the ones that call for talking more, sharing your feelings, loving her cat. But for every one you bomb, there are several others you can pass with flying colors. Lucky for you, they're the simple ones. All they require are a pleasing smile, a lean physique, and a wardrobe that shows you know how to put yourself together. Impress her eyes and you'll be that much closer to impressing her soul—and pressing close to the rest of her. And you may not even have to pretend to like her cat.

THE GUY LIST

15 Things a Man Must Always Remember

To catch your quarry in the pursuit of love, apply these secret principles.

1. Speak softly and carry a big stick. But don't mumble. And don't swing the stick.

2. Telling a woman, "You're a great person," is taken as the lead-in to a confession that you don't love her.

3. Never make any sort of generalization concerning gender, even if it's so true that God Himself would back you up.

4. Never buy a woman (or anyone, for that matter) a gift at a kiosk.

5. Avoid terms like *wigwam*, *crib*, and *love shack* when inviting a woman to visit your home.

6. Never bring out a half-consumed bottle of wine sealed with aluminum foil.

7. When choosing a bottle of wine to take to a dinner party, spend between $10 and $15. That's for a bottle, not a gallon.

8. An ounce of appearance is worth a pound of substance.

9. Wear as much black as you can. It makes you look slimmer and cooler. But avoid black jeans.

10 When running in the park on a hot day, do not take off your shirt if you are a really hairy son of a bitch.

11 Always wear freshly laundered or pressed clothing to work. Even one wrinkle will have certain coworkers creating—and perhaps sharing—scenarios of debauchery or financial distress.

12 Never ask anyone older than age 6 to feel your muscles.

13 Do not get a visible tattoo larger than your penis.

14 Never ask a woman if she wants to have sex by asking her if she wants to have sex.

15 Giving your partner a letter grade after sex is a bad idea. Number grades are okay, but only after complex sex positions.

ASK THE GIRL NEXT DOOR
The honest truth about women from our lovely neighbor

Q: *A woman I've been dating has had many sex partners. I'm nervous I won't be as good as her last. How often do women compare?*
—P. C., Providence, Rhode Island

A: We do have functioning memories, so it's kind of difficult not to make the occasional comparison. Yes, some of my more randy girlfriends reminisce about clitoral magicians who gave them such intense orgasms they felt as if their heads disappeared. But in many years of girl chatter, no friend of mine has ever said she'd rather sleep with an ex than with the new guy she's seeing—no matter how awesome her ex was in bed.

A woman has sex so she can feel closer and more connected to the man in her life. Self-proclaimed tough girls like me may deny it, but all that stuff about women being more emotional about sex is true. Whether she's slept with 3 guys or 30 before you, as long as you're her love interest, she won't think of anyone else as "better," because she won't think of anyone but you.

Q: *Hey, I'm wondering what you ladies think about dating short guys. I'm about 5 foot 5, and most girls have at least 3 inches on me when they're wearing heels.*
—D. H., Boulder, Colorado

A: Any sensible woman would rather bend down for a great guy than get on her tiptoes for a butthead. It's true that few seek out short men. Blame those pesky fairy tales and peskier mothers and the whole "tall, dark, handsome" line. When you're being judged by physique alone—such as across a crowded room—you're a less obvious target than Mr. Six-Two. And, yes, a big hunk of a man does have a way of making a gal feel feminine and protected in a pathetic-yet-pleasurable, damsel-in-distress kind of way. But you know what? Get us out of that crowded room—alone, sitting down, maybe—and it stops mattering. Though my friends never seem to look for short guys, lots have ended up with them, and they love it.

Q: *What immediately attracts you to a guy?*
—T. C., St. Petersburg, Florida

A: When it comes to first impressions, the guy who catches my eye is the one who acts just a little bit like . . . me. The scenario: I'm out at a bar. I get a beer, check out the jukebox, and opt for a spot in the back, away from the crowd. If I see a guy making the same moves, I'll naturally be more interested in him than in the man who pays no attention to the music and seems to enjoy socializing sardine-style. My theory is that if two people are reacting the same way to a situation, chances are they're going to understand each other—and get along—better.

To test my theory, I quizzed a salon full of single women. An upbeat party girl said she's most attracted to guys who look like they're having a great time, while the shyest chick in the place said she finds quiet guys sexiest. So if you want a woman to find you attractive, my advice would be to pay attention to her attitude and adjust yours to match.

Q: *Are there any pickup lines that actually work?*
—D. W., St. Louis

A: If a woman is in the right mood (drunk and horny) at the right time (very, very late) and you happen to have a British accent and look remarkably like Hugh Grant, a line delivered with razor-sharp wit could work. Otherwise, don't risk the humiliation. I've seen guys break the ice successfully by simply making a casual comment that piques a woman's curiosity. A friend of mine fell for a guy whose first words to her were "Hey, doesn't that bartender look just like Redd Foxx from *Sanford and Son*?" Another pal had a one-nighter with a fellow who pointed at the Olestra-soaked chips she was eating and said, "Rumor has it those things take you to gastrointestinal hell and back. Any truth to that?" By keeping it casual and non-cliché, you keep her guard down. If she thinks you're cute, smart, funny, or interesting, she won't let the conversation end anytime soon.

For more honest answers about women, look for
Ask the *Men's Health* Girl Next Door
wherever books are sold.

MUST READS

(Can't Get No) Satisfaction?

So you want a better sex life. Perhaps you're not getting any sex, or you're not getting as much sex as you want, or you're just plain dissatisfied with the sex you are getting. We're with you, pal. We've been there, too.

Greg Gutfeld explains why you're not having the sex you'd like—and what to do about it.

Sure, we're hotshot editors with flashy wheels, great abs, and thick black manes of wild unkempt hair flowing down our well-muscled backs—but even we aren't immune to those barren stretches. It doesn't happen often, mind you. Just enough to send us thumbing desperately through the personal ads and asking ourselves why. Why? Why? Why?

So we did our research, and we found that most sex droughts originate from three basic problems:

① **Not meeting enough women**
② **Meeting women but not getting anywhere with them**
③ **Meeting a woman and marrying her, then wondering
       what the hell happened to all the sex**

We will tackle these three vexing scenarios and uncover the gremlins that can sabotage a sex life. Whatever the reason for the dry spell, we have the rain dance for you. So read on and, as a precaution, stop by the drugstore on your way home. And buy the 12-pack this time.

Why You Aren't Meeting Any Women

You're educated. You make a respectable income. You no longer live in the attic of your mom's place. Yet, for some reason, the closest you get to penetration is plugging in your electric shaver. There may be one very simple reason women aren't swarming over you: You don't know any. Here's why.

● You spend more time on your job than on your gut.
When it comes to attracting women, wealth will not always compensate for a fat belly. In a study, women were asked to comment on the desirability of men based on their waist-hip ratios (WHR), a measure of fat distribution between the upper and lower body. Any deviation from a normal WHR made a man less desirable, regardless of the thickness of his wallet. "The WHR signi-

fies hormone levels, a man's fertility, and resistance to disease," says University of Louisville psychologist Michael Cunningham, Ph.D., who studies the evolution of physical attraction. So women—possibly without even being aware of it—see a pudgy guy and assume he would produce lousy offspring. Moral: Spend less time at work and more in the gym.

● You spend more time on your gut than on your personality.
Then again, let's not go crazy. In a survey of more than 10,000 people living in 37 cultures, both men and women ranked kindness and intelligence as the most desirable traits. "Given the choice, women always pick personality first," says Cunningham. Physical attractiveness came in second and money third—for most, that is. There are, Cunningham adds, roughly 15 percent of women who usually go right for the bucks. But you can spot those. They're the ones on the arms of slow-moving septuagenarians.

● You're wasting time hanging out.
It's Friday night; you meet some pals after work, go to a

The Joke's on You, Pal

Sometime in high school, you learned that the way to win women was to make them laugh. But what's funny to you may not be funny to her—which reminds us of the one about the camel, the bartender, the hooker, and the . . .

● Long, involved joke
A joke that just keeps going and going drives women away, says psychologist Fred Bader. A joke should have at most two parts, the second part sort of funny.

● Dirty joke
"We've found in our studies that while humor enhances male attractiveness, the sexual humor you hear between guys is the exception," says psychologist Michael Cunningham. Don't tell off-color jokes—or make sure the coast is clear before you do.

● Monty Python skit
This may make you a laff riot in the company cafeteria, but most women hate it. Hell, so do we. "Some men have blind spots," says Bader. "They don't realize these things just don't appeal in most contexts." So next time you want to yell, "Nobody expects the Spanish Inquisition!" try coming up with something original.

So what will make her giggle so that her nose scrunches up in that adorable way?

● Poking fun at yourself
"Our research shows that women like men who practice self-deprecating humor," says Cunningham. "That kind of humor isn't threatening and points out that you're confident enough to risk looking silly."

bar, sit down, munch on mixed Asian snacks, listen to another band mangle "Addicted to Love," then go home. You meet no one but the overworked barmaids. Then you repeat the whole dance next week. "Men get comfortable in any repetitive activity," says Boston University School of Medicine health psychologist Stanley Ducharme, Ph.D. (This explains the enduring popularity of high-fiving.)

Sooner or later, you have to ask yourself why you keep putting yourself in no-win situations. "Rather than go out with friends haphazardly, treat your social life like business. Be shrewd," says psychologist and sex therapist Fred Bader, Ph.D., of Fairfield, Connecticut.

If you want to make contact with women who might share your interests, choose places for more than the sheer number of women there. If you like jazz, go to jazz clubs. If you like running, enter local 5-Ks. Broaden your horizon, and your horizon will fill with broads. The only thing people in bars have in common is a look of desperation.

● You don't do any PR.

"In my practice, I've noticed that the most effective way to meet someone is word of mouth," says Bader. "The people who are most successful in romance are those who ask their friends' wives if they know any available women." The wife, more so than your pal, tends to be better at finding suitable women, says Bader, because she generally knows more women. "And if you ask her to act on your behalf, she'll feel obligated to make the effort," he says. It's cheaper and more reliable than a dating service, too.

● You don't bother dating anyone.

You may be holding out for Miss Perfect, so you don't give the time of day to Miss Above Average. Fine. But you may end up with the Jerry Seinfeld syndrome: becoming so damn picky that you find yourself alone, in your forties, hanging out in a tiny apartment with people even more pathetic than you.

"Whether you know it or not, there are opportunities that you turn down quite often," says psychologist Steven Manley, Ph.D., of the Male Health Center in Dallas. Your standards are so high that you find yourself renting movies instead of starring in one of your own.

Realize this: When you date someone new, you expose yourself—to a new environment, new friends, different restaurants, new haunts. "You multiply spheres of opportunity," says Bader. "When you're with someone, you meet more people, and then you're no longer some stranger in a bar." So even if you don't think she's quite your type, take her out. Go to parties she invites you to—if not for the potential contacts, then at least for the cocktail weenies.

⊙ You're aloof.

Most women think it's easy for us to walk right up, introduce ourselves, say something witty, and win them over. "The fact is, most men have a hard time putting themselves on the line like that," says Ducharme. And because women expect us to be social animals, if we hang back, they assume we're stuck up, when all we are is shy. A better move: Ignore the fact that you're attracted to her. The moment you forget you're talking to a woman with the notion of bedding her is the same moment the pressure is off and you can talk to her as you would talk to anyone else—meaning, without staring at her breasts.

⊙ You stare at her breasts.

Stop that.

⊙ You don't eat enough.

Here's some weird science: In a study that looked at the effects of meal size on perception, researchers found that when females were presented with descriptions of fictitious men and their food diaries, the men were perceived as less feminine and more masculine as the size of their meals increased. So on your next date, preserve your appetite by not snacking before the event, then order soup and a salad as well as the entrée. You might eat healthy and get lucky at the same time. (Just leave the food on her plate alone. Gluttony is no aphrodisiac.)

⊙ You spend too much time shaking hands with the unemployed.

If you want to meet more women, as a rule, keep your hands out of your pants. "Masturbation is fine when you're without a partner," says Bader. "But eventually, it may make you less interested in seeking a romantic partnership. There is a certain amount of testosterone-driven desire that pushes us to seek out women, and masturbation damps that desire." Once that drive is diminished, all you'll want to think about is ordering a pizza and watching episodes of *Cops*.

⊙ You're a pushover.

Chivalry is keen. But if you allow any woman to continue to impose on you (acting as her chauffeur, lending her large sums of money, getting pec implants, buying a cat), you're lost. "Women respect men who risk disapproval, and they disdain pushovers," says sex therapist Jeanne Shaw. "If I ask a man to do something unreasonable and he says no, I may be disappointed, but I respect him."

It'sBeenSaid...

❝ Charm is a way of getting the answer yes without having asked any clear question. ❞

—Albert Camus

If you're always compliant, you will always be in what Shaw calls a one-down position. "You make yourself seem like her son instead of her lover," she says.

● You're lacking in the "P" department.
"P" as in "passion." There's a reason women dig Antonio Banderas more than Tony Danza. To ignite her passion, you need some of your own. "A love for skiing, music, or art shows you are capable of passion," says Shaw. "It gives me a clue that maybe you can be passionate about me." So take a look at your life. Other than your abdominal muscles, there must be something about you that instills pride and attracts interest. If there isn't, why not buy a guitar, start skiing again, or volunteer for a cause (preferably one not polluted with celebrities). Do something, anything, that shows you give a damn. Hobbies that don't count: taxidermy, armed robbery, onanism.

Why You Can't Seduce the Women You Meet

You may not understand Morse code, but you can read the messages she's sending out. Winking. Laughing. Touching your arm. The tension between you is thicker than Jerry Springer's skull, and there's no doubt in your mind that tonight, luck is a lady. But just 2 hours later, there you are: staring into your refrigerator, speculating on the safety of that leftover Thai food and wondering why she called it a night. What happened? Maybe you committed one of these common dating mistakes.

● You went from flirtatious to salacious.
She sent you the signal, and you responded with a term that would make Larry Flynt blush. "There's a fine line between sexy talk and coarse language, but when you cross it, you kill any chance you had," says a former features editor of a women's magazine, who conducted an informal poll of women to determine the most common ways guys ruin a sure thing. "You should follow her lead when you flirt, and lay off the offensive stuff."

● You play all your cards.
Maybe it's not your crude words but your hard sell. Exert too much pressure and you may end up shooting yourself in the foot. Women think you're conning them. Here are some of the deal breakers.

- ● Saying "We're so much alike" on the first or second date
- ● Asking her very personal questions
- ● Taking her to expensive restaurants and insisting on paying
- ● Spending lots of money on baubles for her when you've barely dated
- ● Asking her to go away with you for the weekend

○ Asking her to shave your back during cocktails

Wait until after the third or fourth date before springing that kind of stuff on her.

○ **You tell her about your most recent failed relationship.**

Save it for your therapist or your bartender. By laying out a pathetic personal life, you paint yourself as a needy little twerp. "You give the impression that you're the kind of guy who has to be taken care of," says Bader. "And your lack of confidence will most likely turn her off."

So enough about you. Ask about her. Women like men who are interested in what they have to say. And say. And say. And say.

○ **You show off your expertise.**

You like her so much that you want to wow her with your im-

Bad Date Foods

That dinner menu in your hand might just ruin your date. Here's what to avoid when what you want to appear most appetizing is you.

○ **Old-people food**
Order anything creamed, whether it's chipped beef or corn, and you magically turn into Buddy Ebsen. Same goes for those ghastly potpies, whatever they are.

○ **Cornish game hens**
Even cooked, they still look too much like birds. Put your fork in the wrong spot and they fly off the table. Right into her lap.

○ **Anything with a red sauce**
For obvious reasons. That includes ribs, but not pizza or our favorite, shrimp cocktail. Shrimp cocktail is appropriate anytime. Including breakfast.

○ **Anything that comes in a shell**
Crabs, lobsters, snails, tacos, peanuts, gunpowder.

○ **Foods that require work**
Fajitas are a bother. Aren't the chefs supposed to prepare the food for you?

pressive knowledge of 12th-century hygiene practices. Shut up. "Give only a moderate amount of information when talking to a woman you're getting to know," says Bader. "You'll sound less self-centered and confident enough to admit you don't know everything." So it won't hurt to confess ignorance once in a while.

○ **You talk like Don Imus.**

In an attempt to impress, you lower your voice an octave or two, to give yourself a relaxed, confident tone. You may think it's sexy. Nah. Speak at your usual pitch, and don't cup your ear with your right hand when you do.

● **You like to rock out on the ride home.**

You're driving her home, the scent of possibility adrift in the air, and "Radar Love" comes on the radio. You crank up the volume. You do that goofy head-bob thing. Feels good. Meanwhile, she's sinking in her seat. "To men, noise is power, and it's often used as a way to gain status and garner attention," says Cunningham. "It's like screeching your tires as you pull away from a stoplight. Any behavior that draws looks from others, women find obnoxious." Wait until you reach home to break out the air guitar.

● **You're a condom resister.**

Sometimes it helps to have a secret informer in the other camp. The magazine editor says that one woman she interviewed had a special test for a man she thought she might sleep with. "As they were heading to the bedroom, she would tell the man she didn't have any condoms. If he offered to leave and get some, she'd suddenly 'find' one," she says. "But if he didn't make the offer and then tried to get around wearing one, she'd deep-six him."

You Have the Girl, but Still No Sex

Experts claim that monogamous couples get tons more sex than single, disillusioned loners who write articles like this. But you know and I know that there are plenty of otherwise happily married guys who complain all the time about the lack of playing time on the home field. It could be due to one of the following reasons.

● **You're sleeping with your boss.**

If you're hassled on the job, you'll no doubt come home feeling beat. And inevitably, this exhaustion makes sex less desirable and you a less able performer. "I tell my patients to compartmentalize, and it works for them," says Dudley Seth Danoff, M.D., a urologist at Cedars Sinai Medical Center in Los Angeles and author of *Superpotency*. You need to turn the bedroom into an island—and we don't mean by surrounding it with water. "When you get home, disconnect yourself from the work mode with a series of rituals." Turn on some music (something soothing but rhythmic), dim the lights, change your clothes. Then think about heading to the bedroom. Close the shades and take out the cheerleader outfit. Ask *her* to wear it this time.

● **You're always sleeping in the same bed.**

You never realize how much sex is influenced by life's distractions . . . until you have vacation sex. "It's amazing how suddenly a dormant sex life can wake up when you get out of town," says psychiatrist and sex therapist Barbara Bartlik, M.D., of the human-sexuality program at New York Hospital–Cornell

Medical Center. "It's an automatic aphrodisiac. Being somewhere new elevates the excitement level. Some women who have trouble achieving orgasm can do it in a hotel room." (Dr. Bartlik wouldn't tell us which hotel.)

● You've been reading too many sex manuals.
Check out the sex section of your local bookstore and you'd think we were all preparing for an upcoming sexual Olympics. "You read about the female multiple orgasm, the elusive G-spot, the male multiple orgasm," says San Diego State University psychology professor Louis Franzini, Ph.D., who is coauthor of *Eccentric and Bizarre Behaviors*. "The bar is continually being raised. And this pursuit of better orgasms can interfere by creating performance anxiety." So while we agree that self-improvement is a wonderful thing (hey, it's our bread and butter), sometimes it pays to ignore the chattering

Sheet Music

Here's what to play when you want to play.

❶ Any kind of female folk music. Not that we would ever say Mary Chapin Carpenter or Tracy Chapman are romantic, but playing them makes you seem sensitive, and that instills trust in women. Disgust in men, but trust in women.

❷ Brazilian or any kind of highly rhythmic ethnic music. You'll appear culturally hip, and the rhythms are said to be highly stimulating. "Your erection is more sensitive than you realize," says urologist Dudley Seth Danoff, M.D. "You can enhance your erection if sex is accompanied by soothing rhythmic music. Conversely, rhythmic noises like barking dogs can kill an erection." Down, boy!

❸ Roxy Music's *Avalon*. Perhaps the greatest lovemaking music of all time, next to Ravel's *Bolero*.

❹ Marvin Gaye. Effective, but so associated with seduction that it might tip your hand too soon.

❺ Acid jazz. Dreamy, hypnotic. A CD by the Brand New Heavies is cheaper than Dom Perignon.

masses; take down the trapeze wire; put away the oils, creams, and clown suit; and have a carefree roll in the hay. But you didn't hear it from us.

● You think sex should always be spontaneous.
"Spontaneity is often mistaken for a crucial thing," says Dr. Bartlik. The fact is, spontaneous sex requires that she wants it when you want it, that you want it when she wants it, that nobody else wants anything from either of you, and that you're conveniently located near a surface that isn't hard on the knees.

Reel Love

Rent one of these sexy movies.

● **Sea of Love**
Women like Al Pacino; we like Ellen Barkin.

● **Betty Blue**
If your date is slightly bent, take a risk.

● **Breathless**
Your package will look huge compared to Richard Gere's.

● **Body Heat**
We'd throw a chair through a glass door to get our hands on the pre-*Serial Mom* Kathleen Turner.

● **The Big Easy**
If your girlfriend complains about another Ellen Barkin movie, tell her you rented it for the zydeco soundtrack.

That's a lot of variables. "Most couples have better success being strategic instead of spontaneous," says Dr. Bartlik. So don't be afraid to pencil it in. Hire a babysitter for 2 hours on a Saturday or Sunday afternoon, and have sex. (No, not with the babysitter.)

● **She puts on her nightie, then argues about Medicare.**
It's bedtime, and she starts a heated discussion. When it's over, neither of you is in the mood for anything. "She may be doing this—either with a full understanding or subconsciously—because she doesn't want to be sexual," says Franzini. She may have reasons. "It could be she's embarrassed that she's gained weight, she's not happy with the relationship, she's angry for some other reason. Whatever it is, you need to find out," he says.

● **You don't engage in afterplay.**
Afterplay is the opposite of foreplay—that is, it's what you should do right after sex. "After sex, you can make her feel good by telling her what you enjoyed. It makes her all the more willing to do it again," says Bader.

● **You're not renting enough "Thomas the Tank Engine" videos.**
Not for you. For your kids. Give them something you can pop in to engage them, while you run upstairs and hitch a ride of your own.

● **You haven't cleaned the gutters in, like, 3 months.**
Even in marriage, you need to pay a price for sex. "If you aren't making her happy, why should she make you happy?" asks Dr. Danoff. If she's giving you the cold shoulder at night, you might consider that (a) you aren't keeping up your end of the housework, (b) you're not keeping up your end of the parental responsibilities, or (c) you aren't keeping up with the latest advances in hygiene.

Pass Her Home Inspection

Women think that where you live can make or break your relationship. Follow these rules of the house from writer Lisa Jones and you just might have it made.

In my dating and relating universe, I stick to several important principles.

● **First date:**
Wear sexy underwear, but don't let him see it just yet.

● **Universal truth:**
If he listens to Madonna, he will never truly love me.

● **His place:**
No books, no booty. Pictures of him with nephews—I'm smitten. Oh, and, hmmm . . . if I spy an olive-oil brush on his counter, I can't wait to see what he's hiding in his drawers.

See, I know everything I need to know about a man by where he lives. Most women do. Why? Your lifestyle shows us what's important to you—and whether or not we will be. Charm and a clean Google search may glide you safely through the date, but getting her to stick around means she'll have to approve of your place, especially if you're expecting sleepovers. So it's important for you to know the guiding principles of keeping house, at least when a woman's stopping over. Know them and follow them, and you'll be sure to spend more time in the bedroom than anyplace else.

> It's **Been Said**...
>
> " Style is knowing who you are, what you want to say, and not giving a damn. "
>
> —Gore Vidal

Keep the Semi-Scattered Look

Let's start with your kitchen. A guy who eats fruit is healthy and sexy. But if there's a Cézanne-still-life-worthy bowl of fruit on the table, a woman gets worried. How will he handle my imperfect melons? Will I get tossed if I develop brown spots? Can I eat that pear? If everything in your place and life seems too arranged and tidy, she's not sure if there's room for her—or whether she'll meet your standards. Samantha, 24, remembers one guy who had perfectly positioned knickknacks around the room. It wasn't until she opened the kitchen drawer

Show Her Your Stuff?

Leave This Around . . .	And She'll Think . . .
Box of tissues	Sensitive
Electric screwdriver	Handy
Fleece throw blanket	Lovable
Fancy corkscrew	Classy
Piggy bank	Sentimental
Keys to neighbor's apartment	Dependable
Seersucker PJ bottoms	I want to have your babies
Scale	Obsessive
Bedroom slippers	(Cringe)
Mom first on speed dial	Needy
Trophies	Pretentious
Economy-size Vaseline	Perv
Black curtains	Yep, shady
Caller ID	Sneaky

that she felt comfortable. "He had only three forks—one of which was bent. I found this endearing. It showed he wasn't so together after all."

Being scattered also proves that you have better things to do with your time than, well, arrange kiwi. Liza, 31, a photographer, agrees: "Nothing says 'guy' to me quite like a big, fat pile of sweaty, banged-up hockey pads and skates, skis, baseball mitts. It shows he's living life."

Pretend You Have a Heart

The last man I dated had a great apartment (hardwood floors, sunroom), but the Ikea-furniture-per-square-inch density rivaled the store's. He made that forgivable with a couple of personal pieces, like a patchwork quilt from Grandma. So make sure she knows you can care about something (other than Angelina Jolie). The two easiest things that'll do it:

● **Pictures of your pop.**
A man who shows that his friends and family are important to him is at least three times hotter than a handsome loner. Jenna, 34, a public-relations manager, says, "Pictures of family make me feel instantly comfortable, like they're vouching for him, saying, 'John's a good guy.'"

● **Something green (relish doesn't count).**
Buy two plants and put them on opposite sides of the house. It shows you can keep something alive, and that plays to our anthropological instincts.

Once-Over Any Place She May Drop Her Pants

Even if your place is messier than Robert Downey Jr.'s rap sheet, her biggest concern is whether you've detoxified the bathroom. You haven't? Here's the 73-second plan.

- Pour 1 cup of baking soda and 1 gallon of hot water into your toilet before work. When you come home, flush away the stains.
- Open the window. Spray the sink with disinfectant cleaner (or vinegar or lemon juice, in a pinch). Wipe with a wet paper towel. Repeat on the toilet seat. And the floor.
- Put one candle—in a manly scent (like pine) and a manly color (like green)—on the top of the toilet tank. "It shows he's sensitive but still a guy," says Sarah, 25, an editor.

Be Prepared, Not Presumptuous

A lot of men have a single, threadbare gray towel in the bathroom. Did it start out gray, or white, or what? My advice: Don't make her guess what you've used the towel for; make her want you to use it on her. "This man I was dating had a linen bath towel. I couldn't wait to take a shower with him," says Leah, 29, a flight attendant. Other sleepover guidelines:

When You're Not Looking, She Is

All women (except two we talked to, and we think they're lying) snoop. Some are subtle seekers. Others, hard-core privacy invaders. In any case, it's a progressive scale. Here are the places she'll hit and when, plus how she'll react. (Her primary target: any traces of ex-girlfriends.)

When	Target	Freaks Her Out	Impresses Her
First visit	Bookshelves	*Bridget Jones's Diary.* He "understands" what it's like to be a woman. Gag	Any book by Fitzgerald. Romantic, Jazz-age writer who never stopped loving his lunatic wife
First sleepover	Medicine cabinet, under sink, any closed door behind another closed door	Hair-waxing kit. His, or ex's? Either way, it's bad news	Tweezers. Finally, a man who knows the importance of random-stray-hair removal!
One month	Drawers	More than six condoms	More than six pairs of underwear
Anytime she thinks you're lying, stealing, cheating	Mail, voice mail, e-mail, cell-phone directory	Message from any female that begins "Hi, guy"	Just-calling-to-say-hi message she left you a month ago

- Have two bath towels and pillows.
- You'd better have only one toothbrush and box of condoms.

Let the Bed Lure Her to You, Not the Other Way Around

Women give mixed signals. But this much should be clear: If I like you, I'll go back to your place. That doesn't mean I want sex . . . tonight. But I will look into your bedroom and notice . . .

● The position of your bed

"If the bed is up against a wall, I'll assume he wants to remain single because, hey, there's no entrance on my side," says Patty, 23, a drug counselor.

● What's on it

I'm most impressed by a man who has a fluffy down comforter (that increases the chances I'll want to jump in, naked). It should be a solid color or have a simple pattern. And stick to cotton sheets. Naomi, 30, a consultant, says, "Satin sheets would make me think he's a player."

Pay Very Close Attention to Her Butt

I've slept in a lot of sketchy places (Bob's Youth Hostel in Amsterdam, the floor of a science museum, Ohio). The worst place was an apartment that the guys called the crack den. Among its charms: two TVs stacked on top of each other and a perpetually smoke-filled living room. One thing made the place irresistible: It had the most comfortable couch I've ever made out on. It's an easy rule to follow. Make it cozy for her to stay, and she probably will.

The Good-Sex Workout

Remember when you first learned about sex? Remember how you decided there and then that your parents absolutely, positively did not do that, because the thought of your dad and your mom doing that thing was just too horrible to imagine? Those were the good old days. Nowadays, the problem isn't whether kids can imagine you having sex—it's whether you can imagine you having sex.

As writer Mark Roman will tell you, great lovers aren't born, they're trained. Here's a workout plan to power up your sex life.

Your early twenties are over, and those marathon lovemaking sessions are gone. The days off spent in bed ended after your first promotion. It's easy to start wondering if perhaps the party's over, libido-wise.

Well, we have a message for you: The party's far from over. In fact, the dance has just begun. "It's true that the aging process changes all aspects of your physicality. But that doesn't mean you can't be as sexually athletic and daring as ever," says Chicago State University physical-education professor Eric Gronbech, Ph.D., who researches the link between fitness and libido.

In fact, your level of desire—and performance—can be enhanced with a simple program of exercise, one that will keep you as primed and eager as a sophomore on spring break.

Sex is like any other physical activity that involves muscles and sweat. "Training and exercise are at the foundation of peak performance," say Gronbech. "If you're in your thirties, forties, or fifties, your physical performance can be maintained—even improved." A moderate workout regimen designed to add endurance, strength, and flexibility to muscles and joints involved in sex—including those that control orgasm—will keep you lively between the sheets.

perfect figures

BIGGER ISN'T ALWAYS BETTER

Percentage of women who find the physiques of male bodybuilders extremely repulsive: 94

Anyone who works out knows that exercise makes you feel good. But researchers are finding that it's also a turn-on. "Men who work out moderately and regularly report increased libidos, more satisfying sex, and fewer erectile failures," says physical fitness and sex expert James White, Ph.D., professor emeritus at the University of California at San Diego. In a landmark study, White had 78 men follow a moderate aerobic regimen four times per week. After 9 months, the men reported their rate of sexual intercourse had leaped an average of 30 percent, with 26 percent more orgasms. An increased frequency of masturbation was also recorded.

Research suggests that workouts themselves can be a turn-on. In a study of women, Chicago State University researchers learned that almost one in four subjects had experienced sexual arousal, or even orgasm, while exercising. (Kinda makes you want to look into those step-aerobics classes after all, huh?) What about men? Gronbech, who directed the Chicago State study, says that exercise increases the flow of endorphins and adrenaline, hormones that play key roles in the chemistry of arousal for both sexes. Also, moderate exercise boosts levels of testosterone, the male sex hormone. Finally, by increasing the capillary network throughout the body, regular exercise can increase a man's bloodflow. That means there's plenty of blood to spare when the brain signals for an erection.

Psychological factors may be just as important. The process of getting into shape can enhance a man's self-image and confidence. "Even the soreness you feel after working out can give you an intense feeling of self-satisfaction," explains Gronbech. "You feel good about yourself, and that feeling overflows into your relationship with potential partners."

Ready to get lucky? To bolster your desire, performance, and pleasure, we've constructed a three-part better-sex workout, incorporating general fitness, sex-specific training, and exercises that can give you more control over your lovemaking. Here's all you need to go for the gold.

Part 1: Get Fit for Fooling Around

A general fitness regimen should build a solid aerobic capacity and overall strength, tone, and flexibility. "The goal here is not to become muscle-bound but simply to remove physical and psychological impediments to sex, such as flab, fatigue, and stress," says Gronbech.

Another point: Take it easy. In the sex/exercise connection, more isn't better. Too much muscle soreness and fatigue can easily put a damper on romance. Marathon runners, triathletes, and Ironman competitors find that their sexual desire greatly decreases, says White. One theory holds that during heavy exercise, the body channels blood away from the genitals, where the testicles normally promote testosterone production, and into the muscles where it's most needed. The result: a very fit man who always has a headache. Here's how to design a workout that won't wear you out.

LOW-IMPACT AEROBICS

To get through an evening-long lovemaking session, what you need first and foremost is stamina. Unlike in most full-contact sports, you can't call time-out during lovemaking while the team trainer administers oxygen. To build endurance, your best bets are low-impact aerobic exercises, which will do the job without straining your body. Go for three sessions a week of 20 to 30 minutes each. Swimming, stairclimbing, rowing, and running are all fine options.

MODERATE WEIGHT TRAINING

Alternate your aerobic days with a weight-training regimen that covers the full body: arms, legs, abdomen, chest, and back. Use either free weights or a cable system. "The goal is to increase strength and tone muscles, not to lift massive amounts of weight," advises Gronbech. "Remember, you're not trying to bulk up." Work with a moderate weight, maybe half of what you're capable of lifting. Do 2 or 3 sets of 10 to 12 repetitions for each muscle group.

Part 2: Train Your Love Muscles

All right, you've built up stamina, trimmed off flab, and toned your muscles. These are the first steps toward actually *getting* sex. (A nice car and a powerful deodorant help, too.) With a regular workout routine, your energy is up, as is your libido. Now it's time for some target training.

Unless you know some sexual positions the rest of us haven't heard of, bulging neck muscles aren't going to make a whole lot of difference between the sheets. You need to incorporate exercises and stretches that target the parts of the body called into play during lovemaking. The following moves will help boost your performance.

ABDOMINALS

"These muscles are used for the thrusting motions of sex," says White. They also help hold in your belly, which is important when it comes to luring a partner to willingly do the aforementioned thrusting motions with you. Simple crunches are the safest and most effective exercise to develop strength. "If you can get up to 3 sets of 20 repetitions," says Gronbech, "you'll have all the thrusting strength you need for sex."

perfect figures

JUST DITCH THE TIGHTY-WHITIES ALREADY

Percentage of women who like men to wear...

Boxers: 36

Boxer briefs: 28

Briefs: 18

Bikinis: 3

Percentage of men who prefer to wear briefs: 42

CALVES

For your legs, the issue is flexibility, not strength. During orgasm, men sometimes overflex their calf muscles. "Didn't you ever get a knot in one of your calves during sex?" asks Gronbech. Either of these stretches will help.

● Classic runner's stretch

Stand about four steps from a wall. Shift one leg forward about 8 inches, bending it at the knee, while keeping the back leg straight. Then reach out and grab the wall at about chest height, leaning into it as you continue to keep your back leg straight, heel flat. As you lean forward, you should feel the stretch in your back calf, from your heel to the back of your knee. Hold it for a count of 20, then relax and switch feet.

❷ Bedtime calf stretch

Lie flat on your back on the bed with one leg bent, foot flat against the mattress. Keep the opposite leg straight and raise it as far as you can, trying to get it to point at the ceiling. Hold the leg steady and exhale as you slowly flex your foot, pointing your toes down toward your chest. Hold the stretch, relax, then lower your leg and repeat with the other one. Complete this exercise three times.

HIPS AND GROIN

Don't forget to hit below the belt. As the key pivot point in the thrusting motion, your hip joint and the muscles that support it must remain flexible.

❷ Butterfly stretch

To loosen your groin, lie flat on your back in bed with both legs bent, feet flat on the mattress. Reach down and pull your heels toward your buttocks. Then, using your hands to guide them, turn your ankles so the soles and heels of your feet touch together. Your knees will angle out to the sides. Exhale. Let the natural weight of your legs push your knees toward the bed. When your knees are as far apart as possible, hold the stretch for a count of 10.

❷ Hip stretch

Lie flat on your back with your legs dangling off the end of the bed. Pull one knee toward your chest, locking your hands over your upper shin. Inhale and pull the knee closer. Hold the stretch for a count of 10, relax, then repeat with your other leg. Complete this exercise three times.

SHOULDERS

Most people associate shoulder injuries with such activities as hurling baseballs and breaking down doors. But sex takes its toll. "Especially in the missionary position, when the man tries to support his weight on his elbows," says Gronbech. "All that stress ends up in the shoulders." Here's a simple stretch: Sit up in bed, hold your arms above your head, and cross your wrists. Inhale, straighten your arms, and extend them back behind your head as far as you can, keeping your wrists crossed. Your elbows should be behind your ears. Hold the stretch for a 10 count, then relax. Repeat three times.

Part 3: Exercise Control

As an athletic event, sex is more akin to synchronized swimming than to water polo. Timing, in other words, is everything. Here's an exercise you can do to give you more control over, and more intensity during, your orgasm.

The muscle involved is called the *pubococcygeus*. We won't even try to tell you how to pronounce that—let's just use the term *PC muscle*. In men, it anchors the base of the penis several inches within the pelvis; in women, it surrounds the vaginal wall. In both sexes, the muscle surrounds the urethra and controls everything that passes through.

In the 1940s, gynecologist Arnold Kegel discovered that a stronger PC muscle meant better bladder control for women. Dubbed Kegels, his simple exercises—tensing and relaxing the PC—had a welcome side effect: heightened pleasure during intercourse. And during the past decade, sex researchers have realized that men can strengthen their PCs, too. The results: more intense orgasms, better staying power, a greater number of orgasms, and firmer erections.

perfect figures

THIS DOES NOT INCLUDE PORN STARS

Percentage of men who don't wear any underwear at all:
1

Percentage of women:
2

To find your PC, use the men's room. The muscle you clench to stop the flow of urine, or to force out the last few drops, is your PC. Now that you've got the location, try this three-part Kegel regimen developed by psychiatrist and sex therapist Alan Brauer, M.D., of the Brauer Medical Center in Palo Alto, California. The three moves thoroughly exercise your PC in the ways in which it's called upon during sex, he explains. Begin by doing 10 slow reps of each of the Kegel variations five times a day. After a week, increase to 15 repetitions per set. Continue adding 5 repetitions each week until every set includes 30 of all three variations. Once you've reached this level, practice at least 150 Kegels a day.

● Slow clenches
Squeeze down on your PC muscle as if trying to stop urine flow. Hold for a slow three count.

● Flutters
Clench and relax your PC as rapidly as you can.

● Pushouts
Bear down on your PCs as if to force out the last drips of urine. You'll feel your abdominal muscles clench, as well.

What's nice about Kegels is that you can practice them almost anywhere, notes Dr. Brauer. "When you're driving, walking, watching TV, doing dishes, sitting at a desk, or lying in bed. No one will ever know."

What's even nicer is that this technique gives you control over your sexual performance like you've never experienced before. Dr. Brauer explains that after you've followed a routine of regular Kegels for a few weeks, you'll feel an increased awareness of your impending orgasm, so you'll have more time to decide whether to follow through or back off. You'll also be better able to hold back your ejaculation by squeezing—or doing an extended Kegel—as the moment of inevitability approaches. And when you do finally climax, the newly toned musculature will result in heightened orgasm.

EQUALLY DIVIDED

Percentage of women who prefer to wear thongs:
25

Percentage of men who prefer women to wear thongs:
27

• • • • • • • • •

Kegel training may also give you a longer-lasting orgasm, according to Dr. Brauer. Typically, a man feels three to eight pleasurable contractions during orgasm, and the first is the most powerful. By tightening your PC muscle during orgasms, you can stretch out the experience. "Many men eventually double the number of contractions and may reverse their intensity," he says. "The latter ones become the most pleasurable."

About the only body part we haven't talked about is the penis itself. And let's face it, they haven't developed a Nautilus machine yet that can work this baby. But there is an exercise that may help make for a harder and more sensitive erection—though you'll have to do it in the privacy of your own home. Sit on the edge of the bed with your legs spread apart. While you're fully erect, locate the muscles that move your member up and down and from side to side. Practice flexing these muscles—you'll most likely use some abdominal, thigh, and buttock muscles, as well. By exercising these muscles, you'll increase bloodflow to your groin, says Dr. Brauer. And that means a firmer you.

MAN'S GUIDE INTERVIEW

Body Worship

An Interview with sexual-fitness experts Hank Wuh, M.D., and MeiMei Fox

You've heard the expression "Your body is a temple." That means it's sacred ground. So you should treat it that way. Follow these rituals from Hank Wuh, M.D. and MeiMei Fox, authors of Sexual Fitness: 7 Elements to Optimizing Your Sensuality, Satisfaction, and Well-Being, *and turn your body into a temple of love.*

How do you define sexual fitness?

Sexual fitness for men means having an active interest in sexual activity (whether that be with a partner or solo), enjoying it fully, and being able to get an erection whenever you want.

Let's look at the opposite end of the spectrum.
How do you define sexual unfitness?

No passion, as in lack of desire or low libido. A lack of enjoyment, as in no pleasure. And a lack of performance, as in no erection. Most men are primarily concerned with the latter, although we prefer to avoid the term impotence since there's a lot of stigma associated with it. Instead, we use the doctor-approved term erectile dysfunction, or ED.

In adolescence and young adulthood, is almost every man sexually fit?

This is true. Men do experience most of their sexual problems later in life, mostly ED, whereas the majority of women experience sexual problems earlier in life. Many of women's sexual problems are psychological in nature—an inability to enjoy sex or achieve orgasm, but most of all, lack of libido.

How do men become sexually unfit?

The most important cause of sexual unfitness is smoking. Male smokers are twice as likely to suffer from erectile dysfunction as nonsmokers, because nicotine constricts arteries and decreases blood-flow. Smoking also harms fertility. However, getting out of shape definitely contributes to sexual unfitness. When men have high cholesterol levels and are in poor cardiovascular condition due to poor diet and lack of exercise, their sex life is directly and negatively impacted. They'll start having trouble getting erections and will lack the energy and stamina to engage in sexual activity.

If a man doesn't take proper care of himself, when can he expect to see signs of sexual unfitness?

As early as his thirties, and certainly by his late forties or early fifties. This is when men will start to notice health problems such as high cholesterol levels, getting out of breath easily, aches and pains. All of these problems will have a direct impact on sexual fitness.

What's the connection between sexual fitness and physical fitness?

Sexual fitness and physical fitness are intimately linked. A lot of what you shoot for in terms of achieving sexual fitness involves improving your physical fitness. The better shape you're in, the more you'll find that your performance, pleasure, and passion improve. For example, exercise has both immediate and long-term benefits for sexual fitness. In the short term, working out boosts testosterone levels, which means that your juices get pumping and you feel ready for sex. Over the long term, exercise improves bloodflow, which means that you'll be better able to get and sustain an erection.

What's the best kind of exercise for enhancing sexual fitness?

Any type of exercise that you enjoy, makes you feel good, and gets your heart pumping.

Can exercise sometimes be too much of a good thing?

Over-exercising can be harmful to your sexual fitness. Training for a marathon or another extreme event can actually interfere with your sexual health because when you push your body to its absolute limits, you put it into stress mode. It stops producing as much testosterone and other sex hormones. So men who over train may find a decrease in sex drive and possibly even performance. Still, this shouldn't discourage you from exercising. Exercise is one of the single best steps you can take to improve your sexual fitness, now and in the future.

Are there any differences between sexual fitness and physical fitness?

The difference is that there are specific things you can do beyond getting in shape physically that will also improve your sexual fitness. Certain foods and supplements, for example, will help boost your sex drive and might even enhance the sexual experience.

Examples?

Short answer: oysters, asparagus, and chocolate. That's an aphrodisiac lover's feast. Casanova was right about oysters. They're packed with zinc, which is crucial to the formation of sperm. If you eat oysters on a regular basis, you help your body manufacture more active, healthy sperm, contributing to fertility. Asparagus is packed with niacin, a vitamin that causes a sexual flush. Lots of folks take niacin pills to give them more of a rush when they orgasm. Chocolate contains endorphins, the feel-good chemicals in the brain, so feed some to the woman you're trying to seduce.

How quickly do the sexual benefits of these foods kick in?

It's unlikely that eating one oyster-packed dinner will help you make it through a sex session just hours later. Most of the impact of food on sexual fitness is more gradual. Eat more oysters now and you'll be a better lover next month.

What are some other foods on the "good-to-go" list?

Munch on more fruits and vegetables. Doing so will not only cut back your cholesterol and fat consumption, but also give your body the nutritional building-blocks it needs to make sex hormones, healthy sperm, and to boost your overall energy levels. Eat more foods high in vitamin E, which is known as the sex vitamin because a deficiency causes low sex drive. These include beans, seeds, nuts, fruits, and veggies, although vitamin E also can be taken in supplement form. Eat more foods high in folate, which facilitates the production of dopamine, the neurotransmitter associated with sexual arousal and orgasm. These include leafy greens (dandelion greens, chard, kale, spinach), beans, grains, and nuts. Eat more foods high in L-arginine, the amino acid that facilitates bloodflow to the penis. These include meat, nuts, seeds, and grains. Also eat more foods high in niacin, which may enhance pleasure during orgasm. In addition to asparagus, these include fish, grains, peas, beans, figs, avocados, dates, broccoli, and peanuts.

What are foods on the "got-to-go" list?

A high-fat diet raises cholesterol levels, which contributes to ED. Fat also clogs arteries, which will end up blocking bloodflow to the penis. So cut back on ice cream, cheese, packaged food, and fast food.

Should guys avoid any foods that are normally considered healthy?

Any foods containing tryptophan should be avoided the night of the big seduction because they make you sleepy. Foods high in tryptophan include milk, cheese, cream, turkey, pork, veal, beef, halibut, and sockeye salmon.

Any medications we should avoid?

Some antidepressants are known to have a direct negative impact on libido by increasing levels of serotonin, a neurotransmitter that makes you feel happy but unfortunately lowers your sex drive. These include Prozac, Zoloft, and Paxil. Instead, try bupropion (Wellbutrin), which shows no negative impact on your sex drive and may even slightly boost it. Some high blood pressure medications cause erectile dysfunction by decreasing bloodflow to the penis and reducing sex hormone levels. These include antihypertensives that are diuretics (resperine, methyldopa, guanethidine), beta blockers, and alpha blockers. Instead, try the newest generation of ACE inhibitors (Vasotec, Captoen) or calcium-channel blockers (Cardizen, Calan), as they appear to be less sexually disruptive. If you start exercising and eating better, which you need to do anyway for your overall sexual fitness, that'll naturally help reduce your need for medications.

Years ago, doctors said sexual problems were all in a guy's head. Now it's fashionable to say they're all in a guy's pants. Which is it?

Both, really. Except for those first-night nerves that keep you from putting on your best show, ED is mostly caused by physical problems that prevent your body from pumping enough blood to your penis to keep it erect. But lack of sex drive is more often a psychological issue, even with men. When you're stressed, not sleeping enough, working too hard, not getting along well with your partner, worried about money or losing your job, you're simply not going to be as interested in sex. And that is in your head, not your pants.

Even if a man has had ED for a long time, can he become sexually fit?

We are reluctant to say that any man can become sexually fit. If a man has smoked his whole life and destroyed his arteries so badly that they just don't pump blood anymore, there's nothing he can do about that. But most men can regain their sexual fitness. You have as much control over your sexual fitness as you do over your physical fitness—that is to say, a lot. Simply by choosing to eat healthier foods, exercise more, change medications, take nutritional supplements and relax from time to time, you can be begin to see an immediate impact on your sex life. To achieve optimum sexual fitness, however, you've got to follow these new lifestyle improvements for at least 30 days.

**Are there some vitamins all men should take,
regardless of their level of sexual fitness?**

We recommend a multivitamin to ensure that you're getting the crucial vitamins and minerals that are the building blocks of sexual fitness. In addition, we recommend L-arginine, an amino acid that is a precursor to nitric oxide, the substance that facilitates erections.

Are there any herbs men should consider?

We recommend ginkgo and ginseng. Both herbs have been proven in multiple clinical trials to improve men's erections as well as their overall energy levels. Ginkgo relaxes muscles and increases bloodflow, so it may prove particularly effective for men whose erectile dysfunction can be traced to circulation problems caused by high cholesterol levels. Ginseng also works to increase nitric oxide levels. It has been shown to improve libido, sexual satisfaction, and penile size during erection.

**Short of taking Viagra, is there anything a man
can do right away to boost his performance?**

Exercise is the best quick fix because it boosts testosterone levels, which will up your sex drive and improve your erections.

What about preparations advertised as "natural" alternatives to Viagra?

Many are risky. They may contain Spanish fly which, despite its reputation as an aphrodisiac, causes severe allergic reactions and irritation of the urinary tract. Also, watch out for yohimbe, which is the basis of a prescription medication for impotence but can be dangerous if taken as a supplement. It has a long list of side effects, including increased anxiety levels, nausea, sleeplessness, increased blood pressure, and even seizures.

**You emphasize stress-reduction as a key component of sexual fitness.
What are the best stress-reduction techniques for men, besides exercise?**

How about having sex? Seriously, though, while being healthy is great for your sex life, having sex is also great for your health, and a terrific way to reduce stress. When those endorphins and sex hormones start pumping when you get turned on, you can just feel stress slipping away. Other than that, try some "chick" techniques like hanging out with friends, relaxing in a hot tub, listening to your favorite CD, or getting out into nature for a walk with your dog.

You also talk about the importance of sensual stimulation, which also has a "chick" aura to it. How can a guy add more sensuality to his life and not lose his "guyness?"

The best way for a guy to incorporate more sensuality into his life and still feel manly is to do these activities with a partner as a possible prelude to sex. For example, exchange massages, listen to sexy, sensual, seductive music, or enjoy a candlelit dinner. Take a bubble bath. If that bothers you, you're going to have a lot of trouble seducing a woman.

For more on nature's contribution to better sex, see Better Sex, Naturally on page 146.

QUICKIES

EVERY BREATH, YOU REEK

We tested the smart bombs against halitosis. Here are the reults.

PRODUCT	COMMENTS	RATING
Listerine PocketPaks Oral Care Strips; about $2 for 24 strips	Intense fix in a quick-dissolving sheet that you place right on the back of your tongue. You can immediately start talking without fear of spitting mint bits. Nifty dispenser is perfect for bedside	4 lips (out of 4)
Aquafresh Dental Lozenges; $2 for 20 pieces	Fast-acting neutralizer with a powerful, sinus-clearing mint-menthol taste. Good to keep in your desk drawer for freshening up before meetings	3½ lips
Altoids; $2 for 75 pieces	Strong as advertised; refreshing and addictive. Briefly masks garlic odor. Candylike enough to offer someone without offending	3 lips
Dentyne Ice gum; $1 for 12 pieces	A wonderful all-mouth workout; leaves a clean taste and subdues odors. But it's gum— inappropriate in some settings	2½ lips
Mentos Cool Chews; $1 for 30 pieces	Surprisingly effective cousin of the Mentos candy; smaller and stronger, but not quite strong enough on garlic	2 lips
Rembrandt Drops; $1 for 6 milliliter vial	A rush of minty freshness that fades far too quickly. Repeat applications may be required	1 lip

TOO GOOD FOR US

Charity work may do more than help the downtrodden and boost your karmic standing. Women find it attractive, too. A study at McMaster University in Ontario found that women like men to show a little altruism (that means being kind and generous). The flip side: Men aren't so impressed with kind women. Researchers showed men photos of women, with descriptions. When the description listed altruistic tendencies, the attractiveness scores dropped, even though the photo was the same. The study author, Pat Barclay, found these results "very curious. Perhaps men think they're less likely to score with a 'good girl.'"

NOTE ABLE

A love letter can become your season pass to her bedroom. If the name Shakespeare makes you think of that fly rod you've been eyeing, listen to Barrie Dolnick and Donald Baack, authors of *How to Write a Love Letter*.

● Date of delivery
A steamy letter after a second date sets off her creep alarm. But if things are clicking, a flirty e-mail shows interest. Just avoid sexually loaded words—like *fly rod*.

● Content
An ode to her charm goes further than a drooling reference to her bod.

● Tone
Don't fake it—a phony voice will stick out like Steve Martin's nose in *Roxanne*. A little stealing is okay, though. Like her smile? Go to www.bartleby.com. It'll give you 64 quotes about smiles.

● The once-over
Have a close female friend read it. She'll tell you whether you've hit the mark. Just don't let your love interest find out that someone else has read it.

SHELF LIFE

Your medicine cabinet is like your fridge: When something has been in there for a couple of years, you should get rid of it. Defective seals and caps, in particular, offer free entry to fungi and bacteria. So anything that doesn't smell or look okay should be thrown away. Here's your guide:

● Body lotion
Jars provide the perfect environment for mold cultures to thrive. In warm temperatures, creams and lotions can also become rancid.
   Shelf life: 6 to 12 months

● Deodorant
The active substances in deodorant are inorganic and remain good for years.

In case there's any doubt, try a test in the sauna. A top deodorant can withstand temperatures of up to 162°F.

Shelf life: A few years

❍ Shampoo/shower gel

These are germ-free zones. Active fruit acids don't offer a fertile ground for germs. Preservatives take care of the rest.

Shelf life: Several years

❍ Sunscreen

Filtering systems and UV protection collapse during fluctuations in temperature. When that process has progressed far enough, it's definitely time to get some new cream.

Shelf life: 12 months max

❍ Toothpaste

The fluorides remain intact and germ-free behind the plastic cap, so the toothpaste will last virtually forever.

Shelf life: A few years

❍ Acne lotion

Try the sniff test. Acne lotion is still acne-proof after years. However, if the alcohol has evaporated, then the cream's ability to both dissolve fat and act as a disinfectant has been weakened.

Shelf life: Several years

❍ Moisturizer

Old gels and liquids belong in the trash because any product with *hydro* on the label contains water and, under warm temperatures, becomes a breeding ground for all kinds of germs.

Shelf life: 6 months

THE FUNNY PAGE

"Nice buns."

2

DATE HER

With his receding hairline and protruding nose Casanova was hardly good-looking. But he sure knew how to set the stage for a hot date. His strategy went beyond wine and candlelight. He realized that seduction is a dance with a succession of steps involving admiration, attentiveness, and a touch of daring. Your two left feet notwithstanding, you need to master these moves. Why? Because over and over again, women say that one misstep can bring the curtain down on a relationship before the end of the first act. So let Casanova and our 21st-century dating experts prepare you for a grand opening night. We guarantee she'll want an encore.

22 Ways to Tell
If She Wants You . . . or Not

You've spent an hour sharing glances and then conversation with her. Is chatting her up going to lead to something—other than a hefty bar bill? Here's how to unscramble her signals.

1 **She's leaving with you if . . .** her toes, dangling from a cross-legged position, are pointed toward you. (Bonus if her foot is dangling—she's foot flirting with you.)

2 **She's just plain leaving if . . .** her toes are pointed toward the handsome man by your side, or if her leg is crossed in the direction facing away from you.

3 **She's leaving with you if . . .** she asks if you like *Sex and the City* (her excuse to flirt and bring up naughty topics).

4 **She's just plain leaving if . . .** she mentions you seem like an *Everybody Loves Raymond*–type of guy.

5 **She's leaving with you if . . .** she whips out her compact mirror and puts on lip liner and lipstick right in front of you. (Women think this turns guys on.)

6 **She's just plain leaving if . . .** she goes to the ladies' room and returns completely uncoiffed (meaning she didn't even adjust her makeup and hair for you).

7 **She's leaving with you if . . .** she skips a chance to introduce you to her friends (probably because she doesn't need their approval or want their competition).

8 **She's just plain leaving if . . .** she wants you to meet "the girls."

9 **She's leaving with you if . . .** she's asked you a laundry list of questions (three or more), and she's still talking to you.

10 **She's just plain leaving if . . .** she hasn't asked you any questions at all. (Sorry, she's not even scoping you out.)

11 **She's leaving with you if . . .** her hands keep creeping up and tossing her hair—she's telling you she's healthy and playful.

12 **She's just plain leaving if . . .** her body doesn't move or fidget at all—she thinks you're not quite as exciting as *CBS Evening News with Dan Rather*.

13 **She's leaving with you if . . .** she mentions she's not the designated driver. She wants you to know she has no responsibilities that night, and in fact, has designated you as her driver.

14 **She's just plain leaving if . . .** she keeps her keys on the bar and her hands off the booze.

15 **She's leaving with you if . . .** she makes a point of telling you she doesn't have to work the next day. She's ready to pull an all-nighter.

16 **She's just plain leaving if . . .** she makes a point of telling you about a first-thing-in-the-morning job interview, meeting, appointment with her ob-gyn.

17 **She's leaving with you if . . .** she buys you a drink.

18 **She's just plain leaving if . . .** she tells you she's had her share of the swill after you offer to buy another round.

19 **She's leaving with you if . . .** when you tell her you have a dog, she asks you its name.

20 **She's just plain leaving if . . .** she tells you she has a "thing" about dogs.

21 **She's leaving with you if . . .** she avoids the bar grub. She doesn't want you to think she's a pig.

22 **She's just plain leaving if . . .** she gobbles down the bar grub and a triple order of garlic knots.

ASK THE GIRL NEXT DOOR
The honest truth about women from our lovely neighbor

Q: *What do you do to prepare for a romantic date?*
—M. Y., Bath, South Dakota

A: Here's what goes on in the typical woman's apartment 1 to 3 hours before a big night: music blasting, showering, shampooing, pit and leg shaving, pre-thong trimming, exfoliating, walking around nude, snacking nude, beer sipping nude, eyebrow plucking, nail trimming, nail painting, blow-drying, hair brushing, makeup applying, beer sipping, strategic panty and bra selection, outfit choosing, outfit changing, consulting with friends via telephone about outfit, more outfit changing, beer sipping, shoe selection, shoe changing, perfume spritzing, beer sipping, purse filling, mirror dazing, beer guzzling . . . and then, voilà! We're good to go.

Q: *What makes a really great first kiss?*
—D. N., Oklahoma City

A: The ultimate first kisses are always a little overdue. So, if you can, wait until the sexual tension is so high it's distorting the air between you like gasoline fumes. Pick a quiet, cinematic spot: outside a cozy restaurant under the yellow glow of a streetlight, sitting at a little table in a mellow lounge, under a big tree during a post-dinner stroll. Slide your arm around her waist, move toward her slowly, and make soft but decisive lip contact. In my opinion, a first kiss should always be a French one. It sends the message that you can't quite contain your attraction for her, and that is the hottest thing ever.

Q: *What's the appropriate move after a great date?*
Should I send flowers? Call her? Wait for her to call me?
—R.O., Indianapolis

A: You should always call her the next afternoon to let her know you had a good time. If it was an epic first date—you stayed up all night Rolfing, got the same tattoo, became blood brothers—you could send flowers. Otherwise, such a gesture will seem desperate.

Q: *I just started dating a woman 2 weeks ago, and I'm totally confused about what I should do for Valentine's Day. Any suggestions?*
—P. K., Little Rock, Arkansas

A: Hand deliver a small surprise to her office with a note—not a card—saying "Happy V-Day." A new boyfriend did that for me once, and I loved it. Think of something that's either funny or edible. Maybe she mentioned that she's a closet Neil Diamond fan. If so, get her a CD with the cheesiest cover shot of Neil you can find. Did she confess to a weakness for cinnamon buns? Leave a jumbo one in a box with her name on it. Do you know her favorite order at Starbucks? Buy her a skim chai latte (or whatever it is), and have the receptionist call up to let her know there's something hot waiting for her in the lobby. She'll be surprised and flattered in just the right amounts.

Q: *What do women want in a marriage proposal?*
—E. H., Dayton, Ohio

A: In an episode of *Sex and the City*, the world's best boyfriend, played by John Corbett, asked Sarah Jessica Parker's character to marry him, and every cable-subscribing woman in the free world gasped and swooned. He took dog and girl out for a walk in the middle of the night, bent down on one knee under the guise of scooping the poop, but handed Sarah the ring instead. And then he said the magic words: "I love you and couldn't love anyone more. I want to marry you." It was sweet (albeit stinky), intimate, and absolutely non-gimmicky. As a rule, you have to fit the proposal to the woman. If your girlfriend loves road trips and country music, consider taking her on a drive along the coast with Johnny Cash wafting from the speakers before pulling into a scenic overlook and popping the question. If she's nostalgic and you met in a pretty place like a city park or on a ski slope, take her back to the original spot and explain that it was the luckiest moment of your life. Simple but special. Get the idea?

For more honest answers about women, look for
Ask the *Men's Health* Girl Next Door
wherever books are sold.

MUST READS

"Was It Something I Said?"

Ever wonder why your dating universe sometimes seems like a black hole? Plenty of interested women circle around you, but they fall out of orbit and disappear as soon as you open your mouth. Writer Kristen Kemp explains why these 15 dopey comments can make a sure thing more like a space shuttle launch at Cape Canaveral.

He strolled into the bar, and suddenly my friends and I were riveted: Italian suit, wavy hair, body like something out of a Nike ad. He stopped to talk to some friends, then sidled up to us, flashed a mouthful of immaculate calcium, and did something very stupid.

He began to talk.

To this day today, this guy—let's call him Serge—hasn't any idea what he did or said wrong. Most men don't. So I'll take this opportunity, Serge, to point out that when someone tells you she's a writer, the correct response is not "Okay, but what's your real job?"

It drives women nuts when an otherwise attractive man blows his conversational gambit. We don't need you to be a brilliant raconteur; we just want a man who can hold up his end of a discussion and who appears to care about something other than sports and orgasms. We're like an audience watching a performer: We want you to succeed, because it's awkward for everybody when you don't.

Now, granted, we're not the easiest sort to talk to. That's why a panel of my most frequently approached girlfriends got together to give you our take on what not to say when you first meet us. Read on, and you'll never again walk away asking yourself, "Did I say something wrong?" We women have no patience for men who don't get it—so take our clues and be one who does.

1. "So, as I Was Saying about the Logistics of Ego Myopics . . ."

It's nice that NASA called and asked you to save its rocket-science department, but could you save the specifics for later? Even worse: When a guy doesn't have a particularly impressive job but still goes on about it for hours. Last January, I was at a bar talking to a very nice (read: cut and cute) auto-shop owner—let's call him Tony—who was explaining the intricacies of changing F-150 truck transmissions. The more Tony nervously went on about his job, car, life—including his cat named Bob—the more I wanted to rush home to lie on my mattress alone. And to think he may have gotten a look under my hood if he'd just asked me a few questions about me—or at least pretended to be interested in my life.

2. "You Look like Ally McBeal."

I am thin, yes, but I have a full 30 pounds on Calista Flockhart (assuming she weighs about 85). Yet a man at a wedding thought that telling me I looked like the TV character was a compliment. I must've given him quite a look, because he stuttered and said, "I—uh—I—mean, you're a funny professional woman who's lean and trim." Sarcastically, I told him to please go on, I loved being insulted. Another friend of mine was told she looked like Monica Lewinsky, and the man thought he was being nice. The only famous woman you can compare any woman to is Catherine Zeta-Jones—because her face and body are perfect. If we don't look just like her, just say we look nice. If you compare us to your favorite starlet (like, say, Lucy Lawless), odds are two to one that we'll take it wrong.

3. "You Must Work Out a Lot."

"Anytime a guy I don't know starts talking about my body, I think he's making a beeline to my bedroom," says Lisa, 31. "I hate that." The truth is, we don't like comments about our bodies from strangers. First of all, it's creepy. Second, we know you're attracted to us, or you wouldn't have flirted. Third, we hope you're focusing on our minds, not our bodies. (I know, I know, but can't you just play along here?) If at any moment on the first day you meet us you say we have beautiful breasts, all bets for future booty are off. Save the niceties for when you need them—like, the rest of your life. Once you know us well, we need daily—make that hourly—reassurances that you're still attracted to us.

4. "You Probably Won't Want to, But . . ."

One of my best male friends wanted to hit the local watering hole in search of women. He asked me to go along, watch him, and critique his technique. Well, he scored a zero with the two women he hit on, because both times he proposed a date with "I'd really love it if you'd go out with me, but I understand if you don't want to." As gently as I could manage, I asked my friend, "Why did you try to make yourself look like a loser? You're not, but you put yourself down every chance you got."

You don't need to act humble or dis yourself—we women are happy to come to those conclusions without your help. Instead, use self-confident sentences such as "I know you'd have a great time if you went out with me," or "I am good at [insert favorite hobby here—as long as it isn't log splitting or some such]." As a general rule, we like men who like themselves.

5. "Want to Visit My Yacht and See My Heisman Trophy?"

Then again, there's a fine line between selling yourself and putting yourself on blue-light special. At first, my former coworker Michelle, 27, really liked this successful lawyer she was going out with. In the end, she couldn't take his barrage of bragging. "He was always dropping information about his six-figure income, his vacation cottage in the Hamptons, or the Cartier watch his boss gave him as a bonus," she explains. "I felt as if he was desperately trying to prove himself to me—one night of that was enough." We love successful men—don't get us wrong. But women easily OD on bravado.

perfect figures

THE FINE ART OF SEDUCTION

Number of men who lie
to get a first date:
1 in 2

Number of women who lie
to get a date:
1 in 3

Percentage by which the
average guy is more likely to
lie if the woman is pretty:
57

- - - - - - - - - -

6. "Your Hair Would Look Great Spread across My Pillow."

No lie, a guy recently said the following to my best friend: "Do you have a boyfriend? Well, I bet he can't make you scream like I can, or you'd be with him right now." Now, you'd think it would be unnecessary to tell intelligent men like you to tone down the sexual innuendo. Yet seemingly classy guys say this crap all the time. No upstanding woman will ever sleep with a potty-mouthed or -minded guy. She won't even talk to him. So please don't say that you are well-endowed, have superhero stamina, or have a multitalented tongue. (I really heard that once.) One day, if you're lucky—and you don't say, "I'd love your legs wrapped around my head"—you'll get a chance to *show* what you're made of.

7. "Are You Korean, Chinese, or Japanese?"

Avoid all attempts at multiculturalism, suggests Jeannie, a 28-year-old Korean-American. She hates it when men try to guess where she's from. "This happens to me so often—it screams Asian fetish and makes me feel like running for the Himalayas."

Another friend, who is African-American, says she recently had an amazing hour-long conversation with a seemingly great guy when he blurted out, "You're really good-looking for a black woman." "I don't care what he meant—or didn't mean. I didn't even give him a chance to explain," says Jennifer, 25. Don't take chances with easily misconstrued racial comments, no matter what color the girl happens to be.

8. "Do You Like Chicken? Do You Like Music? Because, Really, Who Doesn't Like Chicken and Music?"

This is a real pickup line used by a handsome male of normal intelligence. I know him, and he's still single. Other common lines that I've heard: "Haven't we met before?" "I'm not one of those guys who usually come up to women at bars, but . . . ," and "You have the nicest eyes." Remember that women want men who give good conversation, are original, and intrigue us. So if you catch yourself on the verge of saying anything that could qualify as a line, just go, "Hi, how are you?" instead. It's what you say after hello that matters anyway.

9. "C'mon. Juf Gib Me Yo Nummer."

If you're inebriated, please don't chitchat with us. Talk to a cab driver instead. Nothing is uglier than sour, hours-old beer breath spewing out of a man who can't stand up straight. Now, if we got good and drunk with you during the course of an evening, you may be headed for our apartment. But if you're already lonely and drunk when you start looking for love, you're so out of luck. When we want to hang out with people who slobber, we'll babysit our friends' toddlers.

10. "She Had a Dress Just like Yours."

Please pretend that your ex doesn't exist. If we're interested in you, you can bet that's exactly what we're doing.

11. "Are You Divorced?"

An old friend, Elizabeth, 30, is divorced. "I hate it when I meet men and that's one of the first things they ask about," she says. "When I'm having fun, my divorce is the last thing I want to discuss. It's such a downer topic. And I certainly am not ready to hear his life story, or share mine, until we've been on a few dates."

Divorce isn't the only don't-go-there subject when you're on the prowl. Anything too personal or heavy (read: kids, death, disease, religion, the price of our expensive shoes) will always make us look for a more lighthearted lad.

Learn to Speak Her Romance Language

All it takes to succeed in the art of seduction is a rudimentary understanding of the form. "Courtship is a process, not an event," says psychology professor Monica Moore, Ph.D., of St. Louis's Webster University. Moore has been researching flirting and courtship since 1978, and she says that for men, the key to successful courtship lies in recognizing the subtle signals women send out when they're attracted to you. Act on them and you'll be the healthiest, happiest guy in town.

STAGE 1: FIRST CONTACT

"Most people think it's men who initiate flirting," says Moore, "but two-thirds of the time, women give off a signal of interest first."

Through research, Moore has identified more than 50 "courtship signals" that a woman sends out when she's interested. Some are conscious signs, others are subtle indicators that even she doesn't know she's giving out.

- **Raising eyebrows**

- **Running fingers through hair**

- **Smiling coyly**

- **Licking lips**

- **Giving you short, darting glances**

- **Priming appearance**

- **Swaying to music**

- **Caressing object, like a glass**

- **Hiking skirt to expose leg**

If you have made eye contact and haven't spotted one or more of these actions, it may be better to look elsewhere.

STAGE 2: YOUR MOVE

If someone is sending you signals, approach her, but tread carefully. "A woman can change her mind once she learns more information about you," says Moore. Remember the following.

- **Don't be a wiseass.**

"It's not a good idea to use sarcasm or be mean-spirited, even in joking," advises Moore. You may think you're the next Howard Stern; she'll think you're a creep.

- **Don't say anything about her appearance.**

"That's rushing things," says Moore, "and it can sound too much like a line."

Instead, simply introduce yourself and start talking about where the two of you are and what's brought you there.

STAGE 3: GAUGE HER INTEREST

After you've initiated conversation, a woman will usually send out a signal on

12. "How 'bout Them Yankees?"

Unless the woman you're hoping to score with is wearing a New York cap, your best bet is to avoid any mention of sports. "I was having happy-hour drinks with my coworkers when I bumped into an interesting paramedic and started talking with him," Meghan, 32, says. "He interrupted the conversation and said he had to catch the game, then he invited me to join him at a nearby table. I declined. I mean, there are tons of sporting events on TV, but only one evening when he can meet me. Forget it."

how you're doing. If you're coming on too strong, or if she just plain thinks you're a doofus, the sign may be one of these.

- Avoiding eye contact with you
- Orienting her body away from you
- Crossing her arms over her chest
- Engaging in "private" grooming habits like picking her fingernails and looking at the ends of her hair

If she does any of those, don't panic—yet. Hang around long enough to see whether you receive the bad vibes consistently.

If you elicit only rejection signals, take a hint and work your magic on somebody else.

STAGE 4: SEAL THE DEAL

Here are more positive signs to look for as the night goes on.

- Open body posture
- Exposing her palms as she talks to you
- Illustrating her speech with hand and arm movements

- Whispering
- Gazing into your eyes
- Brushing your forearm ("It may seem like an accident, but a lot of times it's the woman's way of letting you know physical contact is okay," observes Moore)

Finally, if she's interested, she may subject you to a couple of tests.

● The teasing test

"This could be her way of measuring a guy's sense of humor," says Moore. She ribs you, you laugh it off. Got that?

● The damsel-in-distress test

She might linger by a chair to see if you pull it out, or pick up her sweater to see if you help her put it on. She wants to know if you can sense and respond to her needs.

If you do all that and still strike out?

That, friends, is why they call romance a "game."

If your goal is to get into our pants, talk about taking us to the zoo instead. Or pick some other female-friendly topic and humor us.

13. "Why Don't We Go to My Place?"

Molly, 27, was at a mutual friend's birthday party when she met an intriguing architect. At the end of the night, some of her friends wanted to go late-night dancing. "I thought that was a great next step for me and this guy," she says. "Instead, he turns to me and asks, 'Want to just skip it and hang out at my place?'" Molly was furious—she thought some sexy dancing would be enough stimulation. See, one-night stands happen when there's at least the illusion that nothing is going to happen, and women are likely to act against their better judgment when the choice isn't put out there so cold and clear. If you're not sure whether a woman wants to sleep with you or not, take cues from her. If she can't hold back another second, she'll definitely ask you to her place.

14. "Where Did You Get Those Pants?"

Anytime a man asks me this, I know he's not straight. Sure, I'll talk to him for hours, give him my phone number, and make a date to hang out. But I'm not thinking he wants to date or sleep with me; I'm thinking he wants to go shopping. We don't want you to scratch your butt and talk about the best brands of tobacco, but a part of us needs you to be manly, too.

15. "I Just Got Released from a Minimum-Security Prison."

Honestly, I had a close male friend who used this line a lot. (See number 8 for a warning on lines.) Of course, he was kidding. Needless to say, he was a pro at repulsing women. If only he had spoken the truth about himself (for example, he had just completed his master's degree and spent a month hiking along the North Carolina coast), maybe he wouldn't complain about his life in solitary today.

Looking to Click

Online dating isn't just for freaks and geeks anymore. Writer Ron Geraci met dozens of attractive, fun women—and you can, too.

Juliebaby sits there, taunting me.

"I'm about 5 foot 6 inches, 122 pounds, athletic, and I teach Italian in high school," she says.

I zoom in on her face.

She looks like a cross between Salma Hayek and Amy Grant, her lips parted like she's listening.

Her chocolate eyes are smiling. Her skin disappears into a white crewneck that hints it's hugging her just right. It's a good photo.

"Occasionally, I love to purr like a kitten," she continues.

She's selling hard. But, then again, she did come to see me.

perfect figures

CASTING A WIDE 'NET

Percentage of men who think they have a real shot at meeting a fantastic woman over the Internet:

64

Juliebaby found my profile on a dating Web site. She's the latest of dozens of women who have approached me with the intent of finding love or sex. Like many of the others, she's more than pretty.

I tap her back a friendly note. She replies. So forth. A dozen exchanges. Her real name isn't Julie, or Baby. It's Lisa. She works 10 minutes away from my office. Her phone number is waiting in my e-mail in box at work the next morning. Would one more date—to make it a clean 75 in the past half-year—really kill me?

Interesting question. That's exactly why I avoided online dating, and mocked friends who didn't, until very recently.

Kooks. Dog-headed women. Sex offenders and serial killers. Dog-headed serial killers. I'd always figured Web sites like Kiss.com, AmericanSingles.com, and Match.com were rife with such dateless dregs, all desperate to hump something for the first time since Dukakis ran for president.

So about 5 months ago, I dipped into online dating to make fun of it. Now, 74 dates later, I'm open enough to recommend that other single men take a serious look at online dating, and I've even consented to write an advice column for Match.com. I'll pull no punches with them in this article, though, so please send crank e-mails to them if they fire me.

After posting a free guinea-pig profile on five Web sites a few months ago, I've been whacking my keyboard (for a change) almost nonstop. During one ridiculous stint, I went on 33 dates in 46 days. So far, I've been on 74 dates with women I've met online—and by "dates" I mean in-person first dates. I went out with several of these women a bunch of times. This is despite certain drawbacks I bring to the screen: namely, a height of one hand span under 6 foot 2 and a prim corporate photo in which my bloated head looks like a beach ball sitting on a golf tee.

Besides bolstering hope for the future, test-driving an online dating site can pay unexpected dividends. For one, you can learn a ton about single women by rote practice. More important, this experiment can reveal where your weaknesses and strengths lie in making first impressions. That can give you clues about presenting yourself most influentially—techniques you may have lacked (and paid a high price for) your whole life. That's one payoff that transcends meeting a few beautiful redheads.

Profile Decoder

If She Describes Herself As . . .	She's . . .
Curvaceous	Grotesquely obese
Not jaded	Jaded
Smart	Underemployed
Cute	Cute, but almost assuredly has a huge ass
A lawyer and a writer	A miserable lawyer
Slender	Likely built better than women who checked "average"
Sensual	Ready for sex
A free spirit	Not approached by men she likes; she'll likely reply to your e-mail
A hopeless romantic or a dreamer	Probably a normal, well-adjusted woman groping for an intriguing way to describe herself

If She Uses the Phrase . . .	It Really Means . . .
"I like music, dancing, movies, fitness, traveling, restaurants, and reading."	"I have no interests whatsoever."
"Cat" (any mention of a cat)	"You will be prostrate to my neutered children."
"I like curling up with a good book."	"I have an IQ below 85."
"I'm looking for Mr. Right."	"I have an IQ below 80."
"My friends tell me I'm attractive."	"Bring a bag."
"I'll send you my photo if you ask."	"I don't want my ex-boyfriend, sister, or boss to find me online, but don't worry—I'm a dish."
"I love to sleep."	"Forget wine; beer is great."
"Let's become friends and see what happens."	"I get e-mailed a lot, but if you're clever you'll hear back from me."

Who's in the House?

Chiefly, online dating sites have become far more mainstream since their embryonic stages roughly 5 years ago, and they've attracted more normal (read: less ugly and tech-nerdish) people. A December 2001 analysis from Jupiter Media Metrix, a research company that tracks Internet usage, reported that 15.3 million Americans visited dating sites (up from 4 million in June 2000).

What's better, these users aren't just concentrated in densely populated dating hubs like New York City and Los Angeles; you can find datable neighbors (or cousins) in the backwoods of East Jabip, too.

Most online daters are between the ages of 25 and 44. Divorced men and women have embraced online dating because they can seek out similar partners and give their ailing social lives a goose without cruising bars (44 percent of online daters have children). Women make up about 41 percent of the traffic, since the initiative men take in face-to-face approaches is mirrored online. But with millions of women clicking into these sites each month, it's no sausage party. And given that most men shoot themselves in the foot when approaching women online, your odds can be quite good.

A Party of Five

I joined five Web sites: American Singles.com, Lavalife.com, Kiss.com, Match.com, and Matchmaker.com. They all operate in the same basic fashion. First, you post a free profile by clicking self-description checklists and writing mini-essays on what bothers you about starving children. Then you upload digital photos of yourself. (If you don't, you don't have a bloody chance.) At this point, you can sit back and wait for women to e-mail you, or you can pay $25 to $30 a month (or $3 per first e-mail) and go on the offensive. I did both.

The best services let you search through listings of single women by any criteria you want: where they live, their body type, hair color, religion, college degree, and keywords of your choice. Every week, a few sites send me listings of new profiles with photos of 24- to 33-year-old brunettes between 5 foot 4 and 5 foot 8 who typed "Sicilian" in their self-descriptions. Let the cream rise, right?

Don't Look like a Loser Online

Uploading your "profile" is step one. It took me 16 revisions to finally create one that netted a good number of hits for a man: about 25 a month.

One reason your odds can be so good on these sites is that most men post lame profiles that guarantee zero interest. Here's a better formula for success.

❶ **Scan about 20 profiles of men your age.**
Once you see the cookie-cutter nature most share, you'll know what to avoid.

● **Pick a username or screen name that won't scare a thin-blooded virgin.**
Go for Duke9883, not Thonglicker.

● **Post four pictures.**
You should be in different environments that reveal something about you (all of which should require a shirt). Roughhousing with your dog, smiling at a pal's wedding, reclining at work, whatever. A $100 scanner will make a snap-shot digital, or you can have the image scanned by any photo developer for a few bucks.

● **Write at least 100 words for every question.**
Men are suicidally glib. The Clint Eastwood style doesn't work here; women will just assume you're hiding a police record. "Try to be as rich in the de-scriptions as possible," says Peter Housley, CEO of Lavalife.

● **Mention why you posted a profile.**
Quickly and positively. As in, you travel a lot or you're new to the city. You'll seem like a nice catch, so women will be suspicious as to why you're seemingly hard up for a date.

● **Be funny.**
But not sarcastic. "This is all about fun," says Patricia, 29, a 9-plus brunette who regularly gets 200 e-mails a week in response to her online profile. "If your pro-file isn't funny, you'd better be really good-looking."

It's Been Said...

" You can't buy love, but you can pay heavily for it. "

—Henny Youngman

● **Curb bragging.**
You're not writing a résumé, you're writing blurbs intended to interest someone romantically. Think charm and humility. Replace "high-paid profes-sional" with "I have a great job that I love."

● **When listing your salary range, be generously truthful.**
Round up, but never select the highest range. "It seems like every guy on these sites is making 150K-plus, so I assume most of them are lying," says Lisa, 25. By the way, don't opt out of listing your income range; it's one of the top criteria most women look for online—and offline. If this bugs you, welcome to Earth.

● **Write a clever wish list.**
Be creative and brief (about four sentences) in your description of what you're looking for in a potential mate, and never mention physical attributes. You

● **Meet her in a public place.**

Preferably a coffee joint or café . . . or someplace that's friendly for quick visits. You don't know this chick, so don't tempt the 1 percent chance that she'll be drunkenly knocking on your door at 4:00 A.M. next week.

● **Watch out for false intimacy.**

You've traded 88 e-mails before meeting her, and this often causes a bizarre, premature feeling of false intimacy. Some women will hug you like a long-lost lover upon meeting you. Others may reveal odd secrets to you (like their bat-

Geraci's Cyber Scorecard

NUMBER OF WOMEN . . .

I e-mailed online: circa 245

Number of those I met for a date: 43

Who e-mailed me first: 86

Number of those I met for a date: 31

I e-mailed back and forth at least 20 times, but didn't meet face-to-face: circa 115

Who stopped e-mailing me out of the blue when everything seemed to be going well: 17

Who gave me their phone numbers in their e-mail: 33

I wanted to meet but couldn't figure out how to convince: 17

Who were actually better-looking than in their online photos: 12

Who were less attractive than in their photos: 2

Who were an 8 or higher in the looks category: 34

Who were maybe a bit out of my league looks-wise: 23

I dated more than once: 19

I could still date (potentially): 4

With whom I'd gladly grab drinks again, even though it might be just as acquaintances: 1

Who introduced me to a few of their datable girlfriends: 7

Who made me feel like hell when they told me thanks, but sorry: 2

And vice versa, I regretfully speculate: 2

Who struck me as wife material: 4 or 7, depending on the day

tles with bulimia), since you've already killed all the small talk online. However, by the end of the date she'll likely bear no resemblance to the honey you conjured behind those e-mails. She may, in fact, be better, but either way, forget all the e-mails and start now from scratch.

● Limit the first date to an hour.

It's really just a quick meeting to ascertain whether there's a physical attraction and whether one of you has a violent chromosomal defect. Don't give her a chance to yawn. Drink, talk, squeeze-hug, exchange cards, bolt. If she's into you, this will help fan her interest for a great second date. And if you're not feeling it, it'll keep her emotional investment low.

The Fringe Benefits

Online dating requires little effort. You basically hunt for women while you sleep or drink beer. It's like laying crab traps! Plus . . .

● The notion of a dry spell becomes stupid.

You realize there are thousands of perfectly datable women who'd get with you right now. And when they contact you first, you experience something rare: an attractive woman who tries to make conversation with you.

● There's little sting in rejection.

"In face-to-face situations, you have a 'scarcity' mindset, as if the girl in front of you were the only opportunity," says Hogan. If she cuts you off, your guts fall on the floor. "Online, you quickly understand that if one woman doesn't respond positively to you, there are many others who will," continues Hogan. This is the key to getting regular sex, and it's integral to finding and marrying the woman you really deserve, rather than the first one who's nice to you.

● It's dating boot camp.

A lot of single guys suck at talking to datable women because they do it too rarely. Many may have only a 30-second conversation with a potential bedmate every week or so. You couldn't learn to play the kazoo that way. Being forced to confront and amuse a new woman every other day is a crash course in estrogen puppetry. You'll see patterns emerge and be able to test a variety of answers to identical questions to see which of them plays best.

● If a girl snubs you, you can screw her over.

"If we get complaints about a member from two different people, we ban them from the system," says Joe Shapira, CEO of American Singles.com. Of course, she should do something to deserve getting bounced, like e-mailing you repeatedly after you've told her, "No, thanks." But isn't guilt relative?

Is She a Keeper?

As writer Greg Gutfeld discovered, there's only one way to tell. Give her this test.

A well-known theory says that if you want to see what your girlfriend might be like after a few decades of wear and tear, just check out her mom. Unfortunately, this theory doesn't hold up. With the advent of liposuction, self-help tapes, and kickboxing classes, the only thing about her mother that's truly authentic is the contempt she holds for you. So while your mate may be all coitus and curves right now, who can tell whether 5 or 10 years from now she'll still be able to stir a chuckle beneath your buckle? In sum, choosing the right woman puts the "crap" in crapshoot.

We think we've found a way to solve this problem: a quiz that predicts whether your sweet thing will stay sweet, or turn as skanky as the charter-bus toilet on the way home from an AARP chili cook-off.

This test, however, is different from your typical oval-filling yawners. It reveals as much about you as it does about the damsel you're trying to assess. Now, sharpen a pencil; let's fill in the most important blank of all.

The Special *Man's Guide* Compatibility Test

Please note: Her answers may not exactly reflect ours. Look for similarities. By the end, it should be painfully clear whether you should stay with your mate or move on. If you decide to dump her, send us her number. She may need some comforting.

1. AT A PARTY, YOU GET DRUNK AND START PLACING THINGS (ACTUALLY, A POODLE) ON YOUR HEAD. WHAT WOULD SHE DO?

● **She'd leave the room.**

● **She'd tell you, "Knock it off, bozo!"**

● **She'd quietly get you the hell out of there. * KEEPER ***

The real test: Can she actually keep you from soiling your reputation or, worse, the carpet? That, after all, is the mark of a keeper. "If she starts to berate or lecture you—what's to be gained by that?" asks University of Louisville psychology professor Michael Cunningham, Ph.D. "You won't remember anything she's said, and it will only embarrass you further." Not that you don't deserve it, poodle head. But if she can help you—by placing a small reptile on her head to distract attention, or by simply pulling you aside and whispering something like, "Let's get out of here, I'm ovulating"—then she's a keeper. She's protecting you from yourself and the host, who probably invited at least one large, loyal friend to help maintain order in his house. She can lecture you later when you're sober, so come next party you won't pee in the aquarium (or at least you'll do it at close range).

2. YOU ANNOUNCE YOUR PLAN TO QUIT YOUR BRAIN-SURGERY PRACTICE TO FULFILL YOUR DREAM OF BECOMING A VOLUNTEER PARK RANGER. HOW DOES SHE RESPOND?

❍ **If it makes you happy, she's all for it.**

❍ **She wonders, "Have you lost your mind?"** * KEEPER *

The real test: The first response suggests the stupefying "love conquers all" disease. This disorder dissipates once she meets a new guy with a better income (like a pool cleaner). While the keeper sees the romance in your leaving a stable job for something more adventurous, she also sees the inherent foolishness in your misguided antics. So, after questioning your sanity, she sits down with you and asks about a business plan, a career trajectory, and ideas for supplemental income. That's what good women do: They kill your stupid dreams.

3. NOW AND THEN DURING DINNER, YOU SIT SILENTLY WITH A BLANK LOOK ON YOUR FACE. THE ONLY SIGN THAT YOU ARE ALIVE IS THAT FOOD DISAPPEARS FROM YOUR PLATE. DOES THIS BOTHER HER?

❍ **She leaves you alone but wonders if your relationship is doomed.**

❍ **She asks you how you're feeling or how your day was, and leaves it at that. There's no need to talk every second of the day.** * KEEPER *

The real test: Men and women possess different needs for conversation (for men, the need is intermittent; for women, it's frightfully constant). A smart woman realizes this and also knows that men are given to long periods of silence, especially when eating large quantities of meat or meat by-products. She does pursue conversation, because it beats drizzling her pork chops with warm tears. "A socially skilled woman can gently start a conversation—'So, tell me about your day'—but will stop if it isn't working," says Cunningham. She may even follow up with "Maybe we can talk later." Cunningham calls that "leaving the door half open." Men do it, too, especially when using the bathroom.

A woman who believes the relationship is in trouble, however, mistakes silence for unhappiness. Marry her, and surely there will be therapists on the horizon. Some wearing cardigans! The horror!

4. WHICH WOULD MAKE HER MORE UPSET: IF YOU GOT FAT, OR IF SHE GOT FAT?

◗ You got fat.

◗ She got fat. * **KEEPER** *

The real test: Ideally, a woman would keep herself Slim Jim thin while cooing over your expanding flanks. There's more of you to love, after all, and she can keep fit by regularly flipping you over to prevent bed rot.

Okay, not really. A keeper realizes that (a) men appreciate beauty, and (b) men will stay healthy in order to appreciate (and maintain claims on) a woman's beauty. Thus, a smart female realizes that if she gets fat, both of you have a problem. "And a smart woman can stay fit by increasing sexual activity to burn calories," adds Cunningham.

5. BECAUSE OF A CRISIS AT WORK, YOU BREAK A BIG DATE THAT SHE'S BEEN LOOKING FORWARD TO FOR WEEKS. HOW DOES SHE TAKE IT?

◗ She's pissed. It's always about work, isn't it?

◗ She's disappointed, but not after you apologize and promise to make it up to her. * **KEEPER** *

The real test: "This question is a good measure of what I call demandingness," says New York stress and relationship counselor Allen Elkin, Ph.D. Meaning, does she frustrate easily? Can she roll with bad news, realizing it's out of your control? And will she still sleep with you when you return home? "It's the difference between her banning sex for a week or being slightly disappointed but realizing you're disappointed, too," says Elkin. And an apology, followed by an honest effort to reschedule, will pay dividends. If you have to work late, a keeper can always stop by later and both of you can play "powerful executive encounters barely legal cleaning lady." This time, you be the executive.

6. AT A PARTY, SHE CATCHES YOU OGLING A WOMAN'S BREASTS (NOT HERS). ANY THOUGHTS?

◗ She says nothing, but you shouldn't expect any action when you get home.

◗ She knows you can't help yourself. * **KEEPER** *

The real test: The second response—what experts call the right answer—shows the true spirit of a keeper. Happily, a keeper recognizes the psychological concept known as visual capture. "There are some things in the environment that, as an animal, you naturally notice," says Cunningham. "You're biologically hotwired to focus on certain categories of stimuli. Most women look at babies, most men look at the female anatomy."

7. YOU SAY YOU'LL CALL HER ON MONDAY TO GO OUT THAT NIGHT, BUT SHE DOESN'T HEAR FROM YOU UNTIL WEDNESDAY. WHAT DOES SHE DO?

● **No big deal. You were probably busy.**

● **You'd better have a damn good reason. * KEEPER ***

perfect figures

BUT ONLY FOR 5 MINUTES

Percentage of men who would postpone sex with a potential Ms. Right until they really get to know her:
74

Percentage of women who would hold out on Mr. Right:
79

The real test: Beware of the woman who says, "No big deal." She probably harbors deep resentment that will brew until, one day, you come home and all the sleeves of your dress shirts are missing.

"If she was counting on a call and you didn't, she's owed an apology," says Cunningham. "But the real issue here is her problem-solving ability. She must demand a reason, accept your apology if it's legitimate, and then be savvy enough to prevent this from happening again." If she continues to let this happen, she may not mind being low on your priority list. If you dump her, she may barely notice. So enjoy the sex while it lasts, and get to know her cute friends.

8. YOU GET A BIG PROMOTION, WHICH MEANS MORE MONEY FOR LUXURY ITEMS (LIKE HAIR-CARE PRODUCTS). YOU'LL ALSO BE PUTTING IN LONGER HOURS AT THE OFFICE, SO YOU'LL SEE LESS OF HER. HOW DOES SHE FEEL ABOUT THAT?

● **She would worry that she'd never see you anymore.**

● **She'd take [flying, skiing, spin art] lessons. * KEEPER ***

The real test: Independence is the magic word here. While seeing less of you may disappoint her, she should have enough of a life to keep busy. Rather, she should not spend all day nursing the liquor cabinet and agreeing with Oprah (or vice versa). But careful, friend. If she's really independent, you may be left isolated and lonely. "You want a woman who possesses the same level of independence as yourself," says Cunningham. How can you tell if she has the right amount of independence? Is doing the laundry her idea of girls' night out? If not, that's a start.

9. A FORMER GIRLFRIEND (THE ONE WHO TOOK ALL YOUR INXS CDS) IS IN TOWN, AND YOU'D LIKE TO MEET HER FOR DRINKS. HOW DOES YOUR WOMAN RESPOND?

● **She wouldn't be thrilled, but she wouldn't let it bother her if you went.**

● **Fine, as long as she can see her ex-boyfriend (the one her parents loved) when he's in town.** * KEEPER *

The real test: A keeper would stand up for herself, minus the Thai fighting sticks. "And she is right to be jealous, but without jumping immediately to conclusions," says Elkin. With the second response, the keeper rightly expresses the necessary jealousy, as well as a keen understanding that when left alone with a woman he has already slept with, a man may just do it again. After all, this is why we hold on to all our past *Playboy*s. Sure, they're old and tattered, but we can't just throw 'em away. Not with Miss October 1987 staring up at us like that.

10. YOUR POKER, BEER, 'N' GUNS NIGHT WITH YOUR BUDDIES IS SCHEDULED ON THE SAME EVENING AS HER BIG COMPANY AWARDS DINNER (AND SHE'S RECEIVING AN AWARD). HOW DO THE TWO OF YOU RESOLVE THIS?

● **You cancel your stupid poker game.**

● **You reschedule the game, and she makes snacks for it.** * KEEPER *

The real test: Considering that she's getting an award, she's receiving a lot of attention, she bought a new dress that shows off her breasts—you're obligated, buster. If she were to go alone, well, that's how rumors start ("Her husband works nights, as a crack dealer") and why that dress will inevitably come home with a missing button and a stain teeming with DNA.

The keeper expects you to attend the dinner but respects your disappointment over missing the game. So she offers to make up for it later, possibly by cooking pigs in a blanket for a rescheduled poker night, says Cunningham. This displays a keen ability to negotiate her needs and a willingness to accept compromise, which is what makes a successful marriage successful. That, and pigs in a blanket.

11. YOU ASK HER TO PERFORM A REALLY, REALLY KINKY SEX ACT (THINK VACUUM-CLEANER ATTACHMENTS).

● **She's open to new things.**

● **First, let her call her sorority sisters so they can join in.**

● **She wants to know more about what you have in mind. * KEEPER ***

The real test: Being open to new things suggests either she's out to impress you or maybe she wasn't lying about living with Mötley Crüe. (As for the second response, we just threw that in to titillate our boss.) "She should assess how much this act means to you—if it's something casual or something you've been aching to do all your life," says Cunningham. In short, she needs convincing. Depending on how well you explain exactly what you need (don't forget the clown shoes!), she may say, "Let's try it and see how it feels. But if I panic, I'd like to back off."

The reality is she may do it, then complain about it after the fact. But isn't that what she does with regular sex, anyway?

She's a Real Mother

If you want to check out the merchandise, sometimes it doesn't hurt to visit the factory where it's built. It's not foolproof by any means, but here's what you can learn about your mate from her mother.

Her Mother . . .	What This Means
Is really fat	Your mate won't be. She's seen the flab up close, and won't want to grow her own
Has "big bones"	Code word for denial-state fatness. If your mate says this about herself, oncoming blimp ahead
Is hot	Good sign. Just don't sleep with her
Is a drunk	Your mate won't be one. But she won't take your social drinking lightly, either
Is hot and a drunk	May make the holidays more interesting
Is a great cook	This doesn't tell you much—back then, women had the time and the patience to learn the art of cooking
Can't make canned soup	Her family was rich enough to have a cook. Yippee!
Nags her husband	Nagging is genetic. Remember that when you see the old guy cowering in the garage
Wears a housecoat	Hey, don't we all?

12. YOU WANT TO HAVE SEX, BUT SHE'S NOT IN THE MOOD. SHE GRINS AND BEARS IT, RIGHT?

◑ **She would have sex with you anyway.**

◑ **She'd pencil you in for tomorrow.** * KEEPER *

The real test: Sex on autopilot is never the right answer. And she will resent you for it (just ask Donald Trump). While there are sexual alternatives to full-blown intercourse, many of which are legal in your state (visit your courthouse), they're just as much work as full sex anyway (despite the price difference).

Penciling you in for tomorrow is a reasonable accommodation, and one you should accept graciously. "If she realizes sex may be a mild impulse for you and not an overwhelming need that night, then she may whisper something sweet and promise you something memorable for tomorrow," says Cunningham. She understands the twitches in your britches, and who knows, she may even rouse herself, sex-wise. More likely, if she's socially skilled, she will shift your attention from her to something else, like the erotic hand puppets she bought for such occasions.

13. YOU COME HOME DRUNK, WITH FRIENDS, AND YOUR RAUCOUS BEHAVIOR WAKES HER UP. YOU VOMIT INTO THE CD PLAYER. NO BIG DEAL, RIGHT?

◑ **No! She would come down and party!**

◑ **Yes, it is a big deal. She would throw out your friends, and you'd be banished to the couch.** * KEEPER *

The real test: A groovy babe who lu-u-u-uvs to party was fun back at the dorm. You're grown-ups now.

Do you want a woman willing to put up with your adolescent idiocy, especially when you're pushing 30, 35, or 40? The critical issue isn't her behavior but how much of an ass you intend to be for the rest of your life. We're with you on whatever road you choose. If a stable adult life is not what you want, fine. You should have dumped your mate months ago and moved in with Farrah Fawcett.

14. SHE GOES AWAY FOR A FEW DAYS. WHEN SHE RETURNS, SHE EXPECTS TO FIND THE PLACE . . .

◑ **Just as she left it, with no stray hairs on the toilet seat.**

● **Messy, but with attempts made to fix any potentially dangerous structural damage. Feel free to cancel your tee time and help clean. * KEEPER ***

● **With rose petals leading to a candlelit bedroom.**

The real test: A keeper realizes that men and women maintain different standards of neatness—and that men need help in raising theirs. In a typical single-male household, for example, you may enter the residence in bare feet but leave in something vaguely resembling slippers. Don't be fooled. Your feet are still bare.

The second response is best: She wants a neat home, but she also knows what to expect from guys like us. "Of course, you don't want a woman who's neurotic about orderliness," adds Elkin. "My advice: Check out her sock drawer. It may tell you everything." Probably more than you'll ever want to know. (Like, what's that ointment for, anyway?)

As for the rose petals, this means your woman has been watching too much Lifetime Television. Cut her off. Put her on rations of *Sea Wolf.*

15. SHE SEES THAT YOU'RE UNDERDRESSING FOR A DINNER PARTY. HOW DOES SHE HANDLE IT?

● **She says nothing and chuckles later at your expense.**

● **She makes you change into something more appropriate (like maybe long pants). * KEEPER ***

The real test: A keeper spots your fashion discrepancies, then offers a graceful execution of helpfulness. She's like the Red Cross, without the coffee and blankets.

Isn't that nagging? No, friend, a keeper never nags. "A nag points out your failing when you can't do a thing about it," says Cunningham. If she were to tease you about your clothes at the party—that's as evil as Ted Danson talking politics. A keeper says, "I'm not going to let you dress like a jerk forever."

How do you know whether you're being nagged or genuinely assisted? "Ask yourself if you think you should be moving in the direction you're being nagged," says Cunningham. Is it better to bathe than to stink? You know the answer. If you don't, let her go so you can become a performance artist. You'll get to look stupid all the time and receive grant money, too!

16. YOU FORGOT HER BIRTHDAY. WHAT DOES SHE DO?

● **Nothing. It doesn't bother her at all. People make mistakes like that all the time.**

● **She accepts your apology, buys herself a very extravagant gift, and makes it clear this will never happen again.** * KEEPER *

The real test: There is not a woman on earth who would not be bothered by this. Find a crawl space and hide.

The second response is the best you can hope for: forgiveness meted out, appropriate restitution exacted. Here a woman gets what she wants, without having to express gratitude.

17. YOU READ HER A BUNCH OF PROBING QUESTIONS OUT OF YOUR FAVORITE MAGAZINE AND REFUSE TO SHOW HER THE ANSWER KEY. DOES SHE RESENT IT?

● **She feels like you're interrogating her. Plus, she's missing the end of** *Will and Grace*!

● **No problemo. Now she asks you the same questions, smart guy.** * KEEPER *

The real test: After all, a keeper realizes the door to domestic bliss swings both ways, and she, too, has every reason to wonder whether you're the one to hitch or ditch.

Just make her stick to the test questions. If she brings up that small stash of *Swanks* she found in your closet, you're dead meat.

Scoring

Scoring is an important process, so consume no more than four or five beers while totaling the score.

● **14 or more right answers:**
She's a keeper. Propose before she wises up and realizes she can do better.

● **8 to 13 right:**
We say dump her. But, hey, she could improve. Can she cook? That helps!

● **7 or fewer right:**
Tell her that she's much too good for you and that she should move on to better things. If she resists, act quickly to save yourself. Start biting your toenails in public. Run naked through Wal-Mart. If she's still lingering, you don't have a girlfriend, you have a stalker. Which, on the whole, can be entertaining even when you're not famous.

What Would Casanova Do?

No man is more renowned for his power over women. In fact, Casanova's name has become synonymous with seduction. During his 73 years, he made love to noble-women, actresses, dancers, chambermaids, Greek slave girls, a priest's niece, a farmer's daughter, five sisters (plus their mother), a transvestite, a hunchback (with "an excitingly misplaced vulva"), a nymphomaniac, and two unrepentant nuns—132 ladies in all. He was, quite simply, irresistible. All this, says writer Joe Kita, despite a big nose, retreating hairline, puffy countenance, and ribboned ponytail. And the 200-odd years that have passed since Casanova's death have only embellished his reputation. Every man, at one time or another, wants to be a Giacomo Casanova.

The legendary lover would apply his 10 principles of sex and seduction to make any woman quiver in her bodice. Just follow along at home and you can, too.

The ability to entrance a woman, to get her to surrender what Casanova called her "delicious little that," depends mostly on style and sincerity. That's all there is to it. Although you may object to Casanova's morals (he reveled in orgies, abhorred condoms, and once made love to his illegitimate daughter), he was not reprehensible.

"Unlike the fictional Don Juan or the Marquis de Sade, Casanova wasn't a sexual predator," says noted Casanovist Ted Emery, Ph.D., an assistant professor of Italian at Dickinson College in Carlisle, Pennsylvania. "He was very much in love with most of these women, and they with him. He frequently mentions the multiple orgasms he gave them. This is certainly flattering, but the fact that he even thought about their pleasure makes him different and admirable."

To gain a better understanding of this man's genius (without reading all 12 volumes of his autobiography), we attended a Casanova dinner at Sotheby's Institute of Art in New York City. It was a lavishly detailed re-creation (right down to the period cutlery) of a rendezvous in Venice in 1753 between the 28-year-old Casanova and a beautiful nun into whose habit he wished to plunge. It was his finest moment—an evening that exemplified his charm, and one from which all men can learn.

"It was a dinner of seduction," explains Carolin Young, a culinary historian who organized the event. "It was 2 hours of playful flirtation during which they were both waiting to devour each other. Afterward, the nun finally told him she had 'an appetite that promised to do honor to the supper.'"

So what did Casanova do that night? How did he steal the keys to the convent? Before we divulge his secrets, you should understand that Casanova was not an aristocrat. Although he enjoyed projecting that image, he was essentially a gambler and con man who fought duels and even served time in prison. So while this evening may appear highly sophisticated, don't forget that Casanova was, at heart, a philandering rogue who placed fun and love above all else.

Just adhere to the following 10 principles the next time you're with a woman you admire. The results will be delicious.

CASANOVA COMMANDMENT #1
To Make a Woman Feel Special, Do Something Special

For his illicit dinner with the good sister, Casanova rented an elegant five-room apartment. He met her as she stepped off the gondola, and they walked arm-in-arm across a lantern-lit plaza.

◉ Your move:

When you're trying to impress a woman, never utter these words at the cusp of an evening: "So, what do you feel like doing?" A true Casanova takes charge. He has a plan. To devise a memorable one, imagine that you're proposing. What would you do to make the night so special she couldn't possibly say no? Then arrange it (minus the ring and bent-knee thing, of course). After all, you are proposing—only it's something far more enticing than marriage.

"Women are very appreciative of any kind of effort," says Young. "Casanova certainly realized that."

CASANOVA COMMANDMENT #2
Privacy Is Sexy

The nun had a reputation to protect, and Casanova was sensitive to that. The apartment staff did not disturb Casanova and his guest; dinner was served through a window in the wall, allowing the servants to deliver the food without being seen or heard. There were no prying eyes to fear, nothing to distract the two lovers from each other. Privacy gives a woman permission to be herself.

◉ Your move:

Create an intimate atmosphere whenever you can. Invite her to dinner at your place, reserve a cozy table at a fine restaurant, encourage her to slip

It's Been Said . . .

" There is nothing about which men lie so much as about their sexual powers. In this at least every man is, what in his heart he would like to be, a Casanova. "

—W. Somerset Maugham

away from the party for a starlit stroll. . . . Continually search for eddies in the evening where you both can linger and connect. You can bestow no greater compliment on a woman than your full attention.

Let Her Admire You Admiring Her

Casanova's rented apartment was full of mirrors and candles. He wanted his love to be "reflected a thousand times," and he wanted to be able to enjoy her from many different angles during dinner. He knew, too, that a beautiful woman enjoys looking at herself—that the mirrors would become her portraits, and she'd feel even sexier because of it. "There's a magical quality to mirrors, candlelight, and silver," says Young. "Women find it enchanting."

● **Your move:**

If you can't duplicate an atmosphere like this, become a mirror yourself. Let her see the effects of her beauty and charm reflected in you. Every now and then, look at her appreciatively and smile. At opportune times, compliment her—choosing a trait other than the obvious. For instance, pretty women are used to being told they're pretty. That kind of compliment has little effect. But tell a pretty woman that she's smart, and you often win her heart. There's a magical quality to a man's open, insightful admiration that women find equally enchanting.

Ask Her What She Thinks

Casanova's seduction lasted several hours, and he spent much of this time asking questions and listening. In an age when women were considered inferior to men, such behavior was flattering. He treated his guest reverently, and not just because she was a nun. This woman was his equal, and he was genuinely interested in her perspective.

● **Your move:**

The reason women found Casanova so fascinating is that he found them so fascinating. In fact, he believed that without engaging conversation, physical pleasure was uninteresting. "The minute you start thinking of the woman as an object, the instant you become more interested in yourself than in finding out about her, then you're not being a Casanova," notes Emery. "He made women feel valued for things other than their bodies."

It's not difficult to get a woman to talk about herself. Just ask open-ended questions and shut up. But you have to be sincere about it. Casanova's success with women stemmed from his genuine interest in them. He touched their hearts before daring to venture anyplace else.

CASANOVA COMMANDMENT #5
Encourage Decadence

For this particular evening, Casanova spared no expense. The apartment, the dinner table, his own body were all dressed with the finest things available. The meal consisted of eight courses, served in pairs. Many of the dishes—such as oysters, champagne, game, sturgeon, truffles, fruits, and sorbets—were delicacies, considered highly indulgent separately, let alone combined with everything else. Casanova was obviously out to impress, but he also knew that after the first sampling of something sinful, it becomes much easier to sin again.

◉ Your move:

Provide your lady with something decadent. This could be a single chocolate truffle (gift-wrapped) or an ice-cream sundae that the two of you share. Indulgence is the removal of a single brick that significantly weakens the temple.

What Casanova Did

The man himself offers advice on love, life, and getting rid of gonorrhea.

◉ To recover from an orgy:
Have a long, sound sleep. Casanova believed in the laws of equilibrium. Balance overindulgence with diet, rest, and abstinence.

◉ To end a relationship:
Separation should always be by mutual consent. No heartache, no revenge. If she clings, find her a more suitable man.

◉ To mend a broken heart:
Simply find yourself another, more beautiful woman. Casanova was not above using prostitutes to console him.

◉ To be handsome:
Dress handsome, talk handsome, act handsome. If you believe it, if you radiate it, women will see you that way.

◉ To cure venereal disease:
Adhere to a strict diet of nitrate water for 6 weeks.

◉ To tell the difference between true love and sensual pleasure:
Pay attention to how you feel afterward. Real love is the love that sometimes arises after sensual pleasure. If it does, it is immortal. The other kind inevitably goes stale, for it lies in mere fantasy.

◉ To capture a woman's love:
Make her feel beautiful when she's with you.

◉ To live well:
Immerse yourself in the present moment.

◉ To find true happiness:
Reminisce.

CASANOVA COMMANDMENT #6
Appeal to All Her Senses

Casanova scented the apartment with tuberoses because he believed they were an aphrodisiac. He served oysters and champagne as an appetizer because on the tongue there is only one thing more titillating. He asked for his lady's opinions because every woman loves the music of her own voice. He created an atmosphere of lavishness and luxury so her own indulgence would feel less guilty. And he touched her, often and gently, to return her attention to the true focus of the evening. By stimulating every sense, Casanova was able to immerse this woman more fully in the moment, and make her feel more alive and sexual.

● **Your move:**

Be attentive to every one of your mate's five senses. Play background music, touch the small of her back to guide her, make eye contact, give her a flute of champagne to sip, buy her a fresh flower to sniff. . . . Think of each sense as a little engine you need to warm up. When all her senses are purring, she will be, too.

CASANOVA COMMANDMENT #7
Savor the Anticipation

Although Casanova immediately grew "ardent" when he noticed that his lady's breasts were covered by only a dainty chemise, he didn't force himself upon her. He was patient. He accepted her single kiss and cherished her two-word promise: "After supper."

"Casanova appreciated that if you have your pleasure too quickly, you don't suck all the pleasure out of it," explains Young. "Savor the anticipation, because often the anticipation is half the fun."

● **Your move:**

Foreplay doesn't happen only in the bedroom 60 seconds before intercourse. It's organic. It encompasses the entire day. Slip a note into her purse confessing how much you're looking forward to this date, or call her at work and tell her the same. When you meet, take her hands and softly kiss her lips. Most important: Allow the evening to progress at its own pace, remembering that neither of you has to be anywhere except together.

CASANOVA COMMANDMENT #8
Be Playful

Most of the food and drink Casanova preferred was sexually suggestive. Plump oysters, succulent game hens, soft cheeses, ripe fruit . . . On one level, he simply enjoyed watching women put these things in their mouths. But on another, he saw dinnertime as an opportunity for playfulness. When a slippery oyster fell onto an ample bosom, he immediately offered to slurp it off. When the salad arrived undressed, he encouraged the lady to dribble on the oil and vinegar. Casanova realized that sex isn't serious—it's playtime for adults. Games like this are the warmup.

○ Your move:

Whether you're dining at home or at a restaurant, choose something provocative the two of you can share. Put the plate between you and nibble. Eat with your fingers. Feed each other. Make it your goal to keep the evening lighthearted.

CASANOVA COMMANDMENT #9
Be Spontaneous

Casanova was an opportunist. He drifted from country to country, working at ludicrously diverse jobs (among them, priest and pimp). He was a disciple of the moment. Once, while sharing a carriage with a farmer's wife during a severe storm, he found her perched on his lap after a frightening thunderclap. Seizing the opportunity, he deftly rearranged her skirts.

○ Your move:

If the evening isn't going according to plan, abandon it. Be attuned to fate, and go where it directs. The confidence and daring this shows is in itself seductive.

CASANOVA COMMANDMENT #10
Surprise Her with a Gift

After supper, Casanova and his lady retired to a candlelit alcove, where he presented her with a beautiful lace nightcap. She pronounced it "magnificent." It was the final, thoughtful coup de grâce. "She told me to go undress in the next room," writes Casanova, "promising to call me as soon as she was in bed. This took but 2 minutes."

○ Your move:

Women love unexpected gifts. Make hers personal rather than trendy, small rather than large, silly rather than serious—something only she can appreciate. "Casanova's gifts showed a great deal of creativity and thoughtfulness," says Emery. Most important, time your gift's delivery for that critical point in the evening when there remains just one obvious way for her to show her gratitude.

You Casanova, you.

MAN'S GUIDE INTERVIEW

Dream Date

An Interview with Asia Carrera

So, you've always wanted to date a porn star? We're guessing you think the sex would be otherworldly. We asked adult-film superstar Asia Carrera to shed some light on this. Hers may not be such a different world after all.

Do you ever get tired of sex?

I can assure you, most of us aren't getting nearly as much nookie as the public would like to think. I shoot two or three movies a month, on average, with one or two sex scenes per movie, which equates to roughly three or four sex scenes a month. I've also been single since November 2001, and I don't sleep around outside work, so if it weren't for those three or four sex scenes a month, I wouldn't be getting *any*!

Do you think love is a prerequisite for the sex to be really great?

Depends on the person. As for me, I consider sex and love to be separate entities, and I have no problem enjoying sex for sex's sake. An orgasm is an orgasm, whether or not I have some sort of emotional commitment from my partner. But I do enjoy the comfortable familiarity that comes with making love to your significant other. It's always nice when you already know each other's likes and dislikes; you can relax and just have great sex without any of that first-time awkwardness.

What's the most pleasantly surprising thing a male costar has done for you on the set?

Anytime my partner pays me a compliment loud enough for the rest of the cast and crew to hear, that's a great feeling. Knowing that these guys get to work with all the most gorgeous girls in the business can make you a bit insecure, so it's always nice to hear that you're not quite an old has-been yet. . . .

On your Web site, you say that adult-film star Steve Hatcher does and says things that make you feel like you're at home in bed with him instead of on a set. What are some of those things?

Lots of passionate kissing, intense eye-to-eye contact, whispering of sweet nothings in my ear—all the things that make the sex feel like an intimate act, and not just a routine of going through the motions for the camera. Some guys won't kiss or even make eye contact during a scene, and it's hard for me to get into it if I suspect they're busy picturing someone (or something?) else to get the job done.

perfect figures

1234567890
1234567890

Is there anything your male costars know about women that you wish all men knew?

IT HELPS IF SHE HAS BOTH, RIGHT?

Number of guys who say intelligence in a woman is sexier than a great body: 1 in 3

Proper set etiquette dictates that the guy should find the girl on set before their first scene together, just to ask if she has any special likes or dislikes regarding sex, so there's no awkwardness once shooting begins. All guys should take a minute to ask a prospective lover about likes and dislikes before going to town. It saves a lot of embarrassing guesswork and potential mishaps, and makes for much better sex for both parties.

How do you find the energy to be in the mood for sex as much as you need to be?

Well, like I said before, I'm not getting nearly as much nookie as people think, so getting myself in the mood isn't really an issue. But on those occasions when I'm first scene up in the morning (I am *so* not a morning person), I just relax and let nature take its course. After the first orgasm, hormones always take over, and it's all fun and games after that!

Since you've directed a number of films yourself, can you offer any tips for a guy who wants to make a home movie of himself and his partner?

That's a tough one. Making a professional movie isn't the same as just shooting a girl on your own time at home. We've got paychecks and signed releases to make sure everything is on the up-and-up. A guy trying to coerce a girl into having sex on film isn't the same. I wouldn't want to be responsible for telling a guy the best ways to get a girl to agree to doing it, just in case she wakes up the next day and decides to sue his pants off.

You have had a successful career, and you have a tremendous following. How do you keep yourself interesting to people over the long term? How would that translate into keeping a relationship fresh over the long term?

Don't give it all up on the first date. Always leave some things you can do down the road, when interest starts to wane. If you come into the industry and do a monster gang bang [with] all sorts of crazy stunts on your first day, what the heck do you do for an encore? Pace yourself, or you'll get burned out very quickly.

perfect figures

THE OTHER 30 PERCENT WERE TOO DEPRESSED TO FILL OUT THE SURVEY

Percentage of men who have sex on the first date: 19

Percentage who don't get lucky until the second date: 16

Third date: 22

10th date and beyond: 13

· · · · · · · · · ·

What do you look for in a guy?

I've never been one to care much about physical appearances. I'm much more attracted to a guy who's *not* a *GQ* cover model, because I don't want other girls trying to steal my man all the time. I also like a guy who's easygoing, who never says no to me, and who is secure enough to not have a problem with my career.

For guys who think the ultimate in sex is porn, what do you have to say about relationships and real life?

Well, nothing, really. Who am I to dissuade my fans from buying the movies that pay my rent? Seriously, I get a lot of e-mail and letters from fans who are handicapped, physically and/or emotionally, and my movies provide an outlet for them that they wouldn't be able to find any other way. Sure, they know that what they see on the screen is just a fantasy, but it's an enjoyable fantasy all the same, so who am I to take that away from them?

FUMBLE-FREE FIRST DATE

She's finally sitting across from you. Now what do you say?

Be delighted to see her, even if she has kept you waiting for an hour. A simple, "Hi, great to see you," will do. Add a compliment, "Your hair looks great" or "You look fantastic," and you'll be off to a running start.

Next, start querying. The object is to glean as much about her as you can without sounding like Larry King. Start with open-ended questions like "What kind of food do you enjoy?" or "What's your dream job?" Let her do most of the talking.

Avoid concentrating on only one subject. Subtly refocus a train of thought by leaning forward and saying, "Listen, I really want to know . . . how you came to live in Pittsburgh from Montreal. . . . How you do that trick with the wine bottle. . . . What it's like to inherit $10 million."

As the evening progresses, depending on how it's going, you may want to reveal your feeling for her. "I've been thinking about you a lot recently" is enough to spike her curiosity. Clearly, if things are going so well that she's sitting on your lap, you're free and clear. Otherwise, leave her wanting more: "I really enjoyed tonight, and I'd love to see more of you. What do you think?" This promises some sort of feedback, and prompts commitment for another date.

SMOOTHER SEDUCTION

The seduction process is riddled with more hazards than the golf course at Augusta National. These seven tips will lower your handicap.

❶ Take your time.

You won't manage it in the half-hour between *SportsCenter* and *The Tonight Show*. Set aside a whole evening dedicated to the pursuit of your pleasure. Be patient, and ease into it. You've got all night.

❷ Upgrade your bed.

There's no way any self-respecting woman is going to take off her clothes and slip between stained, holey, lime-green polyester sheets. You can find 100 percent cotton sheets at almost any store these days. And the freshly laundered smell is a turn-on for many women.

❸ Warm the place up.
Goose bumps aren't sexy. Period.
❹ Forget clever lines.
They never work. At any time.
❺ Lights, music, action.
Dim the lights. Put on some soft, sexy music—try Al Green or Diana Krall—and pour a couple of glasses of chilled sauvignon blanc.
❻ Kiss to be clever.
Women love kissing. Make sure you do a lot of it. And don't send your tongue halfway down her throat. Try soft, gentle kisses all over her face.
❼ Contraception.
Have a condom handy. This shows respect for her safety as well as yours.

10 TURN-OFFS WORTH AVOIDING

Since it can take ages to get that new object of your desire in the mood, it seems a shame to blow all the hard work with a schoolboy error. We commissioned some detailed research (okay, we spoke to the women we know) and drew up a list of 10 things you must never, ever do when sex with a new partner is on the agenda.
❶ Don't talk dirty.
It'll give the whole situation the intimacy of telephone sex.
❷ Or ask her to talk dirty.
Ditto.
❸ Don't spend ages in the bathroom.
She'll either get paranoid about her own cleanliness or fall asleep.
❹ Don't wear themed boxer shorts.
They're just stupid, okay?
❺ Don't say or do anything you've seen in a film.
Film sex is cliché ridden, which you can forgive only if the scene is beautifully shot and the actors are gorgeous.
❻ Don't mention sex with someone else.
Ever. Even if you mean to compare your current lover favorably, the instant you mention another woman, a ghost starts to hover above the bed. Your real-live woman will be too preoccupied to enjoy herself.
❼ Don't put obvious music on the stereo.
Ambience is good, and soft music is nice, but really obvious stuff prefaced by "This always gets me in the mood" will make her feel that the girl is interchangeable just so long as the CD is right.

❽ **Don't use props.**

Handing her a pair of fishnets and stilettos with a husky, "Would you mind slipping these on?" is a no-no—even if they fit her.

❾ **Don't watch TV.**

❿ **Don't shout.**

Particularly another woman's name, "Score!" or "Mommy."

CONDOM COURTESY

If you're in bed with a woman, you've probably made a decent first impression. (Please, tell us she's not passed out.) But according to an experiment done at Arizona State University, you can improve your already high standing by doing some condom play-by-play. Women watched videotaped scenarios of a man and woman starting to have sex, then they rated the man's maturity in each scenario. They considered the man more mature when he told his partner he was going to put on a condom than when he just let the ripping foil do the talking. A word of introduction reassures her that you're confident enough to be cool about contraception—and that you didn't just take duct tape out of the bedside table.

THE FUNNY PAGE

UNDERSTAND HER

Understanding a woman is like understanding a car. You won't go far if you pay attention only to her chassis. You also have to appreciate the complex machinery of her heart and mind. How does this translate to great sex? Get to know her likes and dislikes, learn to read her moods, and celebrate the differences that make her more than an estrogen-charged version of you. Understand that she's the best thing that's ever happened to you, and she'll take you on the ride of your life. It's that simple.

THE GUY LIST

30 Things
She Wishes You Knew

Lisa Jones reveals some universal truths that all men should—but don't—understand

1 Saying 'I love you' immediately before, during, or following sex doesn't count.

2 I will leave if you lie.

3 I love it when you hug me from behind and whisper in my ear.

4 "Fine" is never an appropriate response when I ask you how I look.

5 Most of the time when I fantasize, it's about you.

6 I get turned on simply seeing that I have an e-mail from you.

7 I expect you to call me.

8 I'm more forgiving of you than I really should be.

9 Oral sex is your get-out-of-the-doghouse-free card.

10 You did something bad. I seem cool with it. I'm not. (See directly above.)

11 Shoes determine whether you're fashionable or not.

12 You should never tell me what to do.

13 If I slept over, you owe me breakfast.

14 I'm very impressed when you ask for my advice.

15 I'm unimpressed with a man who doesn't take the lead.

16 I'm in heaven when you hold my hand.

17 You're sexy when you're shaving, fixing things, wearing a white T-shirt and jeans, driving, eating a peach, holding a baby.

18 I need to hear how you feel about me. Often. Tell me now.

19 Surprises, especially gifts for me = more loving.

20 I want to be the best thing that ever happened to you— and for you to recognize this.

21 If I'm not feeling loved, I will start looking. . . .

22 Discussion of exes (yours and mine) should be avoided at all times.

23 Celebrating our anniversary, even if it's been only a few months, earns major bonus points.

24 I love it when you're sweaty.

25 I like porn.

26 Even nice girls like hushed dirty talk in public.

27 It's cheating as soon as you're doing something with her that you wouldn't want me to see, hear, read. . . .

28 For the record: I'd rather you break up with me than cheat.

29 I remember everything about our relationship.

30 You should know all this and more without my telling you.

ASK THE GIRL NEXT DOOR

The honest truth about women from our lovely neighbor

Q: *What do women do with all those products in the shower and bathroom anyway?*
—J. C., COMPTON, CALIFORNIA

A: Oh, nothing. We all wake up every day with clean, shiny, perfectly sculpted hair (so why would we need shampoo, conditioner, or dozens of tubes and bottles of styling products to achieve different looks?); silky smooth skin (no point in owning a half-dozen exfoliating shower gels and moisturizers made specifically for different parts of our bodies and seasons of the year); ruby-red lips, movie-star eyelashes, and glowing pink cheeks (which could be faked via drawers, baskets, and shelves full of lipsticks, blushes, powders, mascaras, and eyelash curlers); and wrists and necks that smell naturally like fields of daisies or exotic Asian spices (making expensive perfumes or scented lotions redundant). Yeah, so all those products? They're just for show!

Q: *My wife says she doesn't mind when I go out with my friends a lot—but when I do, she clearly doesn't like it. What gives?*
—N. D., TUCSON

A: If she says something is okay and then gets upset about it later, she was never really okay with it to start. The reason why women pretend to be chill in the first place is because we honestly want to be. Unfortunately, once you've done whatever we said okay to, our emotions take over. Are you following me? Anyway, get to the bottom of exactly why your wife is sending you mixed signals. Ask her what exactly it is that bothers her about your going out with your friends so much. (Does she feel left out? Insecure? Afraid you'd rather be with them than her?) It's probably not going to be a fun conversation, but hashing things out is the only way to get her to chill for real.

Q: *Why do women like to talk on the phone with each other so much?*
—Z. B., BALTIMORE

A: Chatting with our friends is a quick, cheap, legal high with long-lasting feel-good effects and zero risk of withdrawal. A couple of common scenarios: (1) I just ate a football-size cheese burrito and the guilt is killing me. Calling a bud and hearing about her Ben & Jerry's binge cheers me right up. (2) My self-confidence is deflated because the guy I'm dating didn't call when he said he would. I phone my sister, she convinces me that he's insane if he isn't itching to talk to a brainy babe like me, and suddenly my ego is like the Goodyear Blimp. Girl-to-girl gossip sessions never fail to make us feel comforted, understood, and supported. So why not have them 10 times a day?

Q: *Why do you cry when we break up—even when it's your idea?*
—A. M., MARION, OHIO

A: Because breakups are sad, and female emotions don't always make sense. When we start dating someone, we secretly hope he'll be The One. So when another relationship gets kicked to the curb, we can't help but feel heartbroken. We've just been sent back to Go, and it sucks. Even though things haven't worked out, that doesn't mean we want to forget all the good things. We'll never wake up in your apartment again. Your friends will no longer be our friends. That thing you do that drives us crazy in the sack—what if no other guy knows how to do that? We may have decided to give you up, but we don't want to lose all of you. Irrational? Yes. But true.

Q: *Why do women go to the bathroom in groups?*
—F. Z., PHILADELPHIA

A: It's fun. Going to the loo with a girlfriend transforms a chore into a mini bonding session. We tell each other how cute we look, bitch a little, confess that we hope we get some action that night, or whatever. It's also a great way to let a new female acquaintance know that we're a girl's girl, not some vixen who's going to move in on her boyfriend the minute she leaves the room.

Q: *Do women who wear tight, revealing clothing want us to look?*
—B. S., Chicago

A: A pushup bra doesn't put itself on. And only the dimmest woman is unaware that a super-miniskirt transforms her bod into a magnet for male eyeballs. If she didn't want attention, trust me, she wouldn't let it all hang out. I've had friends admit that when they walk by construction sites in "hot" outfits and don't hear catcalls, they're disappointed. And I'd be lying if I said I don't take pleasure in receiving a furtive glance from time to time. That said, close-fitting clothes are in style. If a woman seems truly surprised that you're checking her out, she may not have thought of her outfit as suggestive. But if she stands out like Pamela Anderson in a room full of Jodie Fosters and acts shocked that men are drooling, she's simply full of it.

Q: *Every time I'm with a new woman, she asks how many women I've slept with in the past. Does she really need (or want) to know? I feel that any number is the wrong number.*
—E. E., Burbank, California

A: Here's something you may not realize: Women who have slept with more than a dozen or so men seldom, if ever, ask that question. They don't ask it because they don't want to answer it. So if your girl is crunching numbers, hers is probably low. Refusing to answer will only make you look like the gigolo Little Miss Goody Two-Shoes fears you may be. Be truthful, but realize a high number might freak her out. I think the magic she'll-be-okay-with-it number is 10. That covers four or five serious girlfriends, plus a one-night stand, one friend you fooled around with, one vacation fling, one older woman, and one wild card. If your answer is much closer to 20, blow off the question with a joke, like "Do vegetables count? What about pets?" or "Well, there's you, your mom, my kindergarten teacher. . . ."

For more honest answers about women, look for
Ask the *Men's Health* Girl Next Door
wherever books are sold.

MUST READS

Animal Magnetism

Romance isn't a wild game of chance; it's a science. Greg Gutfeld teaches your chemistry class.

The dating scene can be murder. Consider the plight of the male antechinus, a tiny shrewlike marsupial that inhabits the forests of Australia. During his one and only mating season, he must scamper around feverishly, desperately seeking a willing female who'll concede him his single chance to propagate. So overwhelmed is he by the urge to merge that this sad little rodent may go bald, lose his teeth, develop ulcers, and drop one-third of his body weight in the effort to find a date. By the end of the first week of mating season, the forest floor is strewn with scrawny, hairless, toothless corpses.

Not all of these marsupials end up in such a pathetic state. Some actually do find mates, settle down, have a family, invest in slow-growth mutual funds. But these are the lucky ones, the chosen ones, the ones who have what it takes to strike a female antechinus's fancy. Which makes us wonder: What is it, exactly, that makes one tiny, hairless rodent more appealing than the next?

Better yet, what makes one red-blooded American *man* more appealing than the next? After all, we're animals, too—not tiny, no, but increasingly hairless—driven by the same instincts and participating in our own elaborate mating rituals. And when it comes to mating, some of us have our virtual pick of the litter while others struggle endlessly to find a partner. Why is that?

The answer lies in the nature of attraction. In humans, as in shrews, females are biologically programmed to desire certain things in males, and vice versa. "We don't attract women by chance, but rather, women act on cues to certain desirable characteristics," says University of Michigan psychology professor David M. Buss, Ph.D., author of *The Evolution of Desire*. And that's not because of what society tells women; it's because of what evolution tells them. "The rules of attraction cut across all cultures," says Rutgers University anthropologist Helen E. Fisher, Ph.D., author of *Anatomy of Love*. "Women find certain traits more desirable than others, frankly, because these traits enhance their survival."

What all females, forest-dwelling or condo-owning, seek on a purely instinctive level is status, the one factor that signals that this is the guy they want. In the wild kingdom, status can take any number of forms: the amount of food in a male red-winged blackbird's territory, the protein-rich secretions offered by a male insect, or the fullness of some male deer's antlers. For humans, it's

Get a Good Look

You know the hallmarks of feminine beauty. But what physical characteristics do women want in men? And more important, how can you acquire them?

You don't have to be a male model to appeal to a woman. Females look for visual cues that represent you as a viable mate. Display one or two of these traits and chances are you'll have her attention long enough to impress her with that great joke about the bartender and the Shetland pony.

Take the lean approach.

Studies find that women much prefer a lean build to a heavily muscular one. The reason is strictly evolutionary. "Immense guys aren't attractive to women because it signals an odd, endocrinological over-production of testosterone," says *The Evolution of Desire* author David M. Buss, Ph.D. And in ancestral times, mammoth muscles were a burden. "A bulky guy couldn't hunt, and often the best hunters were small and lean."

Dress like you're a success.

When researchers showed women pho-tographs of one particular man either dressed for a shift at Burger King or wearing a white dress shirt, a designer tie, and a navy blazer and Rolex watch, the women rated the nicely dressed ver-sion much more appealing. No surprise here, except for this: Although the women said they were unwilling to date, have sex with, or marry the man in the fast-food garb, they were willing to con-sider all of the above with the better dresser. (And remember, it was the same guy.) Talk about a power suit.

To attract women, your clothes should be high quality, clean, and loose. While a woman in a tight mini sends your hormones moshing, women might gag if it's you in the spandex jumpsuit. They judge men in tight-fitting and revealing clothes unfit for dating because such outfits convey a single-minded interest in sex.

Make eye contact.

Considering that Clark Kent gets Lois Lane hot and bothered only when he re-moves his spectacles, why not follow suit? (Just hold off on the cape.) While studies do show that men in glasses are considered smarter and more sensitive, it's also been shown that most women find bespectacled men less physically appealing. Researchers believe glasses interfere with direct eye contact, a key in attraction.

no different. "It's the hallmark of the human animal—that women pick partners who are going to be good providers—and status is a cue to power, protection, and resources," says Fisher. Volumes of research clearly show that high-status men get more women than low-status men.

But what *is* status, and what marks one man as having it and another as falling short? It's money and power, yes, but it's a lot of other things, too. While having piles of cash and sleek wheels can be impressive, it cannot explain why Joe Schlump in accounting has such a drop-dead beauty queen for a wife when his paltry paycheck and 1975 Pacer aren't exactly big turn-ons. His status may lie not in his looks or trappings but rather in his dependability, his trustworthiness, or his potential to be a good father. These are also signs of status—and they mean a lot more to some women than BMWs and indoor swimming pools.

So perhaps you're a little jealous and you'd like to know what she sees in him. By making subtle, deliberate changes, you can increase your "mate value," the measure by which women subconsciously judge your attractiveness.

◉ Ambition

Ambition is a powerful magnet, not because it signifies status but because it signifies future status. If you don't strive—or at least appear to strive—for something better than you have, your appeal wanes. That's because women are attracted not simply to the resources wealth offers but to the drive that pushes a man to seek wealth in the first place.

◉ Strike a balance.

According to evolutionary psychologists, women are attracted to symmetrical faces (meaning faces in which both sides match perfectly) because this balance indicates a resistance against parasitic infections and other illnesses. The theory is that a history of diseases leaves lopsidedness as its calling card. "Symmetry, in a way, functions as a health certificate in the mating game," says Randy Thornhill, Ph.D., of the University of New Mexico.

Now, while you could invest in some rather complicated plastic surgery to fix facial imbalances, there are cheaper things you can do. Pay extra attention to keeping your sideburns even and your eyebrows even. And if your features are more prominent on, say, the right side of your face (a nose that leans to the right, for example), try parting your hair on the right to add weight to your weaker left side.

When women are asked to list the most desirable traits in a potential mate, ambition and industriousness are rated as indispensable. "Women developed desires for men who show a talent for gaining resources, and a disdain for men who lack ambition," says Buss. In prehistoric times, an ambitious, resourceful man was the one most likely to bring home an elk to feed the family and figure out a way to use the antlers to beat back intruders. If you show the desire to expand your wealth and influence (even if you don't happen to have any right now), you send out the signal that you're desirable. So keep looking for new responsibilities, new challenges; a little button-down derring-do can do wonders for your appeal.

● Balance

While you're out there trying to change your little slice of the world, remember to take some time to relax and enjoy yourself. Women look for balance, and any kind of overindulgence, good or bad, makes them nervous. "If you meet a woman and you give evidence you're a workaholic, that tells her you may not be around to help with the kids and invest in the relationship," says Buss. The same goes for your drinking, your exercising, your football watching: If you eat, drink, and breathe sports, you're not going to score. All things in moderation.

● Modesty

Like a peacock displaying his superior plumage to potential mates, a man who is sure of himself and shows it in his actions has higher success in finding a partner. But self-confidence must be legitimate to have any pull. "Women are quite good at distinguishing false bravado from real self-confidence," says Buss. Exaggerating your power, sexual adeptness, or athletic prowess, which are acts of an amateur, will only signify your lack of status. Even the peacock can run into trouble, as his ostentatious display often attracts predators as well as sex partners.

● Talent

Boast not with words but with actions. Learn a unique talent that sets you apart from other men. By displaying that talent—whether it's playing the piano at a party, building a birdhouse, or performing a few magic tricks (heck, once upon a time that helped David Copperfield snag Claudia Schiffer), you'll come off as a supremely confident guy who's head and shoulders above the competition. "And you garner attention, a potent status cue," says Buss. "Plus, showing off your competence signals a take-charge kind of leadership, which is a cue to status."

● Sensitivity, not simpering

A little vulnerability now and then may actually enhance your desirability and status. In one study, women looked at a set of responses to questions answered

either from a masculine point of view or an "androgynous" viewpoint—
meaning a mix of both feminine and masculine traits. The women rated the
androgynous male as more favorable in terms of intelligence, morality, and
dating and mating potential.

But here men have to walk a fine line. "As the feminine side grew, sexual attractiveness declined," says study author
Robert Cramer, Ph.D., psychology professor at California State University, San
Bernardino. That's because, for all the talk
of making men more sensitive, the truth is
that "women admire men who have firm
beliefs, take control in financial or career
decisions, and protect them when they feel
threatened," says Cramer. The key is to exhibit emotional sensitivity without ex-
hibiting helplessness.

IF HE'S WILLING
TO RE-DO THE WILL

Percentage of women
who find grey hair sexy:
90

Do admit when you're wrong or ask
for directions when you're lost; feel free to
tear up a little during a Meg Ryan movie;
express when you're feeling hurt or sad; show some emotional fortitude when
bad times hit.

Don't act helpless to get out of doing something you don't want to do; get
defensive when you're in the wrong; chicken out after you've made a commitment; brood, sulk, or play hurt to get what you want.

● A cool demeanor

While a quick temper can create an aura of dark sexuality, à la James Dean, in
the real world, it suggests you're as stable as a trailer park during a tornado. In
fact, stability raises your status as a dependable person. "Moodiness signals to
women an inability to handle stress, and that you're undependable," says Buss.
"Being emotionally stable, though, suggests resiliency, an ability to cope with
stress and setbacks." Your best bet is to find a good stress-reduction technique—exercise, for example—that will keep you from blowing your lid at the
slightest provocation.

● A little jealousy

So you're out with a woman so unbelievably beautiful she's causing a parade
of fender benders. You feel uncomfortable and a little overprotective. That's
good. "Women interpret jealousy as a cue that you're as invested in the relationship as they are," says Buss. But don't let your jealousy get the best of you.

Low Ways to Win a Woman

To attract the fairer sex, it helps to be a little unfair. Here are some tactics you never heard from us.

● Be a night owl.

If you're going to a bar, show up late and stay until last call. As the night wears on, magically, you get better looking. In a study of singles-bar patrons, as closing time neared, women's judgments of men's attractiveness increased, and vice versa—even after controlling for the effect of alcohol. The explanation: a psychological mechanism sensitive to shrinking opportunities. As the mating pool thins, what's left looks better and better. Of course, the next morning things may look different.

● Compliment the competition.

Let's say you and Maurice have eyes for Tina. Your first impulse might be to try to convince Tina what a huge dope Maurice is. But doing that could send Tina a cue that Maurice must be worthy of competition, since you have to bash him. Instead, pay Maurice a compliment. A backhanded one. It's a subtle way to demonstrate his inferior status, says *The Evolution of Desire* author David M. Buss, Ph.D.

Compliment	What It Means
"That Maurice, what a nice guy, a real teddy bear."	He's a wimp.
"I really admire how Maurice is happy where he's at, not making a lot of money."	He's going nowhere.
"Maurice is such a great guy. I guess that's why he has women crawling all over him."	He's a womanizer.
"Maurice is a great worker. He does everything I ask him."	He's a real wimp.
"I respect how Maurice seems to be unconcerned with appearances."	He's a slob.

● Get a fake date.

If you have a great-looking female friend, by all means show her off. "There are few things more attractive to a woman than the fact that other women are attracted to you," says Buss. In a study, when people were asked to judge men based on photographs of them with "spouses" of differing attractiveness, unattractive men paired with good-looking women were routinely rated most favorably in terms of status.

● Analyze her romance quotient.

One study suggests that a gaze, when aimed at the right woman, can do wonders. Researchers found that highly romantic women are vulnerable to long, thoughtful gazes.

"Too much jealousy signals lower mate value and status on your part," says Buss. Getting angry at the slightest glances from other men signals to the woman that you think she is out of your league and could find someone better. Chances are she probably will.

Unromantic lasses, though, don't budge. So the key is to measure a woman's romantic quotient quickly.

Early on, bring up a recent romantic flick. Then broaden the topic to love in general. Ask her about her definition of love, whether or not love conquers all, or if love at first sight really exists. (Researchers used these questions to define romantic.) If her answers drip like a Harlequin romance, let the gazing begin. If she comes off cold, tell her how much you hated *Sleepless in Seattle*.

● Steal someone else's.

Buss calls this tactic poaching. "It's an effective strategy frequently reported by men to get women," says Buss. Here's an example.

Make friends with that nice young couple downstairs. You know, the guy in the horn-rims and the college sweatshirt, and the girl who looks like Naomi Watts. Get to know the guy first, gaining his trust by lending him your copy of the swimsuit issue. Soon, he'll have you over for a beer.

There you'll meet her. Be a gentleman. Talk about art. Music. Emphasize how much you want an end to world hunger. Gain her confidence. Listen to her problems. Bring up issues she rarely talks to her guy about. Then keep your eyes and ears open for any rift to appear. When it does—and it will—approach her, not him. Be understanding, because at this point that's what her boyfriend isn't. (Why else would they be fighting?) She'll think the world of you. And you can take it from there.

● If all else fails, move.

Consider Washington, D.C., an option. In cities such as our nation's capital, where women far outnumber eligible men, women will often shift to casual sexual encounters to compete for partners.

Or take Sweden, for example. Because the Swedes provide day care for children, long paid maternity leaves, and many other benefits, women are less financially dependent upon men. With less incentive to marry, maintaining one's virtue prior to marriage becomes less important. Women, thus, are less choosy about their sex partners. And we didn't even mention the meatballs!

❂ Subtlety

"Often, men erroneously think that because they welcome overtly sexual advances, women do, too," says Buss. But one study found that while women might think it's just fine for them to seductively suck on a straw or blow kisses to attract men, they find similar come-ons by men repulsive. "Even if a woman wants a one-night stand, suggesting you want the same is a big mistake," says Buss. That's because coming on like a satyr undermines your status and presents you as untrustworthy and unreliable. In fact, the criteria women use to judge men for a night of casual sex (being self-confident, funny, ambitious) aren't all that different from the standards they use when scoping a permanent mate. Even if all she has on her mind is a quick one, she'd like to think you're interested in much more.

By the way, in almost every scenario, the rule of thumb is, take it slow. Even if you're sure she's interested, let the game play out a little more. Your relaxed patience suggests higher status by convincing her you're neither desperate nor interested solely in a roll in the hay.

❂ Humor

Women love comedians. They love comedy clubs. They love Jerry Seinfeld, and he's no looker by any means. There's a good reason why a sense of humor is rated as a highly desirable trait in studies of attraction. "Beyond displaying a playful, easygoing attitude, a sense of humor conveys a social presence, which translates into high status," says Buss. Being funny in front of others (as opposed to doing it alone in front of a mirror) shows the confidence to command the attention of a group. That confidence suggests you're on top of things without being uptight. And that relaxed self-assurance is usually a by-product of attaining high status.

Now, some guys are funny and some guys aren't. If you're one of those men who can't tell a joke to save his life, fine. At least learn to laugh at yourself and see the humor in a variety of circumstances. Men who never smile are equated with social ineptitude and lower status.

❂ Compassion for children

Why do politicians kiss babies? "To raise their appeal and get attention from women," says Buss. Displaying affection toward children sends a powerful status cue women will respond to in a big way: that you'll be a great dad. Psychologists refer to this as showing high potential for "parental investment." In one study, for example, women were shown slides of one man in three different situations: standing alone, being nice to a baby, and ignoring a distressed infant. Women reported being most attracted to the fatherly type. So even if you consider children to be little more than glorified rodents, pretend you think they're really neat.

"Even a woman uninterested in having kids will notice whether a man is caring toward children, because it suggests whether he is a caring person in general," says Fisher. "And that signifies whether he is willing to provide resources for her in the future."

❍ A small degree of fame

A sure way to attract women is to be become famous. "Fame converts to status, and status converts to resources," says Fisher. Since you may not ever get the chance to guest on *Charlie Rose* or save earth from a crashing meteor, better to cultivate a little fame locally. "It's really in your neighborhood where fame counts," says Fisher. "It's there that you'll meet women and hope to impress them." That means becoming involved in local charities and politics, and keeping a somewhat high profile in social circles. You'll meet more people and be seen by more people, which will add to your prestige. And don't worry if your fame-attained status never gets beyond the city limits. "Status doesn't travel very well, anyway," says Fisher. "You can be an extremely high-status Tongan, but go to New York and see where that will get you."

Easy Answers
to Her Trickiest Questions

She asked you a question. You think it had something to do with shoes. So how did you end up sleeping on the couch? Our guy Tim Dowling tells you what to say the next time she asks.

It is Saturday, a crisp spring afternoon, and you're exactly where you should be: stretched out on the couch in front of a televised sporting event, opening beer number two, relaxed in the knowledge that the pizza you ordered is even now on its way. Nothing could improve this moment, except maybe a bigger television. Suddenly, your girlfriend enters the room and asks, "What exactly do you think you're doing?"

Is this a trick question or what?

Yes, it is. The trick is that no matter how you answer it, you will immediately find yourself driving to the nearest home-improvement center, where you will spend the rest of the afternoon trying to decide the type of curtain rod that's right for you.

How does this happen?

It has as much to do with the nature of the question itself as with anything else. Women are expert at posing questions that seem to have no right answer. Here's a common example.

"Do I Look Fat?"

There is no answer to this question that won't be interpreted as "yes." *No* means "Yes." *Yes* means "Yes." *I don't know* means "Yes." *It doesn't matter* means "Yes." The briefest hint of a pause before speaking means "Yes, yes, yes." Most of us would rather take the SATs again than field this one, yet it may well come up several times a week. Your only real choice is to say no, clearly and immediately, leaving no possibility for any subtext, and making it sound like a widely acknowledged fact and not simply your opinion. This doesn't work, but all the other options are worse.

There are several other questions for which no is the only answer, and several more that call for an emphatic and unqualified yes. In all of these cases, elaboration, justification, or any attempt to be funny is unlikely to pay off. Consult this handy chart.

Just Say No	Just Say Yes
"Is there someone else?"	"Do you still love me?"
"Do you still fantasize about her?"	"Do you ever fantasize about me?"
"Are you tired of me?"	"Do you like my hair this way?"

Unfortunately, many female inquiries require more than a simple yes-or-no response. Some of them are more like riddles. Such as this one:

"Which Shoes Look Better?"

Typically, you're already late for dinner when your girlfriend confronts you with one pair of shoes on and another alongside them. This is no ordinary choice. It's a devious chicken/egg puzzler. If you pick the shoes she already has on, she'll think you're trying to hurry her. If you pick the other pair, she'll think it's because you know you can't pick the ones she has on. Some men try a nonlinear approach and opt for a third, unoffered pair of shoes, but this is inevitably taken as either an attack on her judgment or an opportunity for her to attack yours. On no account suggest another dress. You may as well say, "You're fat."

This raises the question of why she's asking you at all. She knows you don't know which shoes look better, and she knows you don't care, so why is she trying to elicit your opinion? This is part of an ongoing campaign to domesticate you. As part of the same campaign, she will occasionally consult you about alternative table settings or new towels. In these two cases, a disdainful and dismissive "Beats me" should do the trick. Don't try that with the shoe dilemma, or you'll miss your reservation. Instead, suggest that she try on the other shoes, then tell her the first ones look better. This lets you more or less off the hook, as long as you don't raise a fuss when she decides that the second pair is better after all.

"Where Do You See This Relationship Going?"

This could be described as an essay question, since you're obviously not going to get away with snappy little answers such as *Forward* or *Upstairs* or *I dunno*. Another problem is that you and your girlfriend are operating at cross-purposes here. She wants a heartfelt expression of your feelings and an honest assessment of your future together, and you want an easier question. There is certainly no point in answering a toe-curling query like this one without at least a rough idea of precisely what it is she wants to hear. Questions such as this one are a category unto themselves, that being, questions that should be answered with another question. See how easily some of the more difficult leading inquiries can be parried through the simple deployment of reflexive interrogation.

> HER: *Where do you see this relationship going?*
> YOU: *Where do you see this relationship going?*
> HER: *Do you think she's attractive?*
> YOU: *Who?*
> HER: *Will you marry me?*
> YOU: *Where am I?*
> HER: *What if I were pregnant?*
> YOU: *Are you pregnant?*
> HER: *Why? Do I look fat?*

Whoops! You're in a bit of trouble here. You should have seen that coming. Try a more surreal approach:

> HER: *What if I were pregnant?*
> YOU: *What if I were pregnant?*

At the very least, this gives you time to think up a better answer. Some all-purpose question-answers include: *How much is a lot? Why do you ask? Should I be? What are you saying? Does it matter? What's love got to do with it? Are you talking to me?* (Note: *Are you having your period?* is not one of these.)

Let's try a math question.

"How Many People Have You Slept With?"

Hmmmmm. . . . Now, you can tell her the truth, unless the truth is more than 10, or you can have a guess at the number she's more or less expecting. Like most arithmetic problems, the answer is a lot easier once you have a formula. This one should work as long as neither of you has sex for a living: number of people she's slept with + number of people she knows you've slept with + number of people you actually have slept with. Add these up and divide by 2. If you round up to the nearest whole person, you should end up with a realistically healthy but not particularly shocking number. If the result is greater than 10, say 10. Let's move on.

"Why Don't You Lighten Up?"

This rhetorical gem is used whenever you express your disapproval of shoplifting or speeding, or whenever you go to a nightclub and spend the whole time complaining because the music is too loud and there aren't any chairs.

There's no good answer to this one. You could draw attention to her inconsistency in this matter, noting that she doesn't like it when you act like a kid or when you act like your dad; then again, if you do that, she's liable to see your point and break up with you.

Speaking of breaking up, how about this one?

"Are You Saying You Want to End It?"

Women, like lawyers, rarely ask a direct question, unless they already know what the answer will be. As for women lawyers, I don't know what they do, and I'm pretty sure I don't want to know.

The point is, when a woman asks you this question, she knows you're going to say no. Even if you want to say yes, you'll say no. You can't turn the question back on her, because you have no idea what her answer is going to be.

If you are trying to break up with her, you have to say no and start the whole painful process again. If you aren't trying to break up with her, it's best to change the subject. Let's try something easier.

"Notice Anything Different about Me?"

Well, slightly easier. This question is of a piece with two others: "Have you forgotten what today is?" and "Have you been listening to a word I've said?" Apart from being questions that are easier to answer wrong than right, they're the kinds of things women say in sitcoms. They are best treated in an ironic postmodern context—that is, just say what Ward Cleaver would say.

> HER: *Notice anything different about me?*
> YOU: *New apron?*
> HER: *Have you forgotten what today is?*
> YOU: *Of course not. It's Thursday.*
> HER: *Have you been listening to a word I've said?*
> YOU: *That's nice, dear. . . .*

Funny, huh? Well, it's not your fault if she doesn't get it. If she wants a better answer, she's going to have to start asking better questions. Questions such as:

"Have You Taken a Look at Yourself Lately?"

This question and its cousin, the almost always uncalled for "Who do you think you are?" are ways of gently reminding you how much of a factor pity was in her original decision to go out with you, and how that decision could be rescinded if you behave in any way that cannot be described as abject.

You probably brought this rebuke on yourself by mentioning that you reckon Brad Pitt is getting a little chubby or by speculating that Jack Nicholson doesn't have to wait until *his* birthday for oral sex. You're not really supposed to answer either of these questions. You're just supposed to apologize for your wanton self-esteem-having. Instead of apologizing, just smile. Your manifold inadequacies as a boyfriend—nay, as a man—are a kind of revenge all by themselves. Next!

"Do You Believe in Fidelity?"

Like most philosophical questions that seem to pop up out of the blue, this question doesn't pop up out of the blue. This general query about fidelity is in fact a coded inquiry about the extent of your fidelity on a specific occasion or occasions. Your response will also have to be coded. Consult this translation chart before giving your answer.

You Say	You Mean	She Thinks
"Yes."	"How much does she know?"	"He's hiding something."
"It depends."	"How much does she know?"	"I knew it!"
"Why do you ask?"	"How much does she know?"	"Bastard!"
"I dunno. Do you?"	"How much does she know?"	"How much does he know?"

There are several more variations, but they're not worth going into. By the time she asks you this question, you're already in deep trouble. It doesn't really matter what you say, as long as you don't blush when you answer.

Let's look at an example that calls for more straightforward lying.

"What Are You Looking At?"

She means, "You were looking at that girl, weren't you?" And you thought you'd perfected that trick of keeping your neck still and just letting your eyes swivel.

Obviously, the truth is not the best answer here. We all know that the truth can set you free, sometimes before you've found somewhere else to stay. It may seem easy enough to answer this question with a cunning lie, but when men are caught off-guard, their ability to deceive is impaired.

Here are a few of the more common mistakes men make when asked, "What are you looking at?"

○ Too specific
"The rust around the bolts on the handle on the flap of that mailbox on the northwest corner."

○ Not specific enough
"That thing."

○ Too good to be true
"A diamond necklace in that window back there that would be perfect on you."

○ Too true to be good
"A see-through nightie in that window back there that would be perfect on you."

○ Too obvious
"Nothing."

○ Way too obvious
"That blonde babe over there with the big . . . I mean, nothing."

Here's one that requires a little interpretation.

"What Are We Going to Do Now?"

This one crops up whenever some kind of emergency or seemingly unsolvable problem arises. The part that requires interpretation is the mysterious *we* in the middle.

It means two things: In one sense, *we* clearly means "you," as in, "What are you going to do now?" But there is also a sense of "we're in this together," implying that you bear equal responsibility for the fact that she's just dropped her keys down a grate, or that she stores her jack and spare tire in her garage so they won't get stolen.

In such situations, you'll probably find that the only answer to "What are we going to do now?" that you can think of is "We are going to break up. Goodbye." Most likely, you'll decide not to say anything. After which she will probably let loose with the rather ill-advised:

"Why Don't You Say Something?"

Whether you answer this one is up to you. There is only one question that you should never, ever answer. Keep silent, cower behind your Fifth Amendment rights, pretend you didn't hear, run away, whatever, but don't say anything when she asks:

"Should I Get All My Hair Cut Off?"

If you say anything, when she does get all her hair cut off (and let's face it, she's already made up her mind) and she hates it (and she will hate it), it will be your fault. Even if you say absolutely nothing, the best you can hope for is that she will come home with all her hair cut off, stare you straight in the eye, and say:

"Does It Make Me Look Fat?"

You're on your own.

Bedtime Stories

What does it take to get a woman into bed? We asked five sexy women to tell us what works for them.

"Treat Me Right"

EVEN MODERN WOMEN LIKE TRACY QUAN, AUTHOR OF *DIARY OF A MANHATTAN CALL GIRL: A NANCY CHAN NOVEL*, WANT A MAN WHO RESPECTS AND PROTECTS.

My first lover didn't have to seduce me. If anything, I was the predator. It was summer, during my high school years, and I had decided it was time to have sex. Though I didn't suffer the pangs of sexual hunger in any real physical sense, I had been scanning the male population constantly, assessing each guy's desirability. So when I met Peter at a party, I was ready for him. He was more muscular than my previous boyfriend, with blue eyes, square gold-rimmed glasses, and a short beard. And he was the right age—twentysomething—since I was completely disenchanted with high school boys. I had just been fired from my summer job, a stint as a file clerk in a law firm, after the office manager discovered I had lied about my age; and I regarded Peter's job in the Xerox room of the local university as a veritable power gig.

When I felt my body touch the sheets of this college guy's bed for the first time, I said in a tipsy voice, "There's something you should know: I'm still in high school, and I'm not on the Pill." I drifted off to sleep, still a virgin, feeling strangely victorious because I had managed to get myself into bed with a guy who could vote. Things grew chatty and warm as our summer romance progressed. I began to learn the things about sex that I couldn't learn from books. After a few weeks, I lost my virginity and gained a role model for my future lovers.

Back then, I could not put this into words, but what I was feeling with Peter, who resembled a more playful and less soulful version of Nicolas Cage, was much more than a young girl's infatuation with a smooth-talking older guy. It was a woman's budding erotic need to respect her male sex partner. I know it's voguish for sex to occur between peers, and some people disapprove of the unequal scenario—older guy initiates younger girl—but that's my template and I'm sticking to it. Even though 2 decades have passed since Peter, and I've had more sexual experience than some of my lovers, I'm still happiest and most comfortable in the arms of a man who can make me feel like the one who's less experienced.

Some atavistic part of me still divides the male populace into "high school boys" not quite worth my time, and guys with cool jobs. What defines a cool job, now that I've outgrown the glamour of the Xerox room? It's a career, a calling, an identity even. I don't discriminate against artists or bankers, but I do avoid the 9-to-5 Romeo who thinks real life begins when day is done and work ends. A man in love with his work is sexier. The thought that he may even put his work ahead of me makes him more, not less, bed-worthy. If a man has a talent or a diploma that I lack, I'm doubly intrigued because I can look up to him.

I am not out to prove myself the equal of a sex partner. I want a man who is confident enough to treat me like a girl—despite my strength and independence. Instinctively, my entire body relaxes more around a man who helps me through a revolving door or into a cab. Something as chivalrous and reliable as helping with my coat can be surprisingly erotic; it's a protective gesture that draws me closer. I have a weakness for boyfriends who know how to plan a date, pick a restaurant, act a bit 1950s style—despite the fact that I'm a profoundly modern woman in so many other ways.

At least one thing has changed radically, though: If I could revisit it today, my first lover's bedroom would strike me as a juvenile barracks. Then, it was a fantastic bachelor pad that I looked forward to visiting with smug anticipation. These days, I won't get naked for a man on anything smaller than a queen-size mattress. My bed is lovingly designed for comfort, equipped with a thick, fleecy mattress pad and sheets that match both mood and carpet. Any man who invites me to his own apartment reduces the likelihood of sexual intimacy. I long to feel inexperienced, but on my turf.

"Be Exotic"

WRITER PAM HOUSTON, WHO DESCRIBES HER WILDERNESS AND TRAVEL ADVENTURES IN *A LITTLE MORE ABOUT ME*, ADMITS IT'S RUGGED AND ADVENTUROUS MEN WHO WIN HER HEART.

When I was 17, a man's looks alone could do it, and my criteria were very specific. He had to be tall and lean, with hipbones so well-defined that if I stood close to him and looked down, I could see air between his stomach and the fabric of his jeans. It didn't matter whether his hair was dark or light, but it had to be long, with extra points if a big hunk of it flopped across his forehead and into deep-set eyes that had a slightly wolfish tint about them. Forearms have always been (and continue to be) important; I like the sinewy kind, with large, ropy veins. It helped—in those days—if he liked Jackson Browne, which Spider, a lifeguard I hooked up with in Wildwood, New Jersey, did.

Spider had cheekbones to die for and a 1964 Chevy Malibu that said "She's Only Rock 'n' Roll" across the back window. And even though he was a lifeguard, he told me that he sold hot dogs on the beach so I wouldn't think his ego was too big for words. The fact that I remember that detail, after all these years, means I must have been very impressed.

When I was 15, a man's best strategy was to flatter me into bed. "I can't stop looking at you. You smell like black maple trees in blossom. Your breasts are the perfect size to fit in my hand." Some flattery worked better than others. When I was 26, a man tried to tell me I was "like a doe coming out of the forest," and that didn't work even then.

When I was 30, all a man needed to make me want him was an exotic point of origin: the Okavango Delta, for instance, or Estonia. It was at that age that I fell for the old line "I don't like to think about making love to a woman, I like to think of making love with a woman." It didn't hurt that it was delivered in a thick Italian accent. His name was Gabrielle, and he was an architect from Palermo. He spoke five languages fluently and said things like "The most stable point is at the junction of many stresses." That's the kind of statement that makes me want to pull a man straight to the floor.

By the time I got to 35, I had been disappointed enough times in a row that I was better at ruling men out than ruling them in. Don't, for example, assume that because I'm a woman I don't know the difference between cross-checking and high-sticking, between runs scored and runs batted in. Don't read me all the journal entries from the time of your last breakup.

Now I find myself on the verge of 40, newly married, faced with a slightly different question: How will my husband and I find ways to get each other into bed for the long, long haul? The first time, he showed me pictures of his recent trip to Morocco (old habits die hard), climbed a eucalyptus tree in a deserted downtown Santa Barbara park, shed his clothes, and started swinging from branch to branch making noises like an orangutan, then told me an imagined story of our future courtship, which ended (in his mind) with a proposal—live on Oprah. Since then, it's been a little easier, though when I ask myself why I've agreed to go to bed with him every night for the rest of my life, I know it's because he surprises and delights me, every single day. Whether it's by hanging the laundry on the line while wearing nothing but his cowboy boots (the man likes to get naked) or by pulling me into a tango in the lobby of a grand hotel doesn't make much difference.

How will we continue to get each other into bed? Never the same way twice.

"Negotiate the Chasm"

ACCORDING TO JENNIFER WOLFF, A NEW YORK CITY–BASED JOURNALIST AND ESSAYIST, THERE ARE MEN YOU SLEEP WITH AND MEN YOU WON'T SLEEP WITH . . . AND THEN THERE'S THE MAYBE MAN.

William kissed me for the first time in Central Park. It was one of those balmy Indian summer evenings that lent a sense of infinity to the world, and safety in what might be considered an unsafe place: not just the park at midnight, but—with its two front teeth knocked out by terrorists—New York City itself.

I liked that kiss; it was soft and tender and not at all like the tsunami of tongue that most men overwhelm me with on the first go-around. My head felt comfortable resting on his chest, and I imagined that without the leather jacket it might one day make for a nice pillow on which to fall asleep.

I can count on a single glove absent most of its fingers the number of men

I've met whom I have instantly known I wanted naked next to me. I don't have to consult my calendar to know that I haven't felt that way in this millennium. This doesn't mean that in the past 3 years I haven't had sex; it means that, as during most of my life, there have been no yes's, many no's, and a few maybes who have successfully bridged the chasm between the two.

William is currently negotiating that chasm—in my kitchen, where at this very moment he is cooking me dinner. He arrived about an hour ago, his knapsack heavy with a cast-iron skillet and all the fixings for jambalaya. Whilst he double-fists my Calphalon pans, I am on my bed typing this into my laptop, swooning to the sultry scent of paprika-laced warm buttered garlic. They say the way to a man's heart is through his stomach; could it be that the way into my pants is through mine?

Hard to tell. I like William, but I'm not crazy about him. He's attractive, but he looks too much like my dad. Plus, he constantly mixes his metaphors, which to a writer can be close to criminal. However, whenever I peek into the kitchen I can't help but notice that from the side he has a really great ass, albeit popping out from an apron. Ever so slowly my defenses begin to wilt in synchronicity with the collard greens he's sautéing on my stove.

> It's Been Said . . .
>
> **"Men always want to be a woman's first love—women like to be a man's last romance."**
>
> —Oscar Wilde

Little wonder that after dinner William and I don't get through half the video I rented before our tongues start picking rice from each other's teeth. I like how he kisses but not how he touches. He grabs at me with an urgency that feels desperate and starkly impersonal. When we talked, I felt that he was talking with me. When he cooked, I felt that he was cooking for me. But when we fool around, I feel as though he could be fooling around with anybody, a body, but not my body.

I shut down. I don't want to kiss him anymore. He asks what's wrong. I don't want to say, "Nothing," but I don't know how else to explain. I certainly don't want to tell him the truth, which is that he isn't sexy enough to just have sex with and, I sadly realize, not special enough to fall in love with. So I fall silent.

His fingers continue to creep up under my shirt and along the legs of my black capri pants, but they're no longer welcome. I lightly push them away and try instead to hold his hand. I feel him getting confused, then angry. I tell him I have my period, which is true, but we both know that wouldn't make a difference if William made a difference to me.

He reaches for his coat and heads for the door. He pecks me on the cheek and hugs me, but only because I hug him first. Then he leaves.

Somehow William figured out that the chasm between maybe and yes had just widened, and that he had fallen irretrievably deep inside.

"Ask If I'm Wearing Underwear"

LISA JONES, A WRITER AND ASSISTANT EDITOR FOR *MEN'S HEALTH* MAGAZINE, SAYS IT'S THOSE AND OTHER SIMPLE QUESTIONS THAT MAKE A WOMAN TAKE IT OFF.

● January 10, 2000

It starts like this: M. is wearing a blue shirt that perfectly matches his eyes, and we're sitting in a wooden booth at a neighborhood pub drinking pints of lager. He puts a fiver in the jukebox, and we talk for hours. I must be attracted to him, because I'm talking incessantly about nothing; and I can't stop smiling or fidgeting with the saltshaker.

● 1/18/00

He amazes me with kindness. I'm showering at M.'s place, post–sledding date, as he's making dinner. He's put a towel on the radiator so it will be warm for me. I smile and shiver, standing naked in his bathroom, though I'm not at all cold.

● 2/5/00

We're in the city for the weekend, holding gloved hands and stopping on every street corner to smooch. At the museum, M. stands behind me; I can feel his heartbeat on my back and his breath on my neck. And he says, "I can't keep my hands off you."

● 2/11/00

He makes me laugh. He makes me wet with just a glance. He kisses my belly button, and he has perfect eyelashes and those divots some men have on the sides of his bum, which make me absolutely mad with want. I'm smitten-kitten— nearly anything M. does or says can get me naked, and immediately it does.

● 4/10/00

I'm pulling M. into bed as he recites the First Amendment with a deep whisper in my ear. (I can't remember why we were trying to remember the words.) He says, "Congress shall make no law. . . ." (It's much hotter than it sounds, I promise.) By "freedom of speech," I have stripped and am waiting peaceably to assemble. He trips somewhere between "respecting an establishment of religion" and "petition the government," and grabs a pocket-size Bill of Rights out of his bedside table to get the wording exact. I think he doesn't find it at all strange that the greatest protection of word and print should lie side by side with the condoms in his drawer.

◐ 9/10/00

He worships Sunday: the day. It's made for newspaper reading, love and pancake making, and pajama lounging—and he is devout. His love for simple pleasures is completely sexy, and so is he. Sundays with M. have become my favorite time.

◐ 10/29/00

He bribes me with the future. He's taking me on a road trip home to meet his family. He shows me all of his favorite old hangouts—book and coffee shops, college bars, roads he used to bike—and in my girl's mind's eye, all this is a very good sign.

◐ 6/16/01

He intoxicates me (sometimes with alcohol). We're in a cab uptown after drinking at a downtown dive. (I love how he can be at once classy and low-brow.) And he asks, "Are you wearing underwear?" I slide my black bikinis from beneath my black skirt and over my black strappy heels with a simple shimmy, tuck them into my black evening bag, and raise my eyebrows.

◐ 8/12/01

He gets away with it. We're breaking up. Suddenly I can't remember the last time we had sex, and maybe he's reading my mind. I'm wondering if he'll have the nerve to try to get me naked, and hoping he will; he's assessing whether I'm fragile or willing or both. And immediately, our mouths are meeting on the way to the bedroom.

"Read My Signals"

WOMEN ARE PRETTY EASY WHEN YOU DON'T THINK ABOUT IT, SAYS LOS ANGELES CULTURE-AND-SOCIETY WRITER SARAH MILLER.

Seducing a woman is not easy. If it were, all men would be happy; and due to the mass consumption of Zoloft, we know this is not the case. Some people will say that picking up women is an art, but it's easier than art—certainly easier than science.

First, pay attention to signals. Now, please forget almost everything you've learned about what these signals are. As the type of person you want to be picking up (unless you happen to hate smart, stacked brunettes with great teeth

and legs), I'm going to guess that my way is better and more likely to get results. By results, I mean sex, girlfriends, and, if you want, wives.

Let's say you spot me, a woman you would like to talk to, preferably at
some point unclothed. I'm standing there talking to a guy who doesn't look all
that impressive. Yet I keep talking to him, even though I seem to be eyeing you. There's no point in talking to me, because I'm talking to some guy, right?

No. Women are always talking to The Guy We Don't Want. We are terrified that if we talk to The Guy We Do Want, we'll babble about how our mother is crazy and our hair needs to be colored, and you will think, "Why am I not at home watching the Redskins and eating bratwurst?"

You don't need a line; you especially don't need one if you have to think about it. You can just introduce yourself. If I visibly stiffen and start looking around the room, you may want to make a timely and graceful exit. But if I quickly start responding, especially babbling, I'm very relieved and happy that you came over.

Once I start talking, I could be immediately charming. I could also start acting—women have a tendency to do this—weird.

Men think women make fun of them to make them feel bad. What they don't know is that this is actually a dirty little trick with not one but two goals. The first is to see if you can respond confidently and with a sense of humor. The second is just to see if you respond. If we make fun of you and we can tell that you're thinking, "Gee, this girl has an opinion about me, and I feel the need to improve it," then we know you like us.

Also, you should ask lots of questions. Chicks love talking about them-
selves. Correction: We live for it. Questions that allow me to truly reveal my personality are really good. Ask whom I like better, my mother or my father. Ask why I bought my car. Ask where I got my necklace or my cell phone. You are so interested in every thought I've ever had, it is a wonder you survived before you met me.

Now, here's the key: There is nothing wrong with revealing that you want to get into my pants, but I have to know you're interested in my pants and not just any woman's. I can tell when you're just on the prowl. I can hear it in the tone of your voice, when you start to get that game-show-host intonation that screams, "Pussy autopilot!"

The final thing all men who are good at seducing women have in common: They know how to close a deal. You can go with a simple, "Do you want to get out of here?" but only with a woman who is really flirting with you. You can also say, "Look, I want to keep talking to you, but I can't stand the noise/the smoke/another drink/that shirt you're still wearing." This (a) is flattering to her and (b) puts the ball in her court. Because the only thing better than getting a girl to say yes to going home together is getting her to ask you herself.

The Naked Power of a Nude Woman

Writer Susan Bremer's life as a scientist was humdrum and ordinary . . . until the night she discovered she could own any man alive.

Let me tell you about my life as a laser technologist. It was me and a bunch of men—and they made sure I always knew I was outnumbered. I'd spend days, weeks, months at my job at the lab dealing with the daily drain of being on the bottom, the butt of jokes, the one left out when it was time for after-work beers. As a woman trying to find success in purely masculine terms, I wasn't making it.

I'd never been low profile. In fact, for most of my life, I was pretty obvious: a striking blonde, smart and fit. Eventually, life with men robbed me of that. I was still blonde, still fit, maybe even still smart. But I was somehow defeated. I felt more than invisible. I felt completely and utterly powerless.

Then one night, at age 33, I went into a crowded club, went out on a stage in front of a roomful of men, and took off my clothes. I was way past nervous, beyond scared. I was both terrified and, strangely, resigned. But I did it. And everything changed.

I suddenly felt like the most desirable woman on earth. I was certain I could get any man to do anything I wanted. It was a rush of power, and it was exhilarating. Now, after a few years of this, I still can feel my ego swell. I drop my dress, and the whole room goes, "Ahhhh!" I feel cocky and arrogant and excited. I'm happy and elated and having fun. When there's a whole club full of people accepting and applauding just you, there is nothing like it.

I make a production of it, like I'm unwrapping something special, and this causes me to realize I am unwrapping something special: me. I don't understand the fascination with breasts and nipples, but I know it's real. And it gives me the power I need to do my job well.

It's easy for me to tell when I'm doing a good job. Most women think an erection is the true barometer of the power of a naked body. But for me, it's how quickly the money rises from a man's pants. Whether it's a guy who gives me $800 or one who spends all of what little he has, including his cab fare home, I've got him where I want him—by the wallet.

In some ways, things haven't changed much. When I'm at work, I'm still surrounded by men in coats and ties—bosses and underlings, jocks and nerds. All of them are the kinds of men who made me feel so small. Now, I can reduce the top dog to a lapdog by staring at him, opening my top, and smiling. Like the time when a guy from work stopped by a club where I was performing. He was reading a newspaper, just killing time before the next act: mine.

I was scared. For a moment, I was the lone woman at work again, and he was every man who had kept me down. But as I walked toward him, I remembered that in this office the fact that he's a man means that I'm in charge.

"Hi," I said. "I didn't know you came here."

His eyes went wide as they took in my body, breasts, and hips bursting out of my tight leather vest and skirt. Then he recognized my face. Suddenly, he wasn't one of the guys, he was one of my guys. Terrified, he dropped his paper and almost ran out the door.

It's Been Said . . .

" The greatest pleasure in life is doing what people say you cannot do. "

—Walter Bagehot

I can make a man act foolish or macho or boyish, just by dancing. If I feel sadistic, I can do what was done to me: I can ignore him. Make him invisible. Or I can choose any guy out of a group of his friends and make him a lady-killer. When that happens, I know I can take him any place I want, and he'll thank me for the ride.

A lot of things about this surprise me. For example, when I'm in this powerful role, men open up to me in ways they never do with their wives and girlfriends. The odd thing is, I find that when a man expresses himself in mawkish, maudlin ways, I actually care. In the lab, I was surrounded by men who couldn't have cared less about me. As a result, I felt the same way about them. Now I have a different job. Now I'm surrounded by men who care about me very much—even if it's only a temporary, blinding flash of desire. And now, finally, I can afford to return the favor.

Cure Her Headache

An Interview with Pepper Schwartz, Ph.D.

By definition, a long-term relationship should provide lots of long-term sex. Unfortunately, as many of us know, the road to lifelong passion is paved with headaches and other I'm-not-in-the-mood excuses. The reasons why abound. Perhaps the most fundamental? Women remain a complete mystery to men. We talked to Pepper Schwartz, Ph.D., sociologist at the University of Washington and author of Everything You Know About Love and Sex Is Wrong *and* The Great Sex Weekend. *Her insights will help keep your motors running.*

What's the biggest myth that prevents guys from enjoying lifelong passion?

The most destructive myth is that you can't keep sex fresh and interesting. If you believe it, that's the way it's going to go. It's a particularly male fear because men thrive on variety. They've dated this person and that person, and they've settled down to somebody. Then all the jokes come in: Goodbye to sex, goodbye to passion.

What's the second-biggest myth?

That you don't have to work at it. That passion is either there or it isn't. There are some particularly male myths, too, such as "If I don't get an erection as quickly as I used to, something is wrong. That's the end of passion." Men tend to believe their penises too much.

Are you saying the penis isn't such a wise guy?

It's a very fickle friend. Sometimes it's reacting to all kinds of non-sexual things, like work. Or maybe there's a mechanical problem instead of a sexual-desire problem. Trusting too much in what's really a hydraulic system as opposed to one's heart and mind is a very big problem that can get men into significant emotional trouble and, sometimes, sexual dysfunction.

**Still, when a guy has been with the same woman
for a long time, isn't it normal for passion to die down?**

The truth is, it does inevitably cool. The most typical thing is you're in a young relationship, you have kids, they start to absorb you, and you're both distracted. You have sex when the baby's sleeping or at the very end of the night. You're not really focusing and putting in the intensity that passion requires. You're just having bread-and-butter sex, which isn't terrible, but it's not what you could do for each other if you took a getaway, visited a sex store, or saw a good X-rated movie—all the fun things you haven't done for awhile because you're busy playing mommy and daddy.

**Many guys complain that their sex life was once
as rich and varied as a Beethoven symphony . . .**

But now it's more like "Chopsticks." You get efficient. Sexuality is hardly at its best when you get efficient. It doesn't do much for the soul. Yet, that's what people do. They have sex in that last half-hour of consciousness. She gives him a hand-job, he gets her close, they have two and a half minutes of thrusting, and it's over.

So how does a guy make it better?

In a good relationship, there are always embers. You can build a pretty hot fire if you turn your attention back to those little glowing coals that maybe are not a flame but could become one.

Say, "We're going to do something fabulous. I'm taking you to Paris, I'm taking you to the mountains, I'm taking you to the ocean, a cruise, whatever it takes." There are few women who aren't going to think that's one heck of a good idea.

What work can a guy do on himself to become a more passionate partner?

Stay fit. Women will say, "Honey, I love you just the way you are." But the truth is, a lot of them would like you a lot better if you were fit. Nobody is turned on by a partner who has a huge tummy or gets winded after walking up a flight of stairs. You don't have to have a six-pack. But you have to have a body that works for you.

What if *she's* the one with a huge tummy?

Get into an exercise program together. Ask her to meet you after work to run or go to the gym. Even if neither of you has lost a pound, you'll find that the shared physical activity creates a closer bond and makes you feel better. After all, you're not just trying to seduce her. You're trying to seduce yourself. You have to feel like a physical being.

How much of that has to do with attitude?

There are men who carry themselves like they're sexy beings. They look at the world and their eyes twinkle. They've got a sense of self-confidence. They think they're cool without being arrogant. That's something you can totally control with attitude. It has nothing to do with your body or handsomeness. It's like you're telling the world, "I'm a physical person. I like sex. I like myself. I'm okay in my own skin." A guy who projects that is going to be sexier.

What else can guys do to enhance their sex appeal?

Dress nicely. Get somebody to deck you out in European-looking clothes or whatever feels comfortable. Think of those skinny little cowboys who have no butts. They're wiry and thin and they look great in what they wear. Any woman who goes to a rodeo says, "Ooh. I want a piece of that." Of course, personal hygiene is huge. Lots of couples get lazy about the basics: brushing their teeth, using underarm deodorant, and washing carefully around the genitals. Men think it's manly to just jump in bed after they come back from the gym. That can get a little ripe. Ask her if your breath is okay. If she's avoiding your mouth, you might think she doesn't want you any more. But it's not that she doesn't want you. She's become averse because you aren't taking care of yourself.

So even if you've been married since the Carter Administration, you should try to court her like you're on the most eligible bachelor list?

You've got to set the stage. When guys are dating women, they'll bring them flowers. They'll take them to beautifully lit restaurants, admire how they look, ask them to wear sexy lingerie.

What are the little gestures guys can make to get the sparks flying?

Show desire. Go up to your partner, put your arms around her and say, "You're as beautiful as the day we married." If she says, "Yeah, right," say, "I still see you that way." Or just put your arms around her and say, "I'd like a little private time with you." Anything that is tender and that shows desire straight on is usually pretty arousing to a woman. If you can, precede desire with an act of thoughtfulness, like washing the dishes, putting the kids to bed, or fixing a problem with her computer.

What are the little gestures that turn you on?

God, I'm easy. He starts to give me a massage, and says, "Just lie down. I'm going to get your neck and shoulders." OK, I know where that's likely to go. But I love the fact that he's going to tend to me for a little bit. Phone sex turns me on. He calls and says, "I've been thinking about you, and here's what I'd really like to do with you when I come home." Then I'm thinking about it for the next 3 or 4 hours. In a sense, I'm providing my own warm-up.

What kind of lover really ignites a woman's passion?

Any man who thinks of fun suggestions that aren't so far out that they're weird—just far out enough to tease a woman's imagination—is the kind of lover every woman dreams about. If we get one who has any imagination, any sense of fun, any sense or delicacy—who can suggest things that aren't on the known map—we know we've got ourselves a real find.

Can you provide some examples?

Washing hair is really sexy. If it doesn't turn into sex, at least it turns into sensuality, where you wash each other's hair and you wash each other off, then cuddle and pet. Maybe you don't have intercourse, but you feel sexually close and maybe you do have intercourse. One of the sexiest scenes I ever saw—one that a lot of women thought was sexy—was in the movie *Bull Durham* where he paints her toenails. My reaction was, "Hey, let's do that scene!" It's that slow intentionality, that venturing into a woman's world. It's "Let me dress you. Let me undress you. Let's touch in front of a mirror." Anything that's got a little bit of an edge to it, but not pushy as in "I'm going to take you right now no matter what your mood is." We have to feel like we're being seduced and fondled and teased into something really great. A little bit of finesse, a little bit of sensitivity goes a long way.

Is it ever okay to seek passion outside your marriage?

If you've done everything you can to get her to be even a halfway decent sexual partner, then you have to tell her, "I've had it. I'm fed up with our sex life. We need to go to a sex therapist." If she says, "I won't do it," then you have two choices: You can either break up your marriage—and a lot of times that's not possible because there are kids or you care for her in other ways—or you can cheat. Moralists will tell you, "Don't cheat." But it would be cruel and dishonest to say that it doesn't work for some people. But you need to know what you're putting at risk.

What do couples that have successfully achieved lifelong passion have going for them?

First of all, they respect each other. You've got to really like and look up to each other. You've got to have that connection still working. In the beginning, passion can just come from the way somebody looks, smells, walks, or whatever. But over time, it also has to come from attraction to who the person is. I've seen men bored with the most gorgeous women on earth because there wasn't enough between them as people. So there's got to be something serious between you that sparks occasionally. That's part of it.

What's the other part?

The other part is they're still trying to please each other. You can see a good couple. They still look to each other. They still touch each other. They look nice when they're together. They talk about each other in nice ways. They're still relating on at least a slightly romantic basis—a connected basis. They take private time for each other. With a lot of couples, it's all kids. There are no individual vacations. There's no,

"Sorry, this is Mom and Dad's time." They don't hold hands in front of their kids. They've developed themselves into a family as opposed to a couple. Their real allegiance is to their children.

Shouldn't it be that way?

With couples that are passionate about each other, their first allegiance is to each other. That doesn't mean they're child abusers or child neglectors. But as much as they love their children, their highest connection—in terms of ordering their lives—is to each other. They still think sex. They're still conscious about their sex lives. They still think of it as something they want to do with one another. That's something you could lose if you don't treasure and take care of it.

QUICKIES

AS IF WE WEREN'T CONFUSED ENOUGH

That girl who flicked her hair when you met? She likes you. Or maybe not. Research confirms that we are clueless when it comes to reading women's minds, and it's not our fault. Tread cautiously when approaching.

- When a woman first meets a man, she sends out several sexually meaningful signals—tossing her hair, happily chatting, fiddling with her clothes—even if she doesn't find him particularly attractive, Austrian researchers found. Those cues keep him yammering while she evaluates him. After a few minutes, her true feelings start to show.

- The more attractive a guy is, the more likely he'll be the target of someone looking for a shallow, short-term fling, gosh darn it! According to a study of college students, men and women hoping for a longer-term relationship looked for honesty, social skills, and common interests.

SPY ON HER FANTASIES

Our sexual fantasies are predictable: Estella Warren and a couple of her naked friends. Maybe toss in our 10th-grade geometry teacher. That always works.

Daydreaming got us wondering: What goes on in her complex, dirty mind? So we asked women on *Glamour* magazine's Web site to rank their top three erotic sexual fantasies. Turns out a typical woman wants to be carted off to Bali and tied to a palm tree on a public beach. By her boyfriend's brother. Well, read for yourself:

Fantasy #1: Being Taken/Swept Away (Listed by 41 Percent)

- **Why**

Cultural conditioning and romance novels. "Women have been taught to be passive. They're taught that they're not supposed to initiate sex," says Massachusetts sex therapist Gina Ogden, Ph.D., author of *Women Who Love Sex*. The thinking: If she's not in control, she doesn't have to worry about doing the right thing.

O Do this

Be assertive, not aggressive, says Florida psychologist and sex therapist Wendy Fader, Ph.D. Go Fabio on her: Pick her up and playfully throw her over your shoulder.

Fantasy #2: Sex in an Exotic Location (33 Percent)

O Why

The allure of the unknown, or remembering how wild you two were that week in Cancun, says Lisa B. Schwartz, Ph.D., a psychotherapist in Pennsylvania. And it helps her forget work and the daily grind.

O Do this

Tahiti can wait. If you're in Council Bluffs, Iowa, exotic could simply mean the best hotel in Omaha.

Fantasy #3: Being Restrained (29 Percent)

O Why

Another surrender fantasy. If she's tied down—even playfully—she's no longer responsible for what happens, Ogden explains. Once she's in bondage, she may as well submit and enjoy herself.

O Do this

First, talk about it. Agree on a code word she can use to stop things if she gets creeped out. Then try neckties, yarn, even paper towels, says Chicago sex therapist Michael Seiler, Ph.D. Of course they can't hold her, but just "the psychological experience of submitting" can do the trick.

Other Big Winners

- **O Sex in a public place: 26 percent**
- **O Sex with a forbidden lover: 22 percent**
- **O Sex with a famous person: 17 percent**
- **O Sex with a total stranger: 16 percent**

"CALM DOWN?! WE CAN'T CALM DOWN!"

There's a biological reason you walk away from your wife when she confronts you about the cable bill: It's too much for your heart. The male's cardiovascular system takes longer to recover from sudden stress than the female's. For example, if you and your wife are simultaneously surprised by a loud sound, your heart will beat faster and your blood pressure will remain higher longer. Since marital confrontation or arguing evokes a similar response, we're sort of naturally programmed to avoid it. In fact, in more than 80 percent of marriages, it's the wife who has to broach difficult relationship issues.

HOPE SPRINGS ETERNAL

Next time you're convinced every woman in the place is coming on to you, do a quick review of your recent love life. If it's really quick, because there's not much to review, proceed cautiously: The ladies may not be as interested as you think. Princeton University researchers have shown that men who feel they're long overdue often perceive sexual interest where none actually exists. It seems desperation clouds your vision.

Study subjects were presented with hypothetical scenarios, and the men who rated their sex lives as wanting were most likely to think a simple smile meant impending hibbity-dibbity. (Men with satisfying sex lives saw things clearly. And women did, too, no matter what their sex lives were like.)

Our advice for the turgid man is to play it safe: Wait until she's naked and demanding condoms before you assume anything.

THE FUNNY PAGE

"Sometimes a lick on the ear is just a lick on the ear—it doesn't always mean that all I'm interested in is sex."

4

EXPLORE
EACH OTHER

Redefine the lexicon of sex, giving new meaning to such words as spelunk, survey, examine, traverse, and navigate. If you have only a rudimentary knowledge of human anatomy, you'll never realize your relationship's sexual potential. To know each other intimately, you have to know each other inside and out. So go ahead—make like Lewis and Clark. The continents to be explored and mapped: your bodies. Do it right, and you'll be rewarded with the thrill of discovering uncharted territory.

THE GUY LIST

8 Ways to Turn Bench Time into Sack Time

Sex is a full-contact sport, and star quarterbacks don't let minor injuries—especially those caused by their own teammates—keep them on the sidelines. You shouldn't, either. Just use our modified playbook.

1 **Your injury: Back pain.** Have your partner lie back so her butt is at the foot of a low bed or couch. (A futon or beanbag chair works great.) Her feet should be flat on the floor. Kneel between her legs, penetrate, and lean forward. Plant your elbows on the bed to take the weight off your back, and thrust with your leg muscles, not just your hips, says *A Healthy Back* author Lewis G. Maharam, M.D. Or try lying on your back with your partner on top. If you place a few pillows under your legs to keep your hips propped up, you'll feel less pressure on your back. If you're lucky enough to have access to a hot tub, the buoyancy of the water will prevent undue strain in any position.

2 **Your injury: Cricked neck.** You're better off letting her do the work; jerky movement can cause pain. Lie flat on your back, and pile pillows under your head and shoulders to keep your neck supported. Spread your legs slightly and have her slide on top of you in a kneeling position, facing away from you. After you're inside, she should close her legs and slide gently up and down.

3 **Your injury: Pulled hamstring.** Thrusting with your pelvis can aggravate this injury. Try doggie style, where you're both crouched on all fours. Thrust only as much as you comfortably can. Bent knees will help your hamstrings stay relaxed.

4 **Your injury: Broken arm.** Have her lie on her back. Kneel at her pelvis, with her feet resting on your shoulders. Penetrate, rest your hurt arm on her leg, and use your good one to reach between her legs and make circular motions on her clitoris with your thumb.

⑤ Your injury: Bum knee. Put your knee where she'll be able to see it—so she won't jab it by accident. Lie on your back. She should get on her knees and straddle you, facing your feet. Stick a pillow behind your knees to keep them in a bent position. Encourage her to lean back a little as she thrusts—it'll position her G-spot closer to the head of your penis.

⑥ Your injury: Heart attack. Sex triggers less than 1 percent of heart attacks, but it's best to use positions that won't tire you quickly, says David Spodick, M.D., director of cardiology at the University of Massachusetts Medical School. Have your partner lie on her side, and then sidle up to her on your side. After she lifts her upper leg slightly, penetrate by curling your pelvis toward her. Since the mattress supports your entire weight, there's virtually no strain on your heart. Feel better?

⑦ Your injury: Tennis elbow. It's actually outward motion (think of your backhand) that's aggravated by tennis elbow. You shouldn't have problems with a pushup position. Have her lie back with her knees up. Arch your back and support your upper body with your hands—not your elbows—near her chest. A pillow under the small of her back will help. Rock forward so the base of your penis slides against her clitoris.

⑧ Your injury: Sprained ankle. To avoid aggravating a sprain, keep your weight squarely on the flat of your foot, not the side. Try sitting with your feet flat on the bed, knees up, and lean back. Have her straddle you face-to-face with her feet tucked under her butt. She can move up and down by pivoting her knees, and you can help by pushing off the bed with your arms.

ASK THE GIRL NEXT DOOR

The honest truth about women from our lovely neighbor

Q: *What are some secret spots where I can touch my girlfriend to turn her on?*
—G. F., Chicago

A: Peoria.
Just kidding. Here goes: Play with her hair, stroke the back of her neck, kiss her collarbone and shoulders, grab her calves during sex, lick the palms of her hands, suck on her fingers, rub her lower back, grasp her hips when she's on top, massage her feet, run your hands down her sides, tickle her inner thighs, walk your fingertips down her spine, brush your lips between her breasts, nibble her ankles. Then switch all the verbs around and start over.

Q: *I like being fit, and my girlfriend likes the look. But how much muscle is too much?*
—B. W., Penns Grove, New Jersey

A: The line gets crossed somewhere between Brad Pitt in *Snatch* and Jean-Claude Van Damme in anything. Muscles start to look ludicrous when they obviously limit your ease of movement and make you look like a meathead, Mafia heavy, or WWF wannabe. Bowling-ball biceps, watermelon pecs, and abs that a girl could get her forearm stuck between give the impression that a guy's life, like his body, must be out of balance.

Q: *What does the female orgasm feel like?*
—S. B., Austin, Texas

A: Remember the end of *Star Wars*, when Luke sends a shot into a 2-meter opening in the Death Star to make the whole thing blow? Well, imagine that that shot reaching its target is the beginning of a female orgasm. It may start in that one tiny spot—also known as the clitoris—but the intense rush of pleasure explodes through a woman's entire body, her brain goes blank, and muscles deep inside start throbbing ecstatically. At that point, she loses control: Her hips jerk involuntarily, her nipples get hard, and her mouth makes an involuntary O. The blast can last anywhere from 5 seconds to a few minutes. Then it slowly fades, and she feels tingly and satisfied all over . . . kind of like the very first time she saw *Star Wars*.

Q: *I'm clueless about the clitoris: what, why, how, where.*
—T. S., GAINESVILLE, FLORIDA

A: It's a bit of a mystery, even to the women who own them. My advice: Experiment, and ask a lot of questions. When her answers become nonverbal, you're doing fine.

Q: *A woman I'm sleeping with has small breasts.*
I think she's self-conscious about them. I love them.
How do I get her to feel more comfortable with her body?
—B. P., CEDAR RAPIDS, IOWA

A: Giving her hot little A-cups lots and lots of loving attention will definitely help. You're probably already doing that just by touching and kissing them during sex. Right? Reinforce the hands-on appreciation with comments like "You have the most beautiful/perfect/sexy breasts." She may be worried that you secretly wish she had more up front. Sincere, enthusiastic praise will convince her otherwise.

On that note, catching you scoping out busty babes on the street will just add fuel to her big-boobs-are-better fire, so try to keep your eyes in check. That's really all you can do—be positive and don't send mixed signals. Body-image problems are a very personal issue. You being a fan of her figure can kick-start her confidence, but she'll have to take it from there.

For more honest answers about women, look for
Ask the *Men's Health* Girl Next Door
wherever books are sold.

MUST READS

Love Is the Drug

If you need an excuse to have more sex, intrepid reporter Hugh O'Neill tells you how getting physical will improve your health, lower your stress, and help you pay for the kids' college educations.

The following scene happens millions of times a day, in homes from Moosehead Lake to San Mateo.

A man is about to bite into a beauty of a salami-and-cheese sandwich, when the woman in his life walks in and gives him a disapproving are-you-really-going-to-eat-that glance. Sometimes, the fish eye comes with a little cluck, as though she didn't really mean to make a sound but her alarm at seeing her guy about to eat something so bad for him triggered an involuntary hiccup in her larynx.

Now, cynics may claim that a woman's watchfulness stems from some perverse need to act like his mother when he already has a mother. We deplore such skepticism. Rather, on behalf of the men of America, we file a request for more health help from the women in our lives.

The plan we're suggesting offers dozens of health benefits, from cholesterol control to prostate protection, from pain relief to stress reduction.

What is this heretofore unknown road to wellness?

Sex. And lots of it.

It turns out that psychoanalyst Wilhelm Reich wasn't that far off back in the 1940s when he recommended an orgasm a day for optimum health. Here are just a few of the reasons the truly devoted spouse doesn't just snatch the hoagie from her husband's hands but also offers him a medicinal kitchen quickie to boot.

Burn Fat in Bed

"Sexual activity is a form of physical exercise," says Michael Cirigliano, M.D., an assistant professor of medicine at the University of Pennsylvania School of Medicine. True, each individual sex act isn't much exercise. But remember the lesson of the pyramids: Each brick is insignificant; together they amount to a wonder of the world.

If you're lucky enough to have sex three times a week—nothing fancy, just a modest merger—you'll burn about 7,500 calories every year. That's the equivalent of jogging 75 miles. And the calorie-burn count ascends with the amorous effort. If once a week you are a little more athletic, and once a month reenact *The Tropic of Cancer*, your sex life will burn close to 10,000 calories annually. That's roughly the energy you'd use 10-minute-miling it from the Empire State Building to Independence Hall. These are calories spent before you get anywhere near a rowing machine.

On top of its aerobic benefits, sex offers some—yes, a small amount, but some—of the benefits of resistance training. "During arousal and orgasm, there is myotonia—or contraction— of the muscles," says Dr. Cirigliano. The more lifting, spinning, and thrusting, the better, from a muscle-building point of view. No doubt, sex that involves bench-pressing your partner is a greater boon than a snuggle where nobody is clean-and-jerked.

But don't go crazy. "As with any kind of overtraining, sexual overextension can lead to an injury where you want it least," says Dr. Cirigliano.

> **It's Been Said...**
> " Is it not strange that desire should so many years outlive performance?"
> —William Shakespeare

Live Lustier, Live Longer

The French call the orgasm *la petite mort*: the little death. But researchers say a little death now and again can help postpone the big death that's looming later on.

● Love hates cholesterol.
Sex, a form of exercise, helps lower your total cholesterol and tip the all-important good cholesterol/bad cholesterol ratio in the healthier HDL direction. Okay, not much. But maximum wellness is about little advantages—doing all you can.

● Love is like oxygen.
Sex kicks the respiratory system into overdrive. When you breathe quickly and deeply, your blood is enriched with oxygen, which nourishes all your organs and tissues.

● It rallies your testosterone levels.
"Any kind of physical exercise is going to increase testosterone," says clinical psychologist Karen Donahey, Ph.D., director of the Sex and Marital Therapy Program at Northwestern University Medical Center in Evanston, Illinois. Sex is no exception. The magic male nectar has many happy effects. It makes our sex drive robust, and it fortifies our bones and muscles. Some physicians even believe that testosterone may keep our hearts healthy and our good cholesterol high.

● **Amour is the ultimate analgesic.**

There is lots of evidence that the endorphins released during sex are effective painkillers. "Arousal and orgasm can elevate pain threshold," says Beverly Whipple, Ph.D., president of the Society for the Scientific Study of Sexuality and vice president of the World Association for Sexology. "Sex can help relieve arthritic pain, whiplash pain, and headache pain."

Testosterone is a corticosteroid, so its elevation during sex often reduces the joint inflammation of arthritis. Research suggests that some arthritis sufferers have less pain for up to 6 hours after sex. Headaches also can be better managed with sex: The endorphins released during arousal have an analgesic effect. The accelerated bloodflow throughout the body, specifically to the genital area, takes pressure off the brain. The relaxation that comes with orgasm reduces tension in the neck muscles.

● **Sex delivers DHEA.**

DHEA (short for dehydroepiandrosterone) has been a vogue hormone for several years now. The snake-oil salesmen of wellness are pitching it as a miracle elixir, antidote to everything from impotence to bad taste in leisurewear. Though the early hype is premature, there is persuasive evidence that higher levels of DHEA are good for us.

"Just before orgasm and ejaculation, DHEA spikes to levels three to five times higher than usual," says Theresa L. Crenshaw, M.D., author of *The Alchemy of Love and Lust*. According to Dr. Crenshaw, DHEA can improve cognition, ratchet up the immune system, inhibit tumor growth, promote bone growth, and sometimes function as an antidepressant.

Pamper Your Prostate

Some prostate problems that become common once we reach our late forties are caused or aggravated when the fluids in the prostate gland aren't emptied out efficiently. And what hoses out the prostate gland? You got it: s-e-x.

During orgasm, the muscles around the prostate contract over and over, squeezing out the fluids. Though experts differ on exactly how frequent sex should be for optimum prostate protection—some say once a week, others say several times—it's clear that regular sex is a prostate plus. Further, if you currently have an active sex life, it's important to keep up the good work.

"If a man is ejaculating on a fairly regular basis of one, two, three, or more times weekly, and then—for whatever reason—his frequency of orgasm and ejaculation decreases sharply, it is likely that the prostate gland will become overly full of fluid," says Stephen N. Rous, M.D., author of *The Prostate Book*. This is a fancy way of saying that spouses shouldn't let silly arguments interfere with nookie.

One unfortunate note of caution: There seems to be some evidence that any sudden change in the frequency of sexual activity, including a shift from dry spell to orgy mode, may be bad for the prostate, too. So, if for some happy reason, things are picking up, resist the powerful temptation to go from zero to 60 as fast as possible.

Get Excited, Then Calm Down

Question: What's the single greatest cause of stress for men? Financial trouble? Fascist boss? The recurring thought that Bill Gates could buy your house with the money in his couch cushions? No, no, and no. Answer: Not enough sex. There's no formal research to back up this statement only because no self-respecting scientist wants to waste the grant money proving something every idiot already knows.

"Sex can be a very effective way of reducing stress levels," says Donahey. Having sex chills a guy out, suffusing him with a profound feeling of well-being and relaxation. A nooner does wonders for a man's mood. There's plenty of research to indicate that mood matters medically, that optimism is good for your health. And it's much easier to be optimistic if there's a good chance that at any moment your wife may pull you into the hall closet and give you a good going-over.

Avoid Divorce Attorneys

The nexus between sex and love is complicated, but there's science to support the idea that sex makes relationships more durable, enabling you to better weather the moguls that make even a great marriage bumpy from time to time.

The antidivorce drug may be oxytocin, a hormone secreted by the pituitary gland. In one of nature's feedback loops, it both generates our desire to be touched and is boosted by touch. Whenever anybody (even a golfing buddy) touches you affectionately, there's a little extra zap of oxytocin. When somebody (probably not your golfing buddy) touches you so affectionately that you have an orgasm, the level of oxytocin spikes dramatically.

According to Dr. Crenshaw, oxytocin is the "bonding hormone." It makes us inclined to hug and cuddle, and may make us better lovers, parents, or friends. Though

perfect figures

WHO CARES, AS LONG AS HERS HASN'T

Percentage of men ages 25 to 34 who think their sexual peak has passed: 34

oxytocin's effect is more dramatic in women than in men (probably because oxytocin works in conjunction with estrogen, which is much higher in women), it's clear that a man who has an energetic sex life is more likely to be a loving husband and sweet dad than a man who has to beg for carnal crumbs.

Keep Your Wife in Working Order

The women of America should know that the health benefits of sex apply to them as well. Indeed, sex may be even more important for them than for us. "Regular lovemaking can increase a woman's estrogen level, protect her heart, and keep her vaginal tissues more supple," says Donahey. A steady sex life can also help regulate irregular menstrual periods and ameliorate premenstrual syndrome.

"There is increasing evidence suggesting that sex may help you live longer," says Dr. Crenshaw. Touch exerts its power throughout your system by raising the substances that lengthen your life span—DHEA, oxytocin, endorphins, growth hormone—and lowering those that can shorten it, such as cortisol and adrenaline.

Consider this cascade of consequences: You have a terrific sex life. So you're healthy and stress-free. So your performance at work is golden. So you get promotion after promotion, thereby making more money, eventually living in a great house, driving great cars, taking swanky vacations, and having the jack to send your son to Duke and your daughter to Yale. All because two people cared enough about each other and the kids to do it whenever they possibly could.

Now, if you can just figure out how to get your HMO to pay for it. . . .

Your Privates: An Owner's Manual

Sure, they look smart, run smooth, and get great mileage—now. But how do you keep everything well-tuned over the long haul? At last, a guide to the operation and upkeep of the male sexual machine from writer Joe Kita.

Why would any red-blooded American male need an owner's manual for his private parts? There's nothing to program, no wires to splice. Not a shred of assembly is required. If something goes wrong, you just, well, uh . . . ask your cousin Lenny, who did a year of med school before buying that tavern.

To be honest, most men don't have a clue as to what's going on down there. We pee, tuck, zip, scratch, hustle, and, every once in a lucky while, spelunk—all in uninformed bliss. We fully expect the thing to perform flawlessly for 70-plus years without any maintenance beyond a daily lather.

But inevitably, something goes wrong, whether it's a line drive up the middle during a company softball game or a lusty command to snap to attention that goes unheeded. And when it happens, we men are befuddled, embarrassed, terrified—so much so that we often postpone seeking professional help until the pain or anxiety becomes unbearable.

It's Been Said...

“ My brain? It's my second favorite organ. ”

—Woody Allen

Consider this letter from a reader in Los Angeles: "I may well have injured my penis, for all the goofy stuff I've done with it or let be done to it over the years. The fact is, no one told me much of anything about this part of my body. Such ignorance is, in my opinion, criminal when you consider the possible consequences."

That's why we decided to put together this manual, a do-it-yourselfer's guide to understanding, maintaining, and troubleshooting that holiest of appliances, your privates. But because we know there's nothing more boring than listening to a urologist explain the epididymis, we've used garage language and organized it just like that owner's manual you got with your new Hyundai. And we've enlisted the aid of master mechanics Irwin Goldstein, M.D., urology professor and director of the Institute for Sexual Medicine at Boston University School of Medicine, and Dudley Seth Danoff, M.D., a urologist at Cedars Sinai Medical Center in Los Angeles, to make sure your engine stays tuned for years to come.

Introduction

Welcome to the worldwide family of penis owners. We trust that you will enjoy many years of trouble-free service from your apparatus. To help ensure that you will, we encourage you to familiarize yourself with the following equipment descriptions, operating instructions, and maintenance requirements.

Throughout this manual, the words *WARNING!* and *CAUTION!* appear as reminders to be especially careful. Failure to follow instructions could result in serious damage. When it comes to service, remember that your doctor knows your penis best and has the technical training and genuine Private® parts to assure your ongoing satisfaction.

Body and Interior Specifications (All Model Years)

PENIS

Average length & diameter when flaccid = 3.5 × 1.25 inches
Average length & diameter when erect = 5.8 × 1.6 inches
Average percent increase in volume, flaccid to erect = 300
Longest medically verifiable erection = 12 inches
Amount of blood in erection = 8 to 10 times normal
Average erections per night (while sleeping) = 5
Average duration of each nocturnal erection = 20 to 30 minutes
Estimated replacement value = $50,000

● CAUTION!

The following can shrink a relaxed penis by 2 inches or more: cold weather, chilly baths or showers, sexual activity, exhaustion, excitement (nonsexual), illness.

TESTICLES

Average length & width = 1.4 × 1 inch
Average weight = 0.875 to 1.75 ounces
Temperature = 94.6°F
Compartments within each = 400

SPERM

Average body's production = 50,000 per minute/72 million per day
Days to maturity = 84
Number in ejaculate of average fertile man = 200 million to 600 million
Number in ejaculate of an infertile man = less than 50 million
Percentage of total ejaculate = 3
Average swimming speed = 1 to 4 millimeters per minute
Average lifespan of mature sperm = 1 month in you, 1 to 2 days in a woman

● CAUTION!

For optimum sperm production, the testicles need to be slightly cooler than normal body temperature. That's why they hang away from the body. Hot baths and tight underwear can depress sperm count and movement.

SEMEN

Average volume of ejaculate = 0.5 to 1 teaspoon
Chief ingredient = fructose sugar
Caloric content = 5 calories per teaspoon
Protein content = 6 milligrams per teaspoon

Average number of ejaculatory spurts = 3 to 10

Average interval of ejaculatory contractions = 0.8 seconds

Farthest medically verifiable ejaculation = 11.7 inches

Time required for semen to turn from gel to liquid after ejaculation
= 5 to 25 minutes

BLADDER

Average capacity = 7 to 13 ounces

Normal flow = 7 to 8 ounces per 10 seconds

Operation

It's recommended that, before attempting to operate your privates, you thoroughly familiarize yourself with the location and function of all parts and controls. Basically, your penis is designed to do three things.

❶ **Direct the flow of urine**

The penis contains a narrow hose called the urethra that is attached to the bladder. As the urine level approaches the bladder's maximum-capacity line, you get the urge to pull over. When released, urine is flushed through the urethra, out the tip of the penis, and, according to most women, usually onto the floor next to the toilet. Acting as a regulator for this process is the pubococcygeal (PC) muscle. This is what you flex to stop urine flow or rid yourself of those last few drops. (It can also serve as an orgasm regulator. See "Troubleshooting," page 138.)

❷ **Become rigid enough to allow penetration of the vagina during sexual intercourse**

Your penis is equipped with twin hydraulic chambers. During sexual stimulation, these fill with blood until the penis grows firm and erect. After stimulation ends or ejaculation occurs, blood leaves these chambers and the penis softens again. There is usually a recovery, or "refractory," period ranging from minutes to a full day (depending on the equipment's age) before another erection can occur.

About half of the penis is hidden inside the body, even when erect. It is fastened to the pelvic undercarriage for support.

● **CAUTION!**

Any impact to the area where the penis attaches to the pelvis can disrupt its hydraulic function. Be especially careful when bicycling, as numerous cases of impotence have resulted from falling onto a bike's top tube.

❸ **Deposit semen within the vagina during ejaculation**

Sperm is manufactured inside the testicles, those two ball joints below the drive shaft. From there, it passes into a soft, fibrous organ behind each testicle, called

perfect figures

A FERTILE BUSINESS

Sperm donations stored
at the New England Sperm Bank
in 2000: 10,000 vials

Compensation for one usable
vial of donated sperm:
$70

Maximum cost to store
initial specimen:
$180

Sperm withdrawal fee:
$60

the epididymis, where it acquires the long tail necessary for swimming. Sperm then enters the vas deferens for storage. This thin hose loops around and splices into the urethra just below the bladder.

When it's time to shift into sexual high gear, sperm is mixed with liquid from the prostate gland and adjoining seminal vesicles. The resulting transmission fluid, called semen, gathers in a holding tank, which gradually swells to pinch the bladder shut and prevent urine from trickling in. Finally, the semen is expelled from the urethra by a series of muscular contractions.

STARTING THE ENGINE

The key to your sexual ignition is not between your legs; it's inside your head. The brain is man's biggest sex organ, sending nerve impulses racing down the spinal cord to trigger an erection. Keep in mind, though, that since arousal is an electrical spark traveling the neural highway, it can be dulled by a repetitive commute. So vary your starting procedure, explore side roads, stop at a Best Western, let your partner drive, or, when applicable, road-test a new model.

● Hard starting or stalling

If your penis fails to become erect, even after repeated cranking, or if you have trouble maintaining an erection, let it rest for a while. Just about every man experiences an occasional erection problem, so try not to let it bother you. If you worry about it, it can develop into a psychological problem requiring extensive systems analysis to remedy. Chances are you're just flooded with work worries, anxiety, or fatigue—all of which can temporarily foul your engine.

If the problem continues, ask your mechanic about a new fuel injector. Certain drugs can be injected directly into the penis, producing long-lasting (1 hour or more) erections within moments. Also on the market is an erection-producing medication in the form of a small pellet that you insert into the tip of the penis. Another solution is a vacuum constriction device: When the penis is inserted into this cylinder and the attached pump engages, a vacuum is formed that causes blood to flow into the penile shaft. A rubber ring is then slipped onto the base of the penis to trap the blood in the shaft. As a last resort, you may want to consider upgrading to a penile implant (see "Available Options/Upgrades" on page 140).

● WARNING!

Never operate your penis while under the influence of alcohol. Although alcohol lowers inhibitions, most men have less-than-optimum erections when inebriated. The fear this generates may lead to more-frequent bouts of impotence.

BREAK-IN PERIOD

To ensure a long, active life for your privates, it's recommended that you engage in frequent sex. According to noted body mechanics Masters and Johnson, "When the male is stimulated to high sexual output during his formative years and a similar tenor of activity is established for the 31- to 40-year age range, his later years are usually marked by maintained sexuality."

ACCELERATION

● 0–60 mph

Independent testing shows that it generally takes 3 to 5 minutes for the flaccid penis of a young male to become fully erect once sexual stimulation begins. This reaction time at least doubles with age.

● WARNING!

Avoid rapid acceleration on slick surfaces. Failure to do so could cause partial or complete loss of control.

SUDDEN STOPS

Slamming on the brakes while driving at high speed can result in a painful condition. During sexual stimulation, blood gathers in the testicles. If ejaculation does not occur and sexual excitement continues, the resulting congestion in the arteries there can cause a dull pain, similar to that of an aching muscle.

HANDLING

In order to become familiar with the nuances of your equipment and learn how it responds in different situations, high-speed solo driving on a closed course can be helpful. According to one survey, nearly one-third of American men do this weekly. And contrary to rumor, it will not harm your equipment. In fact, it can be viewed as a practice lap for sex, where you're forever flirting with the limits of control.

ENGAGING THE CHOKE

To postpone ejaculation and extend lovemaking, engage "the choke." This technique involves firmly squeezing the tip of the penis, just behind the head, prior to orgasm.

FUEL REQUIREMENTS

Your privates were designed and developed for optimum performance and efficiency using high-quality fuel. Low-quality fuel can cause cholesterol buildup in arteries and veins, thereby reducing bloodflow to and from your privates, and causing hard starting or stalling. In fact, every one-point increase in your total cholesterol correlates to an almost 1½ times greater risk of erection problems. To avoid this, use fuel that has a fat content below 30 percent and is low in cholesterol and high in fiber. Such fill-ups will greatly reduce circulatory-system deposits.

Body Work/Chassis Considerations

Regular exercise gives the body a deep, healthful luster that lends protection, improves performance, and helps it hold its value longer. For example, sedentary men who began an exercise program reported making love 30 percent more often and masturbating 50 percent more often during a 9-month period. Exercise not only makes the body more fit for sex but also stimulates the mind by making you feel sexier.

SPARE TIRE

Your privates did not come equipped with a spare tire. Any roll of fat around your middle was an aftermarket acquisition that will void the warranty if left in place. It not only interferes with sexual performance but also makes the penis look smaller.

Men naturally deposit fat in their abdomens, including the area at the base of the penis. As the spare tire inflates, this pad thickens and eventually engulfs a portion of the organ—1 inch for every 35 extra pounds. Being overweight is also commonly linked to atherosclerosis, or narrowing of the arteries, a primary cause of impotence.

ABS

Your abdominal muscles (abs) are the chief thrusting muscles for intercourse. To strengthen them, do crunches. These exercises are just like situps except that you don't curl up as far. Simply lie on your back with your hands crossed over your chest. Lift your shoulders 4 to 6 inches off the floor, while trying to bring your chin to your chest. You'll feel a tightening in your gut.

ALIGNMENT

One-third of all penile ruptures occur during lovemaking. They're caused by sudden shifts in position or by awkward attempts at parallel parking with the partner on top. The tearing of tissue that occurs within an erect penis is often audible and extremely painful. Such injuries tend to happen where there is a lack of space, such as between the steering wheel and driver's seat. To protect yourself and your passenger, always use turn signals before changing positions.

SAFETY BELTS

It's highly recommended that you wear an athletic supporter for activities that involve running, jumping, and sudden movement. This device tucks the testicles close to the undercarriage to protect them from jarring. For complete security, wear a cup. There are many models to choose from. Beyond the traditional "catcher's" model, there are "soft" cups made of pliable rubber (for limited-contact sports such as volleyball and soccer) and tapered hard-shell cups that offer a more comfortable, anatomical fit.

● CAUTION!

Wearing polyester underwear may contribute to impotence because of the static electricity generated by man-made materials. Loose, 100 percent cotton shorts are recommended.

A Word about Safety

As a supplement to your personal-restraint system, it's highly recommended that you wear a condom. Although such air bags do not guarantee complete protection from sexually transmitted diseases, they are dependable devices that significantly reduce the risk when used properly. One study of prostitutes working in Nevada brothels found just 49 condom breaks in 41,127 uses, a rate of 0.12 percent. An additional 0.25 percent of condoms fell off during or after sex. These are the lowest failure rates ever reported.

CONDOM DEPLOYMENT

1. Use only condoms from a sealed package bearing an expiration date. Be careful of fingernails, rings, and other objects that could puncture or tear the material. Never open a condom package with your teeth or on your partner's spiked collar.
2. Squeeze the air from the receptacle end of the condom and roll it down over the erect penis before penetration or oral sex occurs.
3. With latex condoms, use only water-based lubricants such as K-Y jelly. Petroleum-based brands such as Vaseline and Valvoline can damage latex.

❹ During withdrawal, hold the base of the condom to keep it from coming off. And use each condom only once.

Maintenance

Your privates are the result of centuries of engineering. Before they left the factory, every effort was made to assure they were in good working condition. To keep them running smoothly, regular maintenance is required.

TO BE DONE DAILY

For uncircumcised men, it's especially important to retract the foreskin and wash around the head of the penis every day. Otherwise, yeast infections and other problems may develop. Circumcised men should scrub regularly as well.

TO BE DONE WEEKLY (AT LEAST)

Sex is the best exercise for your privates. Regularly flushing the system with nourishing blood and oxygen assures optimum sperm production, prostate health, and overall good performance. When intercourse is not possible, consider revving your engine manually.

TO BE CHECKED MONTHLY

After taking a warm bath or shower to relax the scrotum, gently roll each testicle between your fingers. It should be smooth and oval-shaped, feeling kind of like a hard-boiled egg without the shell. Compress it gently, searching for any hard areas or lumps that don't feel like the surrounding tissue. (The bump you'll find behind each testicle is the epididymis.) If you detect anything unusual, see your doctor. Although relatively rare, testicular cancer has a 97 percent cure rate when discovered early.

YEARLY INSPECTION

Once your equipment reaches age 40, have your prostate checked annually. This gland surrounds the urethra like a doughnut and, if left to enlarge, can reduce an older man's urine stream to a dribble. Prostate cancer is also a concern. Both of these problems can be avoided if detected early. A complete yearly inspection should include three things: (1) a digital rectal exam (sorry, pal, but we're talking finger here, not computer); (2) a blood test for prostate-specific antigens (PSA), an early warning sign of trouble; and (3) an ultrasound to create a visible image of the tissue.

● WARNING!

Using your privates for anything other than their intended purpose voids all warranties, written or implied.

SERVICING

The frequency of ejaculation/intercourse among:
20- to 29-year-olds = four to five times weekly
30- to 39-year-olds = two to four times weekly
40- to 49-year-olds = one or two times weekly
50- to 59-year-olds = zero to one time weekly
60-plus = one or two times monthly

AUTOMATIC SYSTEMS CHECK

Each night, your privates automatically run a self-diagnostic systems check. Most times, you will be unaware this is happening. Periodic erections will occur while you're asleep, as will an occasional emission. Do not be alarmed. Your privates are simply flushing themselves with fresh blood and oxygen to stay in optimum working condition.

If you have a reason to doubt this is happening, do the following test: Wrap some postage stamps from a roll firmly around the base of your penis and tape the ends together. The next morning, if the stamps are torn along a perforation, you've had an erection. (If you wake up in New Mexico with a postmark, try the test again, but don't sleep so close to the mailbox.)

FLUID LEAKS

After urinating, apply gentle upward pressure under the base of the penis. This will usually squeeze out any remaining drops and prevent embarrassing stains on the upholstery.

CHECKING UNDER THE HOOD

Your penis comes from the factory with its head completely covered by a fleshy protective foreskin. As many as 85 percent of penis owners in the United States have had this foreskin surgically removed via an operation called circumcision. This is usually done for religious or aesthetic reasons. If basic hygiene is followed, the presence or absence of a hood does not affect sensitivity, sexual performance, or susceptibility to disease.

It's Been Said. . .

" Let's forget about the 6 feet and talk about the 7 inches. "

—Mae West

LUBRICATION

Men's Confidential newsletter tested nine popular lubes and rated them according to quality, viscosity, energy savings, and protection from wear. Their overall favorite was a brand called Wet: Classic Platinum, followed by AquaLube and Maximus.

● Checking the oil level

Don't use too much lube. It's not sexy, and it lessens sensation by making working parts too slippery, leading to loss of traction and hydroplaning. Use just a dime-size dab to impart a thin sheen.

● Adding oil

For extra comfort and performance during long drives or when operating your penis in extremely dry conditions, you'll need to relube. Brands such as K-Y jelly and Astroglide can be reactivated with a simple spritz of water.

● Disposing of used oil

When indiscriminately discarded, used oil can foul the bedroom environment. Flavored lubes leave a sticky residue that requires a soap-and-water scrubbing. Most nonflavored brands wipe clean with a towel.

Appearance

Your privates are exposed to the corrosive effects of dirt, perspiration, and vaginal fluids. To protect the finish, trim, and exposed underbody, it's important to wash often and thoroughly. Scrub any dirt and salt from crevices in the undercarriage, and check that all drain holes are free of debris. After washing, allow all surfaces to drain and dry before parking in a confined space. If desired, you may polish your privates immediately.

perfect figures

SNIP DECISION

Number of men who elect to have a vasectomy each year:
500,000

● Minor chips and scratches

The skin of the penis and testicles is remarkably resilient. For chafing and small cuts that cause minimal bleeding, just wash with soap and water, and apply an antibiotic ointment.

● Major dents

If you get hit in the testicles, lie down, apply an ice-packed cloth, and take some deep breaths. If there's swelling and the pain doesn't subside within a few minutes, continue the icing and get to a hospital. A severe groin injury can cause sterility.

Troubleshooting

The diagnoses outlined below are intended to serve only as guides to locate and temporarily correct minor faults or worries. Causes of unsatisfactory performance should be investigated and corrected by your doctor.

◉ Problem

Penis seems small.

◉ Solution

Few men are satisfied with the size of their penises. Keep in mind that the average vagina is just 3 to 5 inches long.

◉ Problem

Left testicle is slightly larger and hangs lower than right testicle.

◉ Solution

Rarely are both testicles identical. In fact, the left one hangs lower in 85 percent of cases.

◉ Problem

Erections do not occur as quickly, nor are they as firm as they once were.

◉ Solution

This is common in older models. However, exercising regularly, following a low-fat diet, avoiding smoking, and limiting alcohol consumption are all antidotes, as is longer and more creative foreplay.

◉ Problem

Ejaculation happens too fast.

◉ Solution

Try strengthening your PC muscle with Kegel exercises. The PC is the muscle you use to stop urine flow. Contract it now to familiarize yourself with the feeling. What you just did was a Kegel. Do 20, 50, 100, or more daily—at your desk or in your car. Since it's the same muscle that contracts for ejaculation, strengthening it will give you more control during sex.

◉ Problem

Ejaculation isn't as forceful or plentiful as it once was.

◉ Solution

Such misfiring often occurs with older engines. In fact, with vintage models, ejaculation may not occur at all, although an orgasm is experienced.

◉ Problem

Pain is felt in testicle.

◉ Solution

Intermittent twinges are common, and anything that lasts less than a minute or so is no cause for worry. Testicular pain that builds gradually is usually caused by an infection or inflammation. Consult a certified mechanic or authorized dealership.

● Problem

Blower operates irregularly or ineffectively.

● Solution

Purchase the 45-minute educational video *Nina's Guide to Fellatio* from Good Vibrations, (800) 289-8423.

Available Options/Upgrades

Customize your privates to fit all your lifestyle needs!

VASECTOMY

Enjoy worry-free sex by having a trained technician cut the vas deferens, thereby preventing sperm from reaching the urethra. It's a safe, quick (7- to 10-minute), effective means of birth control, plus the sensation of ejaculation remains unchanged. Available in traditional snip or modern laser. Price: around $500.

VASECTOMY REVERSAL

Contemplating a U-turn on that vasectomy you had a few years back? No problem. The vas deferens can be spliced so your sperm can backstroke again. The procedure is safe, relatively quick (90 minutes), and, when performed by a trained technician, effective in more than 90 percent of cases. Price: around $6,200.

TESTOSTERONE

Preserve the raw beauty of your libido with testosterone! This potent male hormone, manufactured chiefly in the testicles, is responsible for your sexual desire and, to some degree, your erections. But production declines after age 50. Some men who have no physical problems but experience flagging desire may benefit from testosterone supplements, which can be taken orally, through injection, or via a skin patch. Price: Ask your dealer.

PENIS ENLARGEMENT

Gain valuable inches by expanding your trunk! Body-shop mechanics can make your penis appear larger by cutting the ligaments that attach it to the pubic bone. Once this is done, the penis hangs a bit lower and looks larger. In addition, body fat can also be injected under the skin of the penile shaft to make it thicker. Price: $4,500 to $8,000.

● WARNING!

Most mechanics do not approve of the enlargement procedure, which compromises the penile suspension system and may undermine resale value. Consumers have reported lack of stability and loss of control when operating at high speeds.

PENILE IMPLANTS

If you have chronic difficulty getting an erection and other impotency treatments have failed, consider the new line of deluxe penile implants. These are cylinders that are surgically placed inside the penis to make it firm enough for intercourse. Two models are available.

- A nonhydraulic implant consists of a pair of flexible silicone rods that can be bent up or down by hand. It's the simplest design, but since the penis remains semirigid, some men find it difficult to wear Dockers. Price: roughly $8,000.
- A hydraulic implant includes a pair of hollow rods, a reservoir of saline solution, and a pump, all concealed within the body. For an erection, you simply squeeze your scrotum to inflate the penis. Price: about $12,000.

Roadside Assistance/Customer Support

**American Association of Sex Educators, Counselors
and Therapists (provides referrals for experts in your area)**
AASECT
P. O. Box 5488
Richmond, VA 23220-0488
aasect@aasect.org

Centers for Disease Control National AIDS Hotline
(800) 342-2437

Condomania (mail-order condom source)
(800) 926-6366

Good Vibrations (mail-order sex toys, books, and videos)
(800) 289-8423

National Herpes Hotline
(919) 361-8488

CDC National STD Hotline
(800) 227-8922 or (800) 342-2437

American Foundation for Urologic Disease
1128 N. Charles Street
Baltimore, MD 21201-5559

National Kidney and Urologic Diseases Information Clearinghouse
3 Information Way
Bethesda, MD 20892-3580
(800) 891-5390 or (301) 654-4415

Breasts: A Love Story

Breast owner Sarah Miller tells all! What they're like, what they need, and why you should feel her out before feeling her up.

I have had large breasts for about 20 years. I'm 32, so let's say, roughly, that my breasts were on their path to greatness halfway through the Carter administration. By the time Reagan was sworn in, I was officially stacked.

I first realized I had big breasts when I was about 12, in, of all places, a fish market on Cape Cod. For years, the fishmonger had been showing my buxom aunt marked favoritism. "This is for you," he would say, measuring out what she'd asked for, then, with a wink and a glimpse at her bustline, tossing on a few more shrimp or an extra fillet.

On this particular day, he threw a handful of extra shrimp onto the pile and, ignoring my aunt, turned his gaze on me. "A little extra nutrition for the growing girl," he said. Holy hell, I said to myself, I have big boobs, too! By the time I was 13, I had a C-cup, and by the time I was 15, a D. Today, I hover between a 34 and a 36D, depending on whether I'm on the Pill, and, disgustingly, how much beer I've been drinking. Either way, they garner their share of attention—wanted or otherwise.

There are times when it all seems quite silly to me, when I look at mine in the mirror and think, "What a lot of excitement over two little—okay, enormous—mounds of fat!" Then again, there's the occasional moment when I'll pull an old cotton T-shirt out of the dryer and slip it, still warm and quite tight, over my head, the name of my old university straining across my front. And as I happen to catch a glimpse of myself in the mirror, I can't help but think of Teri Hatcher's line from that old *Seinfeld* episode: "They're real, and they're spectacular."

I know men like to think that women lie around all day touching and staring at their breasts. Well, every once in a while, in fact, we do. But aside from the odd afternoon interlude, most women don't find their own breasts especially sexual. Our breasts kind of have two—well, four—personalities. There is How We See Them. And then there is How Men See Them.

How We See Them

As fashion accessories. When I buy a dress, I don't consciously think, "Wow, this is going to make all the men in the room want me." More like, "How will it offset my best feature?" I know what you're thinking: Nothing low-cut was ever purchased in innocence. I swear to you, my breasts and I, we never conspire. We're just trying to look our best. I feel about my breasts the way Audrey Hepburn felt about her neck. They're just part of my outfit, along with the right shoes, the right hose, the right earrings. All of which, of course, means nothing when confronted with . . .

How Men See Them

Simple: as the very focal point of the entire world. The male gaze flies past all my attempts to craft an individual style and makes a beeline for the breasts.

On the one hand, this is not so bad. I have worn the same tasteful yet cleavage-enhancing black dress to every party I've been to for 3 years. I've thought about buying a new one, but who would notice? Think: Who at your Thanksgiving table will complain about mashed potatoes or squash when your bird is so plump and juicy? I am not always the best-looking or most sought-after girl at the party. But I always look appropriately festive, men tell me that I look nice, and if you ever spot someone waving a twenty at the bartender to get his attention . . . chances are that someone isn't me.

The downside is that many potentially fascinating conversations get lost inside my plunging neckline. For a while, I tried wearing necklaces—I read in a women's magazine (a dubious source of information on any topic other than osteoporosis) that this would "draw the eye upward." Unfortunately, it merely provided an excuse for men's eyes to linger in this general area: "Hey, is that a necklace? It's nice; where did you get it?"

"England."

"I've never been to England, but the longer I look at this necklace, you know, the more I feel I have."

My advice, should you find yourself chatting with an amply endowed female, is to practice restraint. It's not that we mind you looking at our breasts; it's just that seeing you do it is creepy. The stare, obviously, is bad; and the quick, subtle glance is never as quick or subtle as you hope. Try using your powers of reconnaissance: Stare sideways at a woman while you're talking to another man, and then, later, when you start up a conversation with her, look her in the eye while enjoying the mental picture of her breasts.

This may all sound complicated, but it's really not. For those of you who need a little motivation, remember that while prisoners get time off for good behavior, you get shirts off.

Of course, it's during the shirts-off phase that the difference between How

Breasts: A Handling Guide

Breasts are like snowflakes: Every one is unique. Know the right moves, though, and you'll have her melting in your arms. Here are the basics.

● Large breasts

In a study conducted at the University of Vienna, researchers found that large breasts were about 24 percent less sensitive than small ones. "This is probably because the nerve that transmits sensation from the nipple is stretched," says New York City plastic surgeon Alan Matarasso, M.D. Stimulate the outer sides of her breasts, just below the armpits, with your tongue or fingertips. Make flipping motions with your tongue and even experiment with light nibbling.

● Small breasts

They're sensitive, but they can handle more motion because of their size. Use your palms to cup and gently bounce her breasts during sex.

● Surgically enhanced breasts

If done properly, implants won't interfere with sensation. But they will move differently. Concentrate on the surface of her breasts. Use your tongue to make circles that gradually spiral in toward the nipples.

● Droopy breasts

Droopy breasts can be the least sensitive—the nerves are not only stretched but also compressed by the breasts' weight. Have her lie on her back; it'll cause her breasts to shift up and out, relieving the tension on the nerves and helping her focus on the pleasure.

● New-mom breasts

Her nipples will be tender, so focus on the breasts' undersides, which are frequently neglected. Gently cup and support her breasts. It'll feel nice to her after a long day of suckling.

NIPPLES

These handy barometers of desire are simple to read: Up is "on," down is "off." But they're also thermometers, popping up when the weather's cold, like giant goose bumps.

The nipples are important—in fact, for some women, you can induce an orgasm just by doing breast duty. But the sensitivity of nipples varies widely; handle with care.

We See Them and How Men See Them is most interesting. Men are always a bit amazed to see a pair of naked breasts, and their amazement level increases with quality and size. So I come to that naked-from-the-waist-up moment with mixed emotions. On the one hand, I am so totally over these things. On the other hand, hello, you are beholding items of serious quality, and son, you'd better recognize it. If this sounds like just one more damned-if-you-do, damned-if-you-don't chick rule, I apologize. I have always been a fan of the quick, sincere compliment. ("Whoa, nice rack" is not what I have in mind. "Wow, you have gorgeous breasts" is more like it). Living every day with these things, we tend to forget how interesting and sexy they are to people who don't live with them, and it's nice to be reminded.

That takes care of the talking part. As to what you do, well, it's really a matter of personal taste among consenting adults. I was with a group of women lately, and one wished her boyfriend would touch her breasts more when they had sex. Her friend made a face and said her boyfriend was much, much too fixated on hers. I suggested they switch boyfriends.

Bottom line: If you ask most women what they like, they'll be happy to tell you.

After 20 years of having big breasts, I look down at them and ask, "What have you done for me lately?" I do get to walk around as the proud owner of these things that women want and men want to touch. On bad days, when I'm heartbroken or just plain broke, I have consoled myself with this fact. (Yes, I do know that's lame.) I'm aware of the preconception

● Large

Because they have more nerve endings, big nipples are often hypersensitive, so don't be too aggressive when applying pressure, Dr. Matarasso says.

● Small

The areola—the dark-colored circle that surrounds the nipple—is actually more sensitive than the nipple itself. Focus on the sensitive upper quadrant of her breast, between 10 and 2 o'clock.

● Inverted

One study has shown that 3 percent of women have innies. The cause: genetics. The nerve endings in breasts with inverted nipples are no different from those of any other nipples. "Often, women with inverted nipples may be more sensitive emotionally because they may feel that their nipples aren't normal," says New York City sex therapist Shirley Zussman, Ed.D. Reassure her with compliments about her breasts. You can lure the nipples out if you're persistent with touching, kissing, licking, and gentle sucking.

"When I was 11, I thought that women were solid from the neck down."

—C. E. M. Joad

that women with big breasts can coast through life unchecked, but I haven't gotten as much free fish as you might think. Rental-car agents don't neglect to charge me when I scratch the Dodge Neon. When I speed, cops write me massive tickets. I get the same amount of bad news and good news everyone else gets; it's just that whoever delivers it often does so staring at my boobs.

Still, even though women and men—possessors and obsessors—don't see breasts the same way, our two worldviews can coexist. We women need to remember that what we take for granted are two of your main reasons for living. You men need to remember that breasts are flesh and blood, not Fisher-Price toys. Let's cut a deal. We'll wear nothing but low-cut shirts . . . if you promise to listen to everything we say when we're wearing them.

Better Sex, Naturally

Can herbs and other natural ingredients help your sex life? Writer Zachary Veilleux went foraging and found out it's possible . . . if you pick the right ones.

We've always been skeptical about herbal sex boosters and other so-called virility pills. Traditionally, there hasn't been much hard science backing their claims of improved sexual performance. What's more, some pill manufacturers have often resorted to sleazy marketing ploys. For example, around the time that Pfizer introduced the enormously popular erection pill Viagra, a couple of smaller outfits rushed to market with Vaegra and Viagro. Mail-order ads for Vaegra claimed 16,000 customers for the "all-natural" supplement— at $80 a bottle. Pfizer sued both companies for trademark infringement and earned temporary restraining orders that halted production and sales under those names.

Despite such questionable marketing practices, research suggests that some of the herbs found in these pills may be at least moderately helpful for raising erections and stoking tepid libidos. Whether you're an older man battling occasional bouts of impotence or a younger man whose sex drive is sometimes slowed by stress, a sex supplement may be useful.

The key, though, is to read labels carefully and choose a mix of ingredients that offers some promise. Here's what to look for—and what to avoid—if you're considering a natural sex supplement.

Won't Hurt, Might Help

Though herbal cures are seldom backed by the rigorous research typically found behind mainstream drugs, there's evidence that some herbs are at least safe and possibly beneficial in dealing with sexual problems. (Just remember that you may have to take these herbs for several weeks before you see any results. And let your doctor know what you're taking, to avoid interactions with other medications.)

● Avena sativa

This green oat straw has been a staple of sex formulas because it may help alleviate sexual problems (especially low libido) by raising testosterone levels. In one study, 20 men who took 300 milligrams (mg) a day of green oat extract posted a 54 percent increase in frequency of sexual activity.

● Ginkgo biloba

Ginkgo, one of the most studied herbal remedies, improves bloodflow throughout the body by relaxing arteries. Because an erect penis depends on a plentiful supply of blood, this herb can aid potency in men whose poor erections are caused by vascular disease.

In an often-cited 1989 German study, half the men taking 60 mg a day of ginkgo extract regained erections after 6 months. And a small study presented to a national urology conference in 1998 found that overnight erections were slightly more rigid in men who took ginkgo than in men who took a placebo.

The herb is considered safe in doses up to 240 mg a day, but doctors we talked to suggest starting at 80 mg. One caution: "There have been some rare cases of complications associated with the combined use of ginkgo and aspirin, so it's especially important to check with your doctor if you take aspirin regularly," says Tieraona Low Dog, M.D., a family physician at the Tree House Center of Integrative Medicine in Albuquerque, New Mexico.

● Ginseng

This herb contains ginsenosides, compounds that researchers think can improve sexual function by increasing hormone levels. "Ginseng encourages the body to make more testosterone, and it has been shown to increase sperm production," says Dr. Low Dog.

Be sure to check the label for the designation Panax, which means that the herb is of American or oriental origin. Siberian ginseng, found in some products, has not been as well-studied. It's also important to buy a standardized formula containing 15 percent ginsenosides; that means the manufacturers have tested the product to ensure that there are sufficient quantities of the active ingredient. (A *Consumer Reports* test of 10 ginseng formulations found that concentrations varied by 1,000 percent.) Our doctors recommend starting with 1 to 2 grams (g) a day.

L-arginine

Animal studies have shown that this amino acid (it's not an herb, but it is natural) encourages the production of nitric oxide, a chemical some urologists think is crucial to increasing penile bloodflow. In one study, aging male rats fed L-arginine for 8 weeks had significantly better erectile responses than rats in a control group. "The result is a lot like that seen with ginkgo: better bloodflow to the genitals," says alternative-medicine physician Steven Margolis, M.D., of Sterling Heights, Michigan. He suggests taking 500 to 1,000 mg a day.

Supplementing with amino acids can be tricky, though, so you may want to try tinkering with your diet first. An ounce of Brazil nuts, peanuts, or almonds—or a half-cup of cooked lentils or kidney beans—delivers around 500 mg of L-arginine. Soybeans, tofu, and sunflower seeds are good sources, too.

Muira puama

Any remedy nicknamed potency wood gets our attention, especially when it seems to work as both an aphrodisiac and an erection booster. When 262 men took 1 to 1.5 g of muira puama extract daily for 2 weeks, 51 percent reported better erections and 62 percent said it helped their libidos. "I haven't reviewed the original study myself, but I confess that if I had erection problems, I might try this herb," says *The Green Pharmacy* author James A. Duke, Ph.D., a botanist who has spent nearly 30 years studying medicinal plants.

St.-John's-wort

This popular herb has made headlines as a natural antidepressant. So what does it do for your sex life? Nothing directly, but it can be helpful to men whose sexual problems are the result of depression. "Obviously, if someone is depressed, he's going to have a decreased libido, and in that case St.-John's-wort could be very helpful," says Dr. Margolis. For depression, our doctors recommend 600 to 900 mg per day of a 0.3 percent standardized extract.

Saw palmetto

If you have an enlarged prostate (and if you're over 50, there's a good chance you do), the bloated gland could cause sexual problems by interfering with nerves and blood vessels that feed your penis. "Prostate enlargement doesn't necessarily interfere with sexual function. But when it does, relieving the condition may help men attain an erection," says Duke. Studies of men with enlarged prostates have found that saw palmetto significantly relieved their symptoms. Look for extracts that are standardized to contain 85 percent fatty acids.

If you have an enlarged prostate, our doctors suggest taking 320 mg a day. If you don't, says Duke, taking saw palmetto may actually worsen your sexual performance because it reduces the production of testosterone.

Won't Hurt, Won't Help

These herbs, though harmless, are probably a waste of money when it comes to improving your sex life.

> It's **BeenSaid**...
>
> **"** All lovers swear more performance than they are able. **"**
>
> —William Shakespeare

◉ Ashwagandha

Doctors in India believe that this herb can increase potency, enhance libido, and even promote fertility, but there's no proof that these claims are anything more than folklore.

◉ Damiana

Some folks swear by this herb as an aphrodisiac, an erection enhancer, and a cure for infertility. But Duke says that there's no real research to support its reputation.

◉ Dong quai

Since it's one of the most widely used herbs among Chinese healers, some sex-pill makers add this circulation enhancer to their mixes. They hope men won't notice that it's used mostly by women and that the evidence of its effectiveness is mixed at best.

◉ Sarsaparilla

In North America, we use it as a flavoring for root beer, but in Latin America it's used as an impotence remedy. If we had any proof that it works, we'd be drinking A&W by the gallon.

◉ Wild yam

Some species contain diosgenin, a steroid that can be used to produce sex hormones under laboratory conditions. "I'm not impressed," says Dr. Margolis. "Most of the good literature does not support the idea that a plant hormone can be used by humans."

Proceed with Caution

Some products may actually do more harm than good. If you're considering a formula that contains any of the following, consult your doctor first.

● Royal jelly

Some sex pills contain bee pollen or its more exotic cousin, royal jelly, a substance made by queen bees. Its sexy reputation stems from Asian folklore, but there are no data to back it. Journal reports have linked royal-jelly consumption to asthma attacks, severe allergic reactions, and even death.

● Spanish fly

You don't see this sexual stimulant much anymore, and for good reason: The *American Journal of Emergency Medicine* reports that it can cause severe abdominal pain, burning of the mouth, vomiting, bleeding, and painful urination. It's considered unsafe for human use.

● Yohimbe

This is the only herb of the bunch that has advanced from being an alternative-medicine treatment to being a conventional medication (the prescription drug yohimbine). Both the herb and the drug work by dilating blood vessels, allowing more erection-nourishing blood to reach the penis. Both may also improve nerve function in the lower region of the spinal cord, facilitating the transmission of sexual stimuli.

Although studies suggest that yohimbine is effective (in one German study, it helped 71 percent of impotent men who took it), both the drug and the herb have a long list of side effects. "If there is a real herbal erection enhancer, yohimbe is it," says Duke. "Unfortunately, large doses can induce anxiety, increase heart rate, elevate blood pressure, and cause flushing, headaches, and even hallucinations. It's not an herb to mess around with."

Synchronized Schwinging

You're too fast? She's too slow? In this next piece by Zachary Veilleux, we offer you seven moves that can improve your bedroom timing.

You know the fable about the tortoise and the hare. But do you know that their legendary race is a metaphor for sex and reaching orgasm? Think about it. Most couples consist of one partner who's a slowpoke and one who's a jackrabbit. One makes steady progress toward the finish, while the other hurries up and waits. (Or at least tries to. Guess who that is.) It's exciting for both, but it would be even better if they could finish together.

We're here to help—to show you some new positions and techniques that will allow you and your partner to speed up, slow down, or cruise along. By developing a better touch on the pleasure accelerator, you'll be able to compensate for any variation in natural ability and finish in an exquisite dead heat.

Put Your Hands Together

The female orgasm is mostly about clitoral stimulation, and your hands offer the best way to provide that. Invite her to sit on your lap, her back against your chest. Put your hands in front of her as though you're typing, and bring one hand on top of the other. Interlace your fingers and put them between her legs. Use the middle and ring fingers of one hand to gently spread her labia apart, while using one or two fingers of the other hand to make slow circles around her clitoris.

"This will give her a nice 'big' feeling that she won't get when you use just a single finger," says sex educator Lou Paget, author of *The Big O*. "It's also less tiring for your hands."

Once she's aroused, try inserting a finger into her vagina and curving it in and out as you continue to circle her clitoris.

Use Her U-Spot

If your partner needs more time to reach orgasm than you do, oral sex can give her a head start before intercourse even begins. Focus on her clitoris, but use your lower lip (brace it against your teeth) to apply strong, constant pressure to the area of her urethra—located just above the vaginal opening and below the clitoris.

"Stimulating the urethra can be very pleasurable for some women because it's next to the clitoris," says Paget.

Slip and Slide

For you, less friction means less stimulation. "A really slippery lubricant could decrease the amount of friction you feel and allow you to thrust longer before you reach orgasm," says psychologist Gerald Weeks, Ph.D., of the University of Nevada at Las Vegas. (Lubes affect women less since women depend primarily on indirect stimulation to reach orgasm.) Lubes also up the funkiness factor. One of the slickest is Slippery Stuff (available at www.condomsexpress.com).

Work from the Bottom

 Try as you might—and we know how hard you try—you're never going to hit all the right spots exactly the way she wants you to. It's like an engine room—there's simply too much going on down there. So let her climb on top of you so she can take control. Lie down and put your legs together. Have her straddle you, with her knees on either side of your torso. Encourage her to be creative. Suggest she move in circles instead of up and down. Or have her lean forward until her clitoris contacts your pubic bone. Both techniques will increase stimulation for her without driving you over the edge. She'll approach orgasm more quickly, while you'll be able to catch your breath (and enjoy the show).

Establish Rhythm

 Resist the urge to thrust fast, hard, and deep in a repetitive one-two pattern. Instead, try being more creative: Mix slow, deep thrusts with quick, shallow ones. Start with mostly shallow thrusts that target the first third of the vagina—the most sensitive part—but don't create too much stimulation on the head of your penis. As her arousal builds, add a higher ratio of deep thrusts. Go in slowly and come out quickly; the fast withdrawals will generate even more sensation for her clitoris—with no substantial penalty, either.

Adjust Her Legs

 Pole-position and joystick references are so passé. When you're on top, think of her legs as your throttle. Ask her to reposition them based on how much catching up—or slowing down—you need to do. For instance, when she has her knees up and her legs spread, you'll be able to make deep, slow strokes that generate less friction. For more stimulation, have her lower her knees so that she's lying flat on the bed. Need still more friction? Close her legs so that your knees are outside hers.

She's not likely to orgasm with any of these variations. But she's also unlikely to lose much ground, arousal-wise. "The missionary position has been unfairly maligned," says *Sexational Secrets* author Susan Crain Bakos, "but many women enjoy it—and find it more intimate than many other positions."

Thrust toward Her Thigh

 When both of you need a little extra zip, try the dual-orgasm position (or DOG), developed by a British sexologist. Have your partner raise her right leg until her knee is even with your left shoulder. She should leave her left leg flat on the bed. Then direct your thrusts toward the inner thigh of her raised leg.

"By splitting her legs, she stretches her vagina, allowing for tighter penetration and more pressure on the clitoris," explains Bakos.

Mutual Fun

Here are five more tips to help you come together.

❶ She does her best work on top. So do you. To switch positions without losing a beat, lie across the width of your bed instead of the length. Start near the headboard and you'll have enough room to roll yourselves completely over as many times as necessary.

❷ Most men think of oral sex as something they can do only before intercourse. There's no rule that says your tongue can't revisit a favorite stomping ground. When you're miles ahead of her, give your penis a break. Don't worry about losing your erection—her mounting excitement will bring it back even stronger than before.

❸ The longer you spend in one position, the less control you have over ejaculation. Try switching from position to position—sort of like sexual channel surfing. Return to your favorites, but don't spend more than about 30 thrusts in each. Chances are, you'll be able to last two or three times longer than normal. In a study at the University of New Brunswick, researchers found that men who frequently changed sexual positions had better results than those who used other methods (like corks and duct tape) to delay ejaculation.

❹ Finish doggie style. It can give both of you complete range of motion. She can thrust as much or as little as she likes, and however fast or slowly she prefers. You can pick up the slack. Angle your penis up to create more friction. Angle it down to better target her G-spot. Time your finish right before *Monday Night Football* starts.

❺ One of the best ways to tell when she's nearing orgasm is to listen for her breath to become short and shallow. Or ask her to give some prearranged signal. This will help you fine-tune your own finish.

MAN'S GUIDE INTERVIEW

Female Geography 101

An Interview with Beverly Whipple, Ph.D.

With all its peaks, valleys, hidden caves, and whatnot, the female body is one of the biggest mysteries known to man. We asked Beverly Whipple, Ph.D., coauthor of The G Spot and Other Recent Discoveries About Human Sexuality *and one of the world's foremost female-anatomy experts, to give us a lesson on exploring earth's most exquisite terrain.*

If you were to assess American men on their awareness of female erogenous zones, how would they score on a scale of 1 to 10, with 1 being the most clueless?

I'd say about 2.

What are our most glaring deficiencies?

Men are either focusing on themselves or assuming they know what a woman likes without checking it out. They think, "I had a partner once who liked this, so therefore *you're* going to like this." Every woman is different.

Why won't women just tell us straight out what they like in bed?

For most of us, it's hard to communicate about what brings us pleasure. Although there are more than 100 words in the English language for pain, there are fewer than 15 for pleasure. The stereotype is that men are expected to know. Women can't tell them what they like because they're afraid they'll damage the male ego. So we get in this conspiracy of silence. When we're in bed, as women, we wish he'd move his hand a little bit higher or stroke us a little more firmly, but we don't say a word. It's very similar to telling a partner there's something very special we'd like for our birthday, and we'll be so happy if we get it and so disappointed if we don't get it, and we give no clues as to what it is. You know what? We're not going to get what we want for our birthday. The same is true of sexual interactions. We are not going to get what we want unless we can communicate it.

What can guys do to spark this kind of conversation?

Don't have a big discussion. Don't say, "Okay, now we're going to sit down and talk." That can be very threatening to both people. Many couples are afraid to bring up sexual issues, especially in a long-term relationship. If one says, "Why don't we try this?" they're afraid their partner is going to say, "Wait a minute. Whom did you have an affair with?"

What's a better strategy?

Make it part of your normal, everyday communication with each other. Say, "You know, I really liked it when you touched me there. Could you do that again?" Or say, "I didn't get much sensation when you did that. Let's try something different." If that's done in a caring and loving way, I think it's well-accepted. Get specific feedback from your partner and try different things. Don't just hone in on one spot. Honing in on one spot can really be a turn-off to women because it's so goal oriented. It's like, "Okay, I'm going to push this button and you're going to respond."

This doesn't apply to us, of course, but a lot of guys seem to hone in on the clitoris. What other areas would women like men to explore?

With men, they have desire, you touch the penis, they get an erection, have an orgasm and that's it. Women aren't like that. Women have many different areas that give them pleasure. We have the clitoris, which is wonderful. We have the G-spot. We have the cervix. We have the breasts. There are many areas that provide pleasure for women and can produce orgasm other than the clitoris. Some women like to start out with kissing, while other women like to start out with caressing of their back, neck, and breasts. Some women like you to suck on their big toes.

In general, are guys too rough during foreplay?

I think many women feel that men aren't really thinking about what women like. Some women don't like direct pressure onto the tip or head of the clitoris. They like pressure alongside of it or further back.

Your research shows that women have three types of orgasm: clitoral, G-spot, and a combination of the two, or blended orgasm. How can a guy tell which kind of orgasm his partner is having?

When we have an orgasm from stimulation of the clitoris, the end of the vagina balloons out and the uterus pulls up. If we have an orgasm from stimulation of just the G spot, the uterus pushes down in the vagina. It's like a bearing-down sensation, so there's a pushing-out effect. Of course, the best thing to do is ask the woman: "Can you tell me what is happening?"

During intercourse, can a woman have all three kinds of orgasm?

It depends on the position. If the man is on top of the woman in the missionary position, it's very difficult to stimulate the G-spot. Usually, that stimulates the clitoris, if you're in contact with the clitoris. If the woman is on top in the rear-entry position, that would stimulate the G-spot. But if you do clitoral stimulation with your fingers in that position, then it could be a blended orgasm.

Let's talk about breasts and nerve endings. What are the most sensitive parts of the breasts?

The nipples are extremely sensitive in most women. When you stimulate the nipples, there's a release of oxytocin, which is involved in sexual response. Stimulation of the nipples and genitals at the same time can produce very strong responses in women. But it depends on the woman and what she likes. Some women feel that somebody stimulating their nipples is tuning the dial on a radio. It's just a real turn-off. And other women love it.

Are large-breasted women more sensitive to touch than small-breasted women?

The number of nerve endings in large and small breasts is the same, so it doesn't seem to make a difference. The same is true of large and small penises. Having a large penis does not mean the man will feel more stimulation. We don't know that everybody enjoys or uses all those nerve endings. But they're there, whether you like them being stimulated or not.

Are there some erogenous zones that men often overlook?

The big toe. The back of the neck. The back of the knee. Some women love to have their earlobes nibbled. Almost anything has erotic potential for anybody. That's the fun part of it: to find out and experiment.

Some researchers still doubt the existence of the G-spot. How do you respond to this continuing debate?

The research has shown that it's there. It's the female prostate gland. We know from studies of female ejaculate that there is prostate-specific antigen (PSA) released. One researcher hypothesizes that all women have female ejaculation, but because the amount is so small and women are often lying on their backs, it doesn't always come out the urethra during sex. But it does come out the next time they urinate. The researcher got urine from women who had no contact with male seminal fluid for 72 hours. He found no PSA in their urine before they self-stimulated themselves, but found it in all the urine after stimulation.

When a woman ejaculates, is it sometimes noticeable?

In some cases, the man feels the squirt come out. But the amount is not great. What we've collected and analyzed is only about a teaspoonful. It comes out the female urethra, the same as male ejaculate comes out the male urethra. Anecdotal reports show that some men are a little bit surprised by this. Some men think the woman is urinating on them, and they get very upset. The majority of men think it's just a normal phenomenon, and many of them feel kind of excited about it. The important thing is for the woman not to have surgery to correct something that's perfectly normal, or to stop having orgasmic response because she's afraid she's going to wet the bed.

How do you find the G-spot?

The G-spot is halfway between the back of the pubic bone and the cervix—the part of the uterus that comes down into the vagina and feels like the tip of your nose. If the woman is lying on her back, you put in your fingers, palm up, and push up between those two areas with a kind of "come here" motion, the tissue will begin to swell as it's stimulated.

What's the best way to get your partner to go along with this exploratory mission?

It has to be done in a very loving and caring way. Don't just jam in your fingers and say, "Okay, now I'm going to look for this." Incorporate it as part of the sex play. Be sure your fingernails aren't too long. You might also want to use a little water-based lubricant. Since this area surrounds the urethra, many women report that they feel like they have to urinate the first time you touch it. But that usually goes away after a few seconds of stimulation.

Such stimulation also seems to have a pain-blocking effect.

In laboratory rats, it's stronger than 10 milligrams of morphine per kilogram of body weight. In women, pressure on the G-spot produces an elevation in pain threshold of 47 to 50 percent. And if women have orgasm from self-stimulation, the pain threshold goes up over 100 percent. This analgesic effect is also activated during childbirth. We believe that labor and childbirth would be much more uncomfortable without it.

Your research shows that some women can have a tremendous orgasm through mental imagery alone. How do they do that?

Some used fantasy. Some used different breathing techniques. But they got so deep into their imagery that they really couldn't tell us what they did to induce these orgasms. We brought in tape recorders and tried very hard, but we just didn't get the data.

Can men do this?

I've done some studies with men who can have multiple orgasms with multiple ejaculations. But I've never had any men contact me and say they have imagery orgasm.

What role does age play in female sexual response?

If a woman is 35 or older, she is in perimenopause, and some changes begin to occur. The man will think he's doing something wrong or something's wrong with him, when the problem may be organic. If she's not lubricating, it's not because she's not turned on. She may not be getting good bloodflow to her genitals because of decreased estrogen or increased cholesterol. If she smokes, she can have damage to the nerves and small arteries. There are many reasons for decreased vaginal lubrication.

Including medications?

As we get older, we often take more medications that can play havoc with the sexual organs. For example, antihistamines dry up the nose. But they also dry up the vagina. High blood pressure medications can cause problems with orgasmic response. We know that the (SSRI) antidepressants—Paxil, Zoloft, Prozac—are terrible. Most people don't have orgasm with them. In fact, many men are taking them off-label for premature ejaculation.

Does declining physical fitness play a role?

Sure, you get tired easier if you're not keeping yourself physically active. You know what happens when your cholesterol goes up. What clogs the arteries of the heart also clogs the arteries of the penis and clitoris and everything else. So we have to have good, healthy diets. We have to keep ourselves physically fit by exercising. And sex can't be our only exercise. It's not as aerobic as some people think, especially when they get into this boring, one-position-only form of intercourse. That doesn't burn many more calories than sitting on the couch.

Can sex get better as we age?

Yes. I do see more older couples becoming more focused on sensuality and sexuality rather than just on sex and wham-bam. They're much more pleasure oriented than goal oriented. They say they enjoy their sexual interactions more.

QUICKIES

THE SNIFF TEST

Your schnozz can tell what brand of bratwurst is grilling two blocks away. It may also pick up when a woman is fertile, according to a new study. Men were told to smell two T-shirts, then asked which belonged to an attractive woman. In truth, they'd been worn by the same woman—one shirt while she was ovulating, the other when she wasn't. Three out of four men selected the fertile-phase shirt, says the study author, Devendra Singh, Ph.D., of the University of Texas at Austin. Some researchers think the scent may come from pheromones called copulins, produced by vaginal and cervical secretions that peak during ovulation. That's science. We just like to say "copulins."

In another study, researchers found that only about one-third of women ovulate as the textbooks say—that is, between days 10 and 17 of their menstrual cycle. If you're trying to avoid pregnancy, "it's risky to rely on the calendar," says Allen Wilcox, M.D., of the National Institute of Environmental Health Sciences.

WHY SHE MOANS IN THE MIDDLE OF THE NIGHT

You've torpedoed through enough pairs of boxers to know it's common for men to have involuntary nocturnal erections. But you probably didn't know that women have them, too—up to five every night! It's not just her clitoris that reflexively becomes engorged with blood during REM sleep; it's her entire genital area, says Irwin Goldstein, M.D., urology professor and director of the Institute for Sexual Medicine at Boston University School of Medicine. That makes her more likely to have an orgasm. Tonight, try tapping her shoulder to see whether she's already primed for a midnight tryst.

GUESS WHAT SHE HAS!

For years, we've secretly thought that women have a right to feel cheated in the genital department. The clitoris may be one hellcat of a sex organ, but it's, well, tiny—about the size of a collar button, right? Not by a long shot. Helen O'Connell, M.D., a urologic surgeon at the Royal Melbourne Hospital in Australia, found during dissection studies that the glans, or head, of the clitoris is connected to erectile tissue that extends as far as 3 inches inside a woman's vagina, making the entire organ roughly as large as your penis.

How did legions of doctors—and other interested parties—miss this basic biological detail for so many years?

"Historically, there's been little scientific interest in female sexuality," says sexual psychologist Michael Bailey, Ph.D., of Northwestern University in Evanston, Illinois. "It's possible we never looked."

SEX THROUGH THE AGES

Here's what happens to both of you as you get older and wiser

MEN	WOMEN
Delayed erections. As the tissue in the penis ages, it becomes "rusty" and slower to rise to the occasion.	**Erogenous zones.** These stay exactly where they've always been: a little to the right . . . harder . . . faster.
Softer wood. That old tissue thing again. This is usually not serious enough to make insertion a problem.	**No more maculopapular flush.** That's the blush that some women experience on their chests and faces during sex.
Decreased duration of erections. Older weenies have trouble retaining bloodflow.	**Vaginal irritation.** As women age, the labial lips—those protective fatty tissues—grow thinner, making additional lubricants necessary.
Delayed ejaculation. It's a simple truth: The older you get, the longer you last.	**Changes in breast sensitivity.** As women age, their breasts—particularly the nipples—are less responsive to arousal. However, this doesn't correspond to a decrease in overall stimulation or satisfaction.
Force and quantity of ejaculate. This decreases with age. But unless you're an aspiring porn star, you'll never know the difference.	**Lubrication.** Young women jiffy-lube in 10 to 30 seconds. Menopausal women can take 3 long minutes—the length of time it takes Barbra Streisand to sing "People," for heaven's sake.
Refractory periods. When you were 16, you could pop up buster in 10 minutes. By the time you're 80, it'll take you as long as 5 days to make that bronco buck.	**Overall staying power/stamina.** Women's stamina decreases with age, so no more watching the NFL while she leads her cheers from your upper deck.

THE FUNNY PAGE

"Any plans for this evening, hon?"

5

KEEP HER

 Here's an ironic scenario: A woman—we'll call her Angie—decides to get a tattoo. Her man—let's call him Jimmy Bob—wants it to read, "Jimmy Bob forever." Angie figures it would be better to go with "Jimmie Bob for now."

In real life, the woman's logic all too often prevails—the tattoo outlasts the relationship. Over time, the passion that brought two people together craps out, while more corrosive emotions—such as boredom, resentment, and hostility—creep in. But don't assume your sex life and relationship are doomed to fail. We'll show you how to spot trouble faster than you can say, "laser surgery" (which, if you follow our advice, you won't ever need to have).

THE GUY LIST

19 Rules for
a Successful Relationship

Over the years, we have read a lot of memorable things about abs, beer, relationships, and, well, abs. But given that one in two of you still wind up divorced, we suspect that you haven't been reading the same relationship stuff we have. So we dug through our archives and came up with the best advice we could find about how to keep your relationship solid. For just a minute, forget about chiseling your abs. Here's how to chisel yourself permanently into her heart.

① Get pleasure out of giving pleasure—learn everything you can about female sexuality.

② Stop watching the game.

③ Listen to what she's saying.

④ Repeat what she's just said.

⑤ Tell her that what she's said makes sense to you.

⑥ Take immediate action when you sense she's upset. Neglect something long enough—be it a rattle in your engine, a leak in your basement, or a frown creasing the forehead of your beloved—and eventually you're going to pay. Oh, you'll cruise along safely for a while, sure, but the end result will be a crack in your engine block, a crack in your foundation, or a crack in your heart.

⑦ A willingness to play in bed will lead your body to respond instinctively. Sex is one of the few areas in which adults are allowed to play. Take advantage of it.

⑧ Tell her your head hurts, then mention that studies show that genital stimulation can ease pain. Don't mention that the research was done on rats.

9 Don't refer to your wedding ring as a "chick magnet."

10 Don't sleep with anyone whom you can fire—
or with anyone who can fire you.

11 Don't go into a hotel room with a woman unless you
intend to have sex with her.

12 Ask yourself how much ingenuity, improvisation, energy, joy, and
lust you bring to the party. Lots of guys who cheat on their wives
plead sexual boredom with their partners. And, often enough, a
good case can be made. But if your sex life isn't everything you
dream of, make sure that you've given it everything you've got.

13 Compliment her on what she has made, not on what God has
made. Say something like "Terrific memo," "Incredible insight," or
"Great joke!" "You're beautiful" isn't a compliment.

14 Avoid painting team colors on your face or belly
at Giants games, especially if she's rooting for the Redskins.

15 Have two bathrooms.

16 Express concern instead of glee when you hit something
furry on the highway.

17 Use her name when addressing her, letting her know
you actually remember it. Just because the kids call her Mom,
that doesn't mean you should.

18 Put your foot down the next time both of you are making plans
for dinner—or, heck, deciding where to live and whether to have
children. Women rate agreeable men as more attractive than
stubborn ones, but only if the nicer guys have a dominant streak. If
strength and decisiveness are missing, nice guys come off as meek.

19 Remember: A successful relationship is one in which
it never occurs to you that you've compromised anything.

ASK THE GIRL NEXT DOOR
The honest truth about women from our lovely neighbor

Q: *What are the top three things you most want to hear from the man you're seeing?*
—R. N., Phoenix

A: ❶ "I can't wait to see you."
❷ "I brought you something."
❸ "I love waking up with you."

Q: *All of my friends who've been married for a few years complain that their wives don't want to have sex. What's the deal?*
—H. T., Cleveland

A: I've never been married, so I asked around: One of my married friends didn't want sex for an entire year! She was working 12-hour shifts in an emergency room. Another said that the excitement had faded and that neither person was doing anything to revive it—let's chalk that up to laziness. Another confessed she hit a rut when she gained 10 pounds and was feeling like chopped liver.

But several other wives told me their sex lives are better than ever. Are your buddies romantic, or do they just roll over and poke their penis into her thigh at bedtime? Women—unmarried ones, too—stop wanting sex when they're not getting enough emotion or romance. Life is complicated, and sexuality can be easily affected, whether you're married or just dating. Don't let that scare you; just be aware.

Q: *Does a woman enjoy sex even when she doesn't have an orgasm?*
—G. M., Los Gatos, California

A: An orgasm is only the last 15 seconds of what is usually an all-around amazing experience. Okay, it's the best 15 seconds. But if it's just not happening, most women are happy to call it quits and shift down—as long as that's not a frequent occurrence.

Whatever you do, don't give up before she does, or she'll think you don't care about satisfying her. What do you do when you're about to pass Go and collect $200 but she's stuck in Free Parking? Ask if she wants to climb on top—most women climax easier that way. If she declines, she probably doesn't mind sitting this one out. Or, you could let your orgasm rip and then focus the energy you have left on stimulating her manually. If she pushes her body urgently against your hand or starts kissing you passionately, she's still game and is getting close. If she's had enough, she'll gently move your hand away.

As much as women oooh and ahhh over Sting's alleged ability to have sex for 70 hours straight, we'd rather save our energy than exhaust ourselves—and you—over one elusive orgasm.

Q: *I'm planning to buy my girlfriend jewelry for Christmas, but I'm not sure what to get. She has a simple style, so she probably won't like anything big or flashy. Any suggestions?*
—C. G., Taos, New Mexico

A: My pick: tiny diamond stud earrings. If diamonds seem too symbolic, get her a thin necklace (silver or gold, whichever she wears more often) with a small jewel pendant. Think pearl if she's old-fashioned or romantic, black jade if she's exotic or sophisticated, a ruby if she's feisty or sexy, or cat's-eye if she's outdoorsy or rebellious. Just don't buy her a watch. That's what her dad is buying her mom for their 35th wedding anniversary—it's not what she wants from you.

Q: *At which important events or times in your life do you want your man by your side, no questions asked?*
—N. Z., Fair Oaks, California

A: ❶ When I find out I'm pregnant
❷ Midnight on New Year's Eve
❸ On trips to beautiful and/or dangerous places

For more honest answers about women, look for
Ask the *Men's Health* Girl Next Door
wherever books are sold.

MUST READS

You're Asking for It

To get what you want in bed, you'll need her help. Here Zachary Veilleux explains how to make sure she knows exactly what to do.

In a perfect world, great sex would just happen. Loving couples would intuitively know how to please each other, and we'd have no need for sex therapists, divorce lawyers, and the "Is Your Orgasm Overweight?" quiz in this month's *Cosmopolitan*.

But the world of men and women is far from perfect. In most cases, getting what you want in bed takes actual, in-the-flesh communication—a skill men tend to neglect in favor of learning to tie flies, change tires, and make loud noises with our armpits. (Important skills all, but not much help in the bedroom.)

"You don't go to a restaurant and sit there waiting for the waiter to guess what you want to eat," says Chicago sex therapist Michael Seiler, Ph.D. "Yet men have this fantasy that their partners should be able to anticipate their sexual needs with little or no communication."

Sex talk is delicate business. Ask for too much, and you're a drill sergeant; ask for too little, and you're still left hanging. Here's how to strike a balance.

The Pregame

Every sex therapist we interviewed for this article told us the same thing: The best sex begins outside the bedroom. And they weren't talking about an occasional quickie on the kitchen table.

"A lot of sexual communication can be done in neutral territory, where it's less likely to be mistaken for criticism," says New York City psychiatrist Anthony Pietropinto, M.D. Think about it: When she's naked and vulnerable, the merest hint that she's not pleasing you is tantamount to pointing out her cellulite.

Take our word for it. Take her out for coffee, and try one of the following tactics.

The Cab Driver

Now that you actually own furniture on which to have sex, making out in a Toyota has lost some of its appeal. But the car is still a great place to talk about sex. "It's private, there are no distractions, and you can avoid constant eye contact during a potentially awkward discussion," says Los Angeles sex therapist

Linda DeVillers, Ph.D., author of *Love Skills*. (If you're really nervous about eye contact, ask her to sit in the backseat.)

The Alec Baldwin

If you can't string a sentence together when you're under pressure, do what other inarticulate guys do: Follow a script. If past attempts to talk about your sex life have ended in recrimination (hers) and tears (yours), try this neutral approach.

❶ Tell her what you see.
"I've noticed you never:
    . . . initiate sex."
    . . . get undressed with the lights on."
    . . . wear the Tipper Gore wig I gave you."

❷ Tell her how you interpret it.
"I take that to mean:
    . . . our sex life is my responsibility."
    . . . you don't feel good about your body."
    . . . you were only humoring me the one time you wore it."

❸ Tell her how you feel about that.
"I feel:
    . . . pressured to always be in the mood, and to get you
        in the mood, too."
    . . . sad that you don't know how beautiful you are to me."
    . . . that I really miss that wig!"

❹ Tell her what you want.
"I'd love it if you would:
    . . . approach me sometimes."
    . . . let me see you when we make love."
    . . . forget that I ever brought this up."

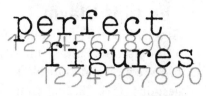

perfect figures

AND THOSE ARE JUST THE GUYS

Percentage of Americans who use lingerie to spice up their sex lives:
49

. . . .

This approach lets you agree on the facts of the situation, while giving her room to disagree with your interpretation of what's happening—a great way to open up a dialogue. Learning to use this approach is worth at least 10 sessions of marital therapy. It's cheaper, too.

The Cliff Clavin

Crave oral sex? There's nothing quite like an impromptu fact or statistic to start a conversation. Putting things in general terms makes a request seem less, well, like a request and more like simple conversation. To begin, use one of our suggestions. (See "Sexual Conversation Starters.") If she laughs, you've lost nothing. If she fires back with a saucy suggestion of her own, you're in business.

Sexual Conversation Starters

If You Want...	Casually Mention That...
More oral sex	83% of men enjoy receiving oral sex and 57% of women like giving it (If she tells you to go find one of those women, quit while you're behind)
Her to be on top	Woman-on-top positions allow for the most clitoral stimulation
To try a sex toy	10% of Americans routinely incorporate toys into their lovemaking (Hint: Don't use the word *incorporate*)
Her to climax sooner	Women who fantasize during lovemaking become more aroused, and they get there more quickly

The E.T.

The next time you're away on business, break out the calling card and ask your mate the same question posed by thousands of other hotel-bound guys every night: "So, what are you wearing?" When the only link between you and your partner is a collect call, you have no choice but to describe—in graphic detail—what you'd do to each other if you were there. "This can be the perfect opportunity to slyly make your wishes known without the risk of insulting her," says DeVillers.

The Roger Ebert

If you're like the average sexually frustrated guy, you take your partner to see big blockbuster flicks at the multiplex and watch skin flicks when you're desperate and alone. Do the reverse. Any movie involving explosives is not going to make your date hot and bothered, so take her to see something sexy. "Even a romantic, R-rated film can have plenty of erotic love scenes. When you find one you like, simply say, 'Wow, that really looks exciting. Why don't we try it that way?'" suggests Dr. Pietropinto.

The Henry Miller

"Often it's a lot easier to write down what you want than to come out and ask for it," says Seiler. Here's a technique he recommends when a couple has trouble making sexual requests out loud.

Each of you gets three pieces of paper. On the first one, write down everything sexual that you currently do together. (Include tame stuff like kissing, taking showers together, talking seductively in bed, or watching sexy films.) Then, make a note of how much you enjoy each activity.

On the second piece of paper, write down all the sexual stuff you don't currently do, but would like to. There are no right answers here—one guy might be dying to sneak a quickie in the armaments aisle at Bargain-Mart, while another guy would settle for making love on colored sheets.

On the last paper, write down anything you definitely don't want to try—not now, and maybe not ever. (This may be a rather short list.)

Next, compare lists. The fact that your partner is also going out on a limb makes the process easier, says Seiler. And while you may be heartbroken to learn that she has no interest in dressing up as Ellie May from the Beverly Hillbillies, you might be surprised at what she is willing to try.

Editor's note: If you can't in your wildest dreams imagine yourself doing this, you're taking it way too seriously. Once you get into it, this exercise can be hilarious as well as educational, reports one of our staffers who tried it with his girlfriend over a bottle of good champagne. They ended up howling with laughter and having great sex.

The Main Event

By happy coincidence, bedside discourse is well-suited to the male communication style: A few well-placed grunts, groans, and guttural monosyllables will give your mate a pretty accurate read on how you're feeling and what you could use a little more of. To nudge her into giving you maximum pleasure . . .

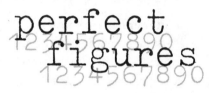

perfect figures

"OOOH, YOU LOOK GOOD IN RED!"

Number of men who have dressed up as Santa Claus:
1 in 5

Number who did it because the wife thought it was a turn-on:
1 in 14

Number who had sex under the Christmas tree:
1 in 4

⦿ **Wake the neighbors.**
"Women love to hear sounds of pleasure, and most men dramatically underdo them," says DeVillers. Go ahead and moan, groan, sigh, and scream. If you're self-conscious about making noise, or if you have kids in the house, a CD player in your bedroom can mask the sounds.

> **"**Love is not the dying moan of a distant violin— it's the triumphant twang of a bedspring. **"**
>
> —S. J. Perelman

● Take matters into your own hands.

"Try wrapping your hands on top of hers and directing her touch in ways you find most pleasurable," says DeVillers. If she's going too slowly, speed her up. If she needs to squeeze harder, tighten her fingers. (The obvious exception is oral sex: Never push her head down to suggest fellatio. Instead, set a good example by being the first to move downtown. You'll earn credits toward your own satisfaction.)

● Talk dirty to her.

Telling her what to do isn't a turn-on. Sexy, silly pillow talk is. "Try starting with 'I'd love it if you'd . . . ,'" suggests DeVillers. If you have a term of endearment for your penis, use it. Unless it happens to be Veronica.

● Shower her with praise.

It sounds obvious, but we men often get so caught up in the moment that we forget to let the lady know when she's getting it right. To really reinforce a successful evening, compliment her again the next morning.

She might even make you breakfast.

The Sex Crusaders

Nearly half the women in America have trouble enjoying sex. But, as writer Joe Kita found out, what two pioneering doctors have discovered—and what they can teach you—could keep everyone smiling.

The Berman sisters, Jennifer and Laura, are giggling. They giggle a lot—much more than you'd expect from two highly regarded UCLA doctors. And even though it's sexist to say so, they're damn cute when they're giggling: white smiles flashing, blue eyes sparkling, cheeks dimpling. If more doctors looked like they do, men would be living well past 100.

Jennifer, 36, is an M.D. specializing in female urology. Laura, 32, has a Ph.D. and works as a sex educator and psychotherapist. Together, they run a clinic in Los Angeles that specializes in the study and treatment of female sexual dysfunction.

Until recently, that's been a bit of an oxymoron. After all, a woman's privates don't have any apparent moving parts, nothing that requires complex hydraulics. If a couple was having trouble in bed, the guy had to be the culprit. The Bermans are helping to change that assumption. They're showing that men aren't the only ones who can become impotent. In fact, they're giving Viagra to women.

Before we get into that, let's find out what all the giggling is about.

"Hmmm. If we could change one thing about sex, what would it be?" says Laura, repeating my question. "That's a tough one."

"I know!" says Jennifer. "I wish we could be like those lizards. You know, the ones that are both male and female. Hermaphrodites. Then we wouldn't need partners. We'd always be satisfied. We could have sex whenever and however we wanted."

"And you could read your own mind," adds Laura.

They giggle.

The Bermans are like tag-team wrestlers in conversation. Each continually hands off incomplete thoughts for the other to expand upon. At times, it seems as if they can read each other's minds, although that shouldn't be so surprising. They've been working closely together for the past decade, first as codirectors of the Women's Sexual Health Clinic in Boston and now as founders of the Network for Excellence in Women's Sexual Health, at UCLA.

Along the way, they've garnered a reputation for being intelligent, opinionated, and disarmingly frank when discussing sex. (During our lunchtime interview, they talked about premature ejaculation while munching egg-salad sandwiches.) These are traits the media and the public can't resist. Their book, *For Women Only*, is a bestseller, and publications ranging from *Newsweek* to *People* to *Harper's Bazaar* have written about them, bestowing such nicknames as the Viagra Twins, Doctors of Desire, and Baby Ruths (in deference to Dr. Westheimer).

"Our main mission is to get the word out about female sexual dysfunction," says Laura. "Women shouldn't be embarrassed about seeking help."

The Bermans estimate that 43 percent of American women suffer from some type of sexual problem. This compares with 31 percent of men. "Yet for most of the past 100 years, doctors have dismissed women's sexual complaints as either psychological or emotional," they note in their book. "The problem is not just 'in our heads.'"

Sound familiar? This is the same thing a few forward-thinking urologists

❝Sex without love has its place, and it's pretty cool, but when you have it hand in hand with deep commitment and respect and caring, it's 9,000 times better.❞

—George Carlin

were telling men back in the 1990s. In fact, the Bermans worked for one of these pioneers, Irwin Goldstein, M.D., at Boston University Medical Center, and consider him their mentor.

At their UCLA clinic, the sisters work in tandem. Laura interviews and evaluates patients before Jennifer examines them. And this isn't your usual gynecologic inspection. The Bermans use special probes to measure clitoral sensation, vaginal compliance, and genital bloodflow. (Erotic videos, a vibrator, and 3-D surround-sound glasses are provided.)

What they've found, after examining thousands of women, is that common sexual complaints such as low libido and the inability to reach orgasm often have distinct physical causes that can be remedied medically, in addition to therapeutically. Women no longer have to resign themselves to a life of numbness. And let's face it, if your partner doesn't want sex as often as you do or doesn't enjoy it as much, that's eventually going to affect your relationship and maybe even cause you to doubt yourself.

So here's a look at some of the new things the Bermans are uncovering about female sexuality—facts that'll help you not only understand your woman better but also keep her giggling with pleasure.

Vibrators Are a Girl's Second-Best Friend

In their practice, the Bermans dispense vibrators like aspirin. They regard them as the quickest and easiest way for a woman to bring out her latent sexuality. But most men are secretly distrustful of the things. To us, every vibrator is a tall, trim lifeguard who's making eyes at our date.

"For women, sex is more than just orgasm," says Laura. "It's about connecting and sharing with someone you care about. A vibrator is never going to replace that. However, it's great for enhancing sex. A lot of couples enjoy going to an erotica shop, picking one out, and experimenting together. Or you can buy her one and say, 'Have fun with this while I'm away on my trip.' Giving your approval without pressure is vital."

Actually, the Bermans are experimenting with a device that's capable of producing even more grins than a vibrator. It's an electronic implant for women. This tiny electrode stimulates the part of the spine associated with genital arousal. It may one day make climaxing as easy as pushing a button.

"But don't worry," says Laura. "Women will always want the connection, intimacy, and value that a partner provides."

To Make a Woman Feel Precious, Find the Key to Her Treasure Chest

This has nothing to do with unhooking her bra. Rather, the Bermans claim that every woman has a treasure chest inside her that most men don't know exists. It's that special, secret part of her that she cherishes.

"Typically, it's a nonbody trait," explains Laura, "like her intellectual curiosity, her sense of humor, her outlandishness. But it could be the color of her eyes or even her laugh. It's when a man discovers this, when he comes to appreciate and love that part of her, that he really gets the girl both emotionally and sexually. That's when she feels she's being loved as a complete person."

If you don't have a clue what's inside your woman's treasure chest, listen closely the next time she's with her father. Dads are usually the ones who instill these gems in their little girls. Note what he compliments about her and what makes her sparkle.

Men Feel Intimate as a Result of Being Sexual; Women Feel Sexual as a Result of Being Intimate

This is the basis of the entire war between the sexes. If you can grasp the wisdom of these 18 words, you'll forever be blessed.

"A lot of women come into the clinic complaining of low libido," says Laura. "They tell us they've lost the intimacy in their relationship. They want to cuddle with their husband, but the second they do, he thinks it's an invitation for sex. Then the woman has to reject him because she's not in the mood, and the whole process begins again."

To break this cycle, the Bermans recommend VENIS, or "very erotic noninsertive sex." This can be as tame as washing her hair, then massaging her with warm oil. Or, if that makes you feel too much like John Gray, "erotic wrestling with maximum body and genital contact" is also okay.

"All these things are examples of fun, engaging, romantic, sensual activities that will encourage playfulness and intimacy," says Laura. "The point is to have one night when intercourse isn't the focus."

Her Hot Zone Is Twice as Big as Originally Thought, and It Has More Nerve Endings Than Your Penis

The clitoris is merely one part of a recently discovered subterranean complex called the cligeva, which also includes the urethra and the G-spot. Jennifer calls it a "very important, erotic, sexual organ." The whole thing becomes engorged during stimulation, hardens like an erection, and, in some cases, even ejaculates a clear fluid.

Obviously, then, it's worthy of your attention. To titillate it properly, you'll need guidance. "Some women like direct stimulation of the clitoris; others prefer the area around it," explains Laura. "Some have a clitoris that's too sensitive; others have one that's not sensitive enough. So it really comes down to communication."

To foster this, create a no-pressure atmosphere in which she feels comfortable talking about what gives her exquisite pleasure. Queries with yes-or-no answers, such as "Does it feel good when I touch you here?" are better than open-ended ones such as "What would you like me to do next, dear?"

A Woman Can Make You Impotent

The inability to achieve an erection is not entirely physiological. If a woman has an undiagnosed condition that's causing her to lose interest in sex or be unresponsive, her partner often starts to question his virility.

When this happens, the male mind can compound the situation, resulting in low libido, early ejaculation, and erectile dysfunction. The Bermans contend that a large number of men are in this predicament.

Even when such a situation doesn't affect the man physically, it often causes a rift in the relationship. That's why the Bermans encourage women to bring their partners to the clinic. Men need to understand that it's not entirely their problem.

"All this research into female sexual dysfunction will help solve problems in male sexuality," says Jennifer. "The thinking used to be that all a man needed was an erection satisfactory for intercourse. There was never any thought given to his relationship, his level of satisfaction, or his emotional connection. Now we're realizing that these things are just as important to a man's sexual performance as they are to a woman's."

It's**Been**Said. . .

" Sex is the most civilizing force on the planet. It is the life force. "

—Hugh Hefner

Women Experience Not One, Not Two, but Three Different Types of Orgasms

They are clitoral, pelvic floor, and blended. One is not any more pleasurable than another, but each feels distinctive. A clitoral orgasm is more localized and results from direct stimulation of the clitoris and surrounding tissue. A pelvic-floor orgasm resonates from much farther down and involves vaginal and uterine contractions triggered by deep penetration. A blended orgasm contains elements of both.

Unfortunately, it's pretty difficult (if not impossible) for a man to detect the difference between these. And in case you're wondering how many types of orgasms men have, you'll have to be content with just one.

Only 20 to 30 Percent of Women Reach Orgasm through Vaginal Penetration Alone

As amazing as it sounds, intercourse just doesn't do it. "Women need foreplay," says Laura. "To get her really excited, you need to slow down and smell her rose."

If you're like most guys, though, you view foreplay as a delay-of-game penalty. So here's a timesaving trick: To satisfy your partner and yourself, try the missionary position with a pelvic tilt. Have her lie on her back with knees bent, feet on the floor, and one or more pillows beneath her butt. This satisfies your urge for action while giving her clitoris maximum stimulation. With a bit of practice and adjustment, the two of you should climax simultaneously.

70 Percent of Women Have Faked It

There's a story in the Bermans' book about a 32-year-old woman who has been faking orgasms for years because, she says, "you have to be delicate with the male ego." Rather than be honest with her husband and face her own sexual shortcomings, she has become deceitful. And apparently there are lots of women doing this. Jennifer says faking is so widespread because of the importance men attach to orgasm. Since it's the end-all for us, we assume it must be for women. And we unwittingly pressure them toward that conclusion.

"Most women don't have orgasms every time they have sex," states Laura. "That's the biggest misunderstanding men have about us. We don't need to be swinging from the chandeliers to be satisfied."

Unfortunately, there's no easy way to know whether your partner is being truthful about her pleasure level. There are physical signs of climaxing, such as vaginal contractions, increased heart rate, accelerated breathing, and facial flushing, but in the heat of the moment, we don't recommend taking measurements. If you suspect that your partner is regularly faking for your benefit, then you need to remove the pressure she's evidently feeling to validate you.

The Bermans recommend two things: (1) Tell her that you won't be offended if she doesn't have an orgasm, and (2) emphasize that an honest, open, loving relationship is what's most important to you. Say it this way: "If there's something I can be doing differently, anything that would help you respond the way you want to, I want to know."

For Good Sex, Women Need Good Bloodflow—Just like You

When you fall asleep in an awkward position and your arm or leg goes numb, it's because you've pinched off bloodflow to the area. The same thing can happen over a lifetime to sex organs. As circulation gradually decreases, performance, sensation, and enjoyment decline as well. This process has been understood for some time in men, but the correlation was never made in women.

"A decrease in bloodflow to the vagina and uterus, whether as a result of aging or surgery, can diminish sexual response," say the Bermans. Health conditions that inhibit circulation, such as diabetes and arteriosclerosis, can also impact a woman's sex life, just as they can yours.

To treat such problems, the Bermans prescribe Viagra and the Eros clitoral-therapy device (CTD). Both draw blood to the genitals—one chemically, the other mechanically. Although use of Viagra by women has yet to be approved by the FDA, a recent study by the Bermans found that 67 percent of those using it over a 6-week period enhanced their ability to reach orgasm, and 70 percent felt more sensation in their genitals during foreplay and intercourse. (See "Chicks on Viagra!" on the opposite page, for a first-person account.) Meanwhile, the Eros CTD works on the same principle as a penis pump. It's placed over the clitoris, and its gentle sucking action draws blood to the area. Short-term, it enhances arousal. Long-term, it may keep clitoral and labial arteries from atrophying, or even help regenerate them.

So if your partner doesn't seem to want or enjoy sex as much as she used to, it could be an indication of a developing health problem. Even if she's experiencing no difficulties, the Bermans claim that sexual sensation can be amplified with moderate aerobic exercise. In fact, exercise could be the poor woman's Viagra. Done before sex, it can stimulate overall body circulation and have just as pronounced an effect. One study found that women who watched erotic videos after exercise experienced 168 percent more genital engorgement than when they watched them before exercising.

To Fully Enjoy Sex, Women Need Nerve—Lots of Them

A woman's pelvic region is a vast, interconnected nerve field that has yet to be fully mapped. The Bermans have found that women can often trace diminishing sexual enjoyment back to when they had surgery in this area (Cesarean section, hysterectomy, tubal ligation) or some other trauma (difficult childbirth; bicycle or balance-beam accident). The Bermans suspect that nerves and blood vessels central to sexual function were damaged. They're working to pinpoint the processes and also develop nerve-sparing surgical techniques similar to those being used with prostate-cancer patients.

Until this happens, the Bermans recommend that women avoid sitting on

Chicks on Viagra!

Here's what happened to one 30-something woman when she popped the little blue pill.

❶ The experiment

Though Viagra isn't FDA-approved for women's use, some researchers theorize that if it increases bloodflow enough for an impotent man to get and sustain an erection, then maybe the same boost in bloodflow can heighten sensation for sexually dysfunctional women.

❶ Our lab rat

Though our female writer has no complaints about her sex life, she wanted to see if the 25 milligram pill would change the intensity of her orgasms.

❶ Husband's reaction

Insulted, then interested.

❶ Time to take effect

25 minutes.

❶ The effects

"Whole-body flush, breasts swelling (in a good way), massive lubrication, clitoris engorged and erect. His penis thrusting against me caused plenty of sensation. I had one intense orgasm and a number of lesser ones," she says.

❶ Conclusion

"I've always found orgasms easy, but this was way over the top—rushing, intense, extreme sexual frenzy." She tried it again (twice), just in case the first trial was a fluke. It wasn't.

❶ Caution

Viagra has potentially dangerous side effects, especially in people with heart conditions. Do not take it without a doctor's prescription.

narrow bicycle saddles for long periods, take extra care when participating in sports with equipment that must be straddled, and, most important, think twice about having any elective surgery done down there. This especially includes genital cosmetic surgery, such as vaginal tightening and labia reconstruction. These have become increasingly popular among older women within the past decade, and they're often done at a partner's prompting. But what the couple doesn't realize is that it may eventually hurt, not help, their sex life.

Women Need Testosterone, Too

Of all the things they're researching, Jennifer says this is the most exciting. Testosterone is a hormone that influences sexual desire. Most people assume it's a male thing because it's responsible for such manly characteristics as facial hair and a deep voice. But women (and not just the ones with mustaches) have some testosterone, too. In fact, the Bermans say, "Testosterone is so central to a woman's sexual function that no lover and no amount of sexual stimulation can make up for its absence."

One of the first things they do when treating a woman with low libido is to measure her testosterone. The body naturally produces less with age, but stress, depression, anxiety, and childbirth all can inhibit production. If it's low, the Bermans supplement it, working to administer the perfect restorative dose without making the patient look like Joe Torre. So far, they claim to have had significant success. Indeed, they're hopeful that one day they'll wipe out libido problems entirely. And here, too, their work may have an impact on men, since our testosterone levels also decline with age.

Check In to the Love Lab

Can your relationship survive the G forces of modern matrimony? A Seattle psychologist says he can predict divorce with 90 percent accuracy. In this next piece by Joe Kita, Joe and his wife put their relationship to the test. Maybe it's time you do the same.

This doesn't look like a typical marriage counselor's office. For one thing, there's equipment—huge, floor-to-ceiling banks of instruments designed to troubleshoot a relationship the way national-defense radar spots bogeys. Switches, cords, dials, and blinking lights abound, and there's a library of nearly 1,000 VHS tapes of previously probed couples. This is objective analysis. This is marriage science. This just may be the closest anyone has come to dissecting love.

That's why our mouths are dry and our moods apprehensive as my wife and I are wired into the Love Lab of John Gottman, Ph.D., at the University of Washington in Seattle. The fingertip sensors measure perspiration. The ear clips monitor bloodflow. The electrodes on our ribs trace heart rate. The tubes around our chests track respiration. The cameras in the corners scrutinize body language. The chairs record nervous movement.

There is no hiding here, no escape from the monsters that may surface as we discuss our relationship. Each dial in the control room indicates a measure of our discomfort, our honesty, and, I guess, our love. It feels as if we've been wired for execution . . . and perhaps we have.

Marital B.S. Detector

Next to *Is it in yet?* the four most unnerving words for men are *Let's discuss our relationship.* The Love Lab's John Gottman, Ph.D., says the reason guys dread this phrase is because by the time a "discussion" is needed, the problem is hopelessly big. "Every marriage ought to be equipped with a built-in early-warning system," he says. "This allows you to talk about issues while they're still minor." The following marital B.S. detector will help you to do just that. More than two yes answers means trouble is brewing, and you should talk about it now.

1. When I'm with my partner, I often want to be somewhere else.   Yes   No

2. There is tension between us.   Yes   No

3. My partner has little idea what I'm thinking.   Yes   No

4. I wish we were closer right now.   Yes   No

5. My partner has wanted to be alone a lot lately.   Yes   No

6. We've been fighting more often.   Yes   No

7. There hasn't been much fun or joy in our lives lately.   Yes   No

8. Small issues have a tendency to escalate.   Yes   No

9. We have been hurting each other's feelings.   Yes   No

10. We really need to talk.   Yes   No

Maria and I aren't here because our marriage is in trouble. We've been happily wed for 15 years, but lately couples we know have started dropping like soldiers at Normandy. Nowadays, the chance of a first marriage culminating in D day is 67 percent. Half of these divorces occur within the first 7 years, but the second most dangerous time is at 16 years, when middle-age regrets intensify and bored libidos open a lustful eye.

That's what has us worried. We're concerned about our future together. Based on almost 2 decades of research, Gottman claims to be able to predict divorce with 90 percent accuracy. His expertise lies in analyzing all the physiological data while

Will Your Marriage Fail?

This quiz is based on the seven principles of making marriage work that have been identified by the Love Lab's John Gottman, Ph.D. Answer true or false for each, then score yourself at the conclusion. If you're feeling brave, have your partner take the test to see how you compare.

1. I can list my partner's major aspirations and hopes in life.   T   F
2. I know my partner's current major worries.   T   F
3. I know the three most special times in my spouse's life.   T   F
4. I can easily list the three things I most admire about my partner.   T   F
5. I often touch or kiss my spouse affectionately.   T   F
6. Our sex life is generally satisfying.   T   F
7. I look forward to spending my free time with my partner.   T   F
8. My partner is one of my best friends.   T   F
9. My partner tells me when he or she has had a bad day.   T   F
10. I am genuinely interested in my spouse's opinion.   T   F
11. I usually learn a lot from my spouse even when we disagree.   T   F
12. I feel that I have an important say when we make decisions.   T   F
13. I can admit that I am wrong.   T   F
14. Even when we disagree, we can maintain a sense of humor.   T   F
15. My spouse is good at soothing me when I get upset.   T   F
16. My partner and I are a good team.   T   F

watching a couple argue. This is a unique approach to marriage therapy. He's brought science to the aid of matrimony.

In preliminary interviews, assistants have helped us identify hot spots in our relationship. Once they leave, we're to pick one hot spot and have at it for 10 minutes.

The argument Maria and I have chosen involves religion— the fact that I put little faith in it and play a meager role in our children's spiritual upbringing. Maria, a lifelong Roman Catholic, feels it's unfair for her to be alone in this responsibility and wishes I would take it more seriously. It's an old battle

Marriage Fact #113

An unhappy marriage increases your chance of getting sick by 35 percent and shortens your life by 4 years. "I often think that if fitness fanatics spent just 10 percent of their weekly exercise time working on their marriages instead of their bodies, they would get three times the health benefits," says the Love Lab's John Gottman, Ph.D.

17 When we argue, winning isn't my objective.		T	F
18 I accept that there are issues we will never resolve.		T	F
19 We share many similar values in our roles as husband and wife.		T	F
20 We share many happy memories.		T	F

SCORING

● 13 or more true answers

You have a solid relationship that will probably endure until both of you are toothless and incontinent. Fortunately, you'll still be so in love that neither of you will notice.

● 7 to 12 true answers

This is a pivotal time in your relationship. There are many strengths you can build upon, but there are also some weaknesses that need tending. It's time to put down that remote and get away for the weekend.

● 6 or fewer true answers

You may be in danger of divorce. If this scares you, you probably still value the relationship enough to try to save it. Honest talk is needed. If that's not possible, you may want to consult John Gottman himself. Call the Gottman Institute (888-523-9042) or visit www.gottman.com.

that never fails to rankle me and disturb her, and this time is no exception. Ten minutes goes by like 10 seconds. We're not even aware of the instruments.

Not surprisingly, it's during disagreements that the most serious relationship damage occurs. But it's not so much the topic as the way in which it's debated. While we're arguing, Gottman is in the next room watching for what he calls the Four Horsemen of the Apocalypse. They generally march through an argument and a marriage in the following order.

● Criticism

There's a big difference between complaining and criticizing. "A complaint," says Gottman, "focuses on a specific behavior, such as 'I'm angry you didn't clean the kitchen.' But a criticism throws in blame and character assassination, like 'Why are you so lazy?'"

The Better-Marriage Workout

A relationship can be built just like a body in a gym. But it doesn't require that much sweat. According to real-life research done by the Love Lab's John Gottman, Ph.D., it takes only 5 hours per week. Here's the training plan.

EXERCISE 1

Before saying goodbye to your partner in the morning, learn about one important thing that's happening in her life that day. This will break the "habit of inattention" that eventually turns couples into strangers.

● **Repetitions**
2 minutes per day × 5 working days

● **Time**
10 minutes per week

EXERCISE 2

Decompress after work by discussing the most stressful parts of your day. This will prevent job frustration from spilling over into your home life. When it's her turn to talk, resist the urge to give advice. Instead, be supportive and say you understand.

● **Repetitions**
20 minutes per day × 5 working days

● **Time**
1 hour 40 minutes per week

EXERCISE 3

Once a day, spontaneously tell your partner that you appreciate something she's done or that you admire a certain quality in her.

● **Repetitions**
5 minutes per day × 7 days

● **Time**
35 minutes per week

◐ Contempt

Too much criticism leads to conversations tainted with sarcasm, cynicism, and mockery. "Contempt is poisonous to a relationship because it conveys disgust," Gottman says. "It's fueled by long-simmering negative thoughts about your partner." A contemptuous extension of the previous exchange would be "Your laziness makes me sick. You're an inconsiderate pig."

◐ Defensiveness

In the face of persistent criticism and contempt, it's natural to defend yourself. But rather than defuse the attack, this response usually escalates it. "Defensiveness is really a way of blaming your partner,"

Marriage Fact #212

If your heart rate exceeds 100 beats per minute during an argument, you'll have a hard time processing what she's telling you.

Gottman explains. "You're saying, in effect, 'The problem isn't me, it's you.'"

◐ Stonewalling

When there's no hope of progress, one partner (the man in 85 percent of cases) simply tunes out. He doesn't care; he doesn't even appear to hear. "Stonewalling usually arrives last," says Gottman. "It takes time for the negativity to become overwhelming."

After our argument ends, we're led into the control room to face our judge. Gottman is a 56-year-old psychology professor and the codirector of the Gottman Institute, where he counsels couples and trains other therapists. He's also the coauthor of *The Seven Principles for Making Marriage Work*. When he addresses us, his tone is sincere, but he has the steely facade of an insurance-company claims adjuster about to allocate fault.

"You didn't have any of the predictors of divorce," he begins, immediately quelling our fears.

EXERCISE 4

Show affection outside the bedroom by occasionally kissing or touching her.

◐ Repetitions

5 minutes per day × 7 days

◐ Time

35 minutes per week

EXERCISE 5

Plan a date once a week, just like when you were single. Go someplace, just the two of you, and get reacquainted with each other.

◐ Repetitions/time

2 hours, once a week

"I didn't see contempt, not much in the way of criticism, and very little defensiveness. Generally, both your heart rates stayed low, except for one time when Maria's went to 104. There was a lot of tension then. Let's examine that." He cues his assistants, and we cut to tape as if we were analyzing last week's Packers game.

"Now Joe," he says, swiveling his chair toward me, "there's a moment when Maria starts to open up, but you roll over her. You do that a lot, and it prevents you from really finding out where she's at."

I immediately saddle up the third horse and become defensive. Who does this guy think he is? Just because he has a Ph.D. doesn't mean he knows my wife and me.

World's Worst Marriage Advice

"YOU CAN IMPROVE YOUR MARRIAGE BY LEARNING TO COMMUNICATE BETTER"

Relationship experts encourage couples to become "active listeners." When discussing a problem, experts advise you're supposed to repeat what your partner has said, empathize with her, then express your opinion, which she then repeats and empathizes with. Theoretically, this process continues until both sides feel heard and validated, and wild make-up sex can begin. Realistically, though, it's a stilted style of conversation that's tough to master. Besides, says the Love Lab's John Gottman, Ph.D., "successful conflict resolution isn't what makes marriages succeed."

"A COUPLE HAS TO WORK OUT THEIR DIFFERENCES"

According to Gottman's research, there are two types of marital conflict: solvable problems and perpetual ones. Surprisingly, 69 percent of disagreements fall into the latter category; they simply cannot be resolved. But that needn't threaten a marriage. More important than whether you solve a problem is how you treat each other while dealing with it.

"MEN ARE FROM MARS, WOMEN ARE FROM VENUS"

Among the couples Gottman has interviewed, 70 percent of wives say the quality of friendship they share with their spouses is the determining factor in how satisfied they are with the sex, romance, and passion in their marriages. Seventy percent of husbands say the same thing. "So men and women are from the same planet after all," Gottman says.

"Watch," he says, pointing at the monitor. "Did you just see that? Maria was starting to talk about her religious doubts. Her heart was racing, and she was turning toward you, but you didn't give her a chance."

That right there is the difference between traditional marriage therapy and Gottman's. This isn't his stroked-goatee perception. It's verifiable fact.

"Most of the time when couples reach out, their partner isn't there," he

Marriage Fact #671

In happy marriages, couples tend to have fond memories. Couples in failing marriages recall bad times or, even worse, nothing at all. Happy memories point to a happy future 94 percent of the time.

"YOU NEED PROFESSIONAL HELP"

Research shows that only 35 percent of couples see meaningful improvement in their relationships as a result of conventional marriage therapy, says Gottman. And a year later, only 18 percent say that it helped.

"MARRIAGE IS A 50-50 PROPOSITION"

"A happy spouse does not keep tabs on whether her mate is washing the dishes as a payback because she cooked dinner," says Gottman. "If you're keeping score, you're probably not in love anymore."

"MEN WERE NEVER MEANT TO BE MONOGAMOUS"

The male's job is to propagate the species, to have sex with as many women as possible, this theory goes. So when we stray, it's simply a matter of boys being boys. Not true, says Gottman. "The frequency of extramarital affairs does not depend on gender so much as opportunity. The number of affairs among young working women now slightly exceeds that of men."

"AFFAIRS ARE THE REAL CAUSE OF DIVORCE"

"Eighty percent of divorced men and women said their marriages broke up because they gradually grew apart," says Gottman. "Only 20 to 27 percent of couples said an extramarital affair was even partially to blame."

Five Common Marriage Problems Solved

Like an auto mechanic who can zero in on engine problems after being under the hoods of umpteen cars, the Love Lab's John Gottman, Ph.D., has pinpointed the most common marriage snags based on discussions with nearly 1,000 out-of-tune couples. No doubt you'll find that your relationship has misfired over many of the things listed here. What will surprise you is how easily these problems can be fixed.

PROBLEM: IN-LAWS

● Cause

When there's trouble, it's typically between a guy's wife and his mother. That's because both women are subconsciously competing for the attention of their man: you.

● Solution

Because solidarity is essential to the success of a marriage, you must side with your wife in any disagreement. If Mom gets offended, gently remind her that you're a husband first and a son second.

PROBLEM: MONEY

● Cause

Most couples, especially newlyweds, don't know how to balance the freedom and power that money brings with the security and trust that it's supposed to foster.

● Solution

View yourself as a financial team. Decide what's important to both of you (home, kids, college, retirement), and open a joint account to manage these areas. Deposit 90 percent of both paychecks there. Then, to keep each of you happy and to prevent arguments about "frivolous" spending, open two individual accounts. Agree that the remaining 10 percent each of you deposits every month can be spent however the earner wants. No questions asked.

PROBLEM: HOUSEWORK

● Cause

Because so many of us were raised in traditional homes where the father did only the hard labor, we often unwittingly model that behavior. We may cut the lawn and clean out the downspouts, but we don't often dust or vacuum. This causes our wives, who are orderly by nature, to feel unsupported.

● Solution

The only way out is to do more housework. There are a few tricks, though. First, there's no need to split the chores equally. In most relationships, the mere perception that you're doing something is enough to please a mate. Second, women find a man's willingness to do

continues. "They're busy thinking about something else or what they're going to say next. You need to work on listening more closely.

"And Maria," he says, swiveling toward her, "you need to pay attention to how you're feeling. When your heart is beating faster, recognize that this is a difficult subject and that you need to talk. Don't let Joe bulldoze you. Speak up."

Gottman has one more recommendation for us. He suggests we try to create a "culture of appreciation" in our relationship. One of the reasons mar-

housework extremely erotic. According to Gottman's research, "when the husband does his share to maintain the home, both he and his wife report a more satisfying sex life." The key: Make sure she notices what little you're doing. Example: Do the dishes when you've used only two plates.

PROBLEM: SEX

● Cause
Rarely are a couple's sexual desires perfectly matched. Passion compensates initially, but over time, differences emerge. Because sex is such a difficult thing to discuss, unfulfilled desires can fester and eventually be perceived as personal rejection.

● Solution
Trust is the best foreplay. It frees you to be yourself without fear of embarrassment or hurt. Start cultivating more in your relationship by taking an empty tissue carton and making it your "fantasy box." Write five secret sexual desires on individual slips of paper (hold off on the

ménage à trois for a while), have your partner do the same, then deposit them in the box. Take turns drawing one whenever you make love.

PROBLEM: BECOMING PARENTS

● Cause
Seventy percent of women report being significantly less satisfied with their marriages in the year after the first baby arrives. This is because they have gone through a life-altering experience, but their husbands are lagging behind.

● Solution
Stop pining for the carefree life you used to have. It's over. The two of you won't be able to go out spontaneously for happy-hour margaritas for at least 14 years. Instead, find new enjoyment in this little family unit you've created. Begin by getting involved in small ways. For instance, become the official burper. When your wife finishes feeding, share the nurturing. Rate each expulsion on a scale of 1 to 10.

riages crumble at 16 years is that partners take each other for granted. They live in an environment of niggling complaints rather than heartfelt thanks.

"Little compliments are very important," he explains. "The masters of marriage we've studied do this routinely. It's sort of Thanksgiving every day for these couples."

Even during an argument, it's still possible to acknowledge the good in the other person. It's obvious from watching our tape that we don't do much of this. Again, it's the ability to see my flaws that makes the most impact. And it's evidently what appeals to other men. Gottman claims that 80 percent of the initial calls to his marriage clinic come from guys. He attributes it to his technical approach and basing diagnoses on science rather than intuition.

Indeed, 6 months after our visit, his advice has stuck with us. I'm trying to listen better and let Maria have her say. And although it may sound trite, I try to find something to thank her for every day.

Overall, getting hard evidence of what we were doing wrong was a surprisingly constructive experience. For the first time, I feel that I have solid proof of my marital goofs and what we need to do to avoid D day.

Eight Signs It's Over

Are you noticing a certain chill in the air? Here's how to tell when your squeeze is becoming a death grip, from writer Malia McKinnon.

Men generally know when love has left town. All the bloody details aside, the basic checklist has three items: talking to her is torture, listening to her is even worse, and then—one depressing and fateful day—the sex is no longer worth suffering through the first two.

The sad part is, by the time you reach that point in a romance, it's usually too late to do anything about it. Indeed, if only there were some warning signs that your relationship was going bad, you could take steps to save it—or at least put it out of its misery before you experience the flying toasters, restraining orders, and other end-of-love-affair ugliness.

Well, you're in luck, pal, because there are some steps you can take. What follows are eight subtle clues that your relationship is heading nowhere fast—

along with some ways to tell if you should try to save it or just get the hell outta Dodge while the getting is good.

Warning sign #1: The sex is great. Especially when you fantasize about Angela, your college fling.
Nostalgia's just nostalgia, right? Maybe. Fantasizing about other lovers can be healthy. But if Angela always pinch-hits when you're in the clutch with Jane, it's a sign your relationship is in trouble. "If you hardly ever fantasize about

Five Ways to Cut Bait

She's given you five of the signals in this chapter, and that's just since breakfast. It's time to give her the heave-ho. But don't be ruthless; she has a lot of date-worthy friends. Here are a few ways to send her gently into that good night.

Be a sympathetic broken record.
Meet with her alone, and repeat why you want out over and over, says psychologist Steve Brody, Ph.D. Listen politely while she reacts, then give her the same spiel again, verbatim. She'll know you're resolute.

Read your "Dear Jane" aloud.
This reeks of honesty. Write a long, sentimental letter (riddled with "I," not "you" or "we") and read it in front of her. It'll stop you from becoming tongue-tied and keep her from interrupting, advises psychologist Susan Heitler, Ph.D.

Make it mutual.
You'll both fare better if she helps pull the plug. Get confirmation that there's at least one big reason you can't stay together, advises sex psychologist Lonnie Barbach, Ph.D. Starter: "This isn't working. Don't you agree?"

Do it in public.
Unless absolutely necessary, never break up over the phone. (Faxes, letters, and e-mails are also for cowards.) Be a man and tell her eye-to-eye. But if she might claw out that eye, break up in a public place—say, a Mexican restaurant during Cinco de Mayo. It's far from perfect, but it should help stifle her reaction, says Barbach.

Emphasize that distance doesn't always make the heart grow fonder.
Long-distance romances are looser—and more dangerous. She can't catch you with Debra, so you may try to have it both ways. But she'll find out. "Make sure she hears it from you first," warns Barbach. In this case it's okay to dial the phone and spend $186.29 to tell her the distance is too great.

your partner when you're with her, it could mean you're ready to move on," says Isadora Alman, a syndicated sex columnist and certified sexologist in San Francisco.

To make sure, visualize your current partner in a way that turns you on. There's probably something about her you still find sexy. It could be the first thing you noticed about her. Whatever it is, find it. Fixate on it. If that still doesn't help, it may be time to give Jane her walking papers and scare up Angela's phone number.

It'sBeenSaid...

" I never knew what real happiness was until I got married, and by then it was too late. "

—Max Kauffman

● **Warning sign #2: You go to a party together. She works the room. You man the bar. Upon leaving, you've barely spoken.**
Many couples mingle untethered for hours. But if they're in love—whether for 5 days or 50 years— they'll connect throughout the evening: a sustained glance, a hand on a back. "If these rituals of flirting are gone, it's a sign that the relationship may be in some trouble," says Louanne Cole Weston, Ph.D., a sex therapist in Fair Oaks, California. If you'd rather be cornered by a chatty insurance salesman than make small talk with your main squeeze, your love flame is fading. And if she doesn't flinch at being ignored, she's not exactly pining for you, either. "Women are very attuned to this signal," says Weston. "If she doesn't ask you what's wrong, she's distancing herself."

You can melt this ice with a little fire of your own. Be forthright, advises Weston. Face your mate and say, "If this is winding down, I'd like to be the first to know." Your move should force her hand.

● **Warning sign #3: You bolt right after sex.**
You say you can only sleep in your own bed? Please. You slept on the gearshift of an AMC Pacer when Suzette spied a rat in the motel. It's motivation, boy. "Some people can take others only in small doses," explains Weston. If that dose is nothing but eros, you or your partner are purposely limiting the relationship. Couples who don't sleep (meaning "sleep") together are usually struggling over who's in control of the relationship, says Weston. One partner feels he'll lose the upper hand, or the other fears committing herself too deeply to a cause that might be futile. As long as they wake up alone, they don't have to relate to each other in nonsexual ways.

To put your relationship to the test, stay the night. Or suggest an extended jaunt where you'll see her in the morning. You'll know right away if there's hope for the two of you in the future.

● Warning sign #4: **You finally get that promotion, so you immediately call Phil and head out to celebrate.**
That's a sneaky one. Phil may best understand what you've gone through, and he may have known you longer, so in some ways he deserves first hurrahs. But if this woman is inside your soul, you'll call her first. "When something significant happens and you don't share it first with your mate, the romantic connection needs to be investigated," says Alman. "It may be a sign that you don't see that person as a lifelong partner."

To avoid paying hell tonight, ask your mate to go along, too. Chances are she won't outlast Phil. To avoid paying hell for the rest of your life, picture rushing home years from now—with news of fortune or tragedy—and seeing her face. If that leaves you longing for Phil, end things now, not later.

● Warning sign #5: **She forgets your birthday.**
Ouch. Forgetting birthdays, anniversaries, and any of those 342 faux holidays created by Hallmark may be an honest, excusable mistake for you, but not for her. "Women generally place a much higher priority on significant dates than men do," explains Steve Brody, Ph.D., a psychologist in Cambria, California, who specializes in couples therapy. "Chances are if she forgets your birthday, she's either angry or indifferent."

To see which it is, nonchalantly mention that you have a free birthday dinner waiting at Denny's. If she suddenly explodes—figuratively, that is—she was probably trying to get back at you for something. See if you can work it out, then have great make-up sex. On the other hand, if she just plumb forgot for no reason, that means you don't register with her. Don't be surprised if she soon forgets other details—for instance, that you prefer not to find strange men hiding behind the suits in your closet.

● Warning sign #6: **She's unfazed when Angela calls you unexpectedly—at midnight.**
This sounds like a utopian situation, a cake-and-eat-it-too scenario. It's not. No matter how confident she is, a woman who's genuinely interested in you will pose a few pointed questions regarding this phone call. If she truly doesn't care, she's probably fixing to forget your birthday, too. *Capisce?* "It's an even worse indicator if the relationship is fairly new," says Brody. Women are more likely to be jealous over new mates who haven't been around long enough to earn their trust yet—though a wife of 30 years will shoot you an evil look, too.

Vocal or not, a little paranoia is a wonderful thing. "A man took me to see his old girlfriend perform in a ballet," says one 25-year-old woman. "She was lithe and beautiful, and she did the most seductive dance I've ever seen. The truth was, it didn't faze me at all, and that night I broke it off with him."

Ask your mate if the phone call from your ex bothered her. If her resounding no doesn't convince you that it did, even a little bit, lose her before she runs a personal ad to replace you.

Four Marriage Savers

If you think marriage is tough, try divorce. It has all the problems of your current entanglement, plus lawyers, settlement costs, a lingering sense of failure, and confused kids. To help you avoid that fate, we've identified four strategies to help get your marriage back on track. If your union is strong, try these tips anyway: Kathie Lee and Frank used to be a fun couple, too.

● Turn off the television.

"If the TV is always on, that indicates that neither partner has an interest in what the other has to say," says Atlanta psychiatrist and family therapist Frank Pittman III, M.D., author of *Private Lies*, a book about infidelity.

One solution: Pry yourselves out of the matching La-Z-Boys at least once a week and go looking for adventure, suggests Michael Perry, Ph.D., a marriage and sex therapist in Encino, California. Trade off: One week you take her to the amusement park or check out the seedy juke joint on the edge of town. The next week you do something she wants to do—take a Szechuan cooking class, go to the opera. You may have to grit your teeth, but those arias may save your marriage in the long run.

● Up your civility quotient.

"The heart of marriage is good manners," says Dr. Pittman. "A marriage is in trouble when partners stop treating each other with respect."

If you've both been less than chivalrous lately, dust off the manners you displayed when you were courting, advises Perry. It's a small thing to offer your wife a little more wine with dinner, or to open her car door before you open your own, but these things set a tone for the marriage. Too often, we reserve our best manners for work contacts and present our worst side to the ones who matter most.

If your fights tend to disintegrate into insults, choose a "safe word" with your partner, recommends Perry. Uttering the word in the midst of a fight means that

⊙ Warning sign #7: Since when did she stop shaving her legs?
"A relaxed attitude is common when a relationship reaches a certain point," notes Brody. But he warns that it can also be a big, fat clue that the novelty— and the romance—are gone. Watch for other signs that someone is biding time. You plan an evening at the theater followed by a stop at the Waldorf, and she's content to wear her casual Friday garb (though she looked finer than Jessica Alba when you met her last New Year's Eve). You notice that you forgot to brush your teeth and put on deodorant—several hours ago—and you don't make a pit stop at the drugstore. When she no longer has any motivation to increase her "mate value" by dressing well, or you couldn't care less about impressing her, one of you is probably just treading water until somebody more interesting comes along.

So plan another paycheck-gutting night, and ask her to wear that black dress she wore last December, heels and all. If she balks or somehow forgets the

you immediately cease and desist. (Don't choose *stop*. The word should be completely out of context, such as *peaches* or *sassafras*.) "When either of you says the word, that means it's the end of that round," says Perry. "Physically separate yourselves, and don't talk for a half-hour." That should be enough time to cool down—and clear the way for a truce.

⊙ Stop giving yourself a hand.
Consistently preferring masturbation over sex can be a distancing maneuver, says Dr. Pittman.

To break down physical distance, start giving each other full-body massages with the works: candlelight, oil, soft music. Getting the kinks out of one another's tensed-up muscles makes each of you feel cared for. Also, kneading

each other's naked bodies—and hearing those guttural sighs of satisfaction—will soon trigger your lust, says Perry.

⊙ Bring her up to date on your bottle-cap collection.
The most common sign of a troubled marriage—and the deadliest—is apathy, says Perry. "It's a bad sign if you don't care what she did at work today, or if she's not interested in the progress of your hobby."

To cut through that fog of indifference, learn to ask specific questions about each other's interests and day-to-day lives, advises Perry. Don't ask, "How was your day?" Perry says. "That's just too general. You're going to get, 'Fine.' Ask your partner for specific details, and you're bound to learn something of interest."

rouge, lip liner, and sleek legs that rightly accompany that dress, she's saying you're not worth the trouble.

● **Warning sign #8: You come home one particular evening,
and she has nothing nice to say to you.**
We all know couples that bicker, criticize, and belittle one another. They think it builds sexual tension, and it may—for a while. But after a few rounds, those love jabs can draw blood.

Forget about what you've seen on all those stupid sitcoms set in New York high-rises. In strong coupleships, people don't look for ways to goad each other. In fact, they hunt for points to stroke. "If your partner becomes more critical of you, it may mean that she's becoming more critical of the entire relationship," says David Olson, Ph.D., professor emeritus of family social sciences at the University of Minnesota in St. Paul. If she starts to greet you with a daily list of your inadequacies, and you soberly end every compliment with ". . . for a girl your size," you're headed for Splitsville.

The only detour? Gush over her for a week. The more compliments you give her, the more you should get back. If you're rapidly increasing your own charm quotient but you're not getting anything in return, it means that either she just doesn't like you anymore or she can't focus on the positive aspects of the relationship. Either way, it may be time to say goodbye.

Unnatural Commitment

An Interview with David Barash, Ph.D., and Judith Lipton, M.D.

Despite what you've been told, monogamy is not a natural state. According to David Barash, Ph.D., and Judith Lipton, M.D., the married, Seattle-based coauthors of The Myth of Monogamy: Fidelity and Infidelity in Animals and People, *almost all animals— including people—are natural-born cheaters. Here's how to keep infidelity from wrecking your relationship.*

You dismember the widely held notion that swans, geese, and other animals are monogamous.

BARASH: We've known for a long time that monogamy is unusual in animals. Now it turns out that it's really rare—much more so than we ever dreamed. Whenever we examine a species in any depth, it turns out to show a fair level of not just male philandering but also female philandering. It should be a wake-up call that it's not biologically natural for humans to be monogamous, either.

We're crushed. We figured if a swan could mate for life, so could we.

BARASH: That does make people crestfallen. But we don't have to look to swans or geese for our own sexual behavior, and even if we did, we'd find that we'd probably philander at least as much as we do today. Part of the crowning glory of being human is that we are in fact able to make our own decisions. We can do what we want, but we need to understand what our inclinations are.

What are they?

BARASH: If you're a male, and you don't find yourself sexually aroused—at least on occasion—by attractive women, that's probably an indication that there's something wrong with you.

LIPTON: It's also healthy for women to notice interesting men. Often, what's interesting to women isn't as much pretty men as men who have other kinds of traits. Very successful men, very smart men, very talented men. Women sure notice, and if they don't notice, they may be ill or depressed.

This would seem to guarantee perpetual conflict between men and women.

LIPTON: Competition and conflict are part of the fabric of life. The war between the sexes is so painful because we'd all like to think that we could have a partner with whom we could gang up against the rest of the world. We'd all like to think, "It's you and me, buddy. We'll stick together."

So if our partner strays, who deserves our anger more: she or the other guy?

LIPTON: It's between you and the female because she broke a promise.
BARASH: But it's also between you and the other guy, between your sperm and his sperm.
LIPTON: That's where sperm competition comes in. If your girlfriend sleeps with another guy, you could see it as a war *among* the sexes.

That's depressing.

LIPTON: It is somehow disappointing when you think of the brutality that you see in men against men that there's a more subtle kind of brutality going on within the reproductive tract of females. But it shouldn't be all that surprising. It confirms a lot of beliefs that men have, and makes them more explicit.

How so?

LIPTON: We all know that the rich and powerful men in our society simply have access to more females and more desirable females.

Yet you point out that monogamy has helped level the playing field for men . . .

BARASH: Although many men think of monogamy as a constraint on their lives and behavior, it's very much to the benefit of men in terms of male-male competition. It's sort of an exercise in egalitarianism, a democratic movement that benefits men at least as much, if not more, than it does women.

Is it healthy—even in a playful way—for partners to acknowledge their interest in other people?

LIPTON: It would be healthier to say, "Yum, that person looks good enough to eat," than to either notice and feel self-loathing or guilt, or pretend that your partner didn't know that you noticed. I met a New York cab driver once who told me his wife was always pointing out pretty girls. She'd say, "Did you ever see a skirt like that?" or "Did you notice our neighbor has nice tits?"

What if a guy actually develops a crush on someone else?

LIPTON: The minute you have serious feelings about a third party, you're in dangerous territory. If your mind is preoccupied when you're not seeing the person, it's not just physical arousal. If you have repetitive thoughts about the person, longing for the person, fantasies about the person, dreams about the person—all that stuff—you've got trouble.

Even if you haven't admitted it to anyone?

LIPTON: Yeah, because a crush in that sense is a variant of an obsessive-compulsive disorder. That kind of preoccupation means your own mental state isn't free. Admitting it or not admitting it, you're already in it.

What if the object of your affection is a coworker or a friend of the family?

LIPTON: If you have a crush on a coworker, it's a really loaded situation. For one thing, it can be illegal. It can be the source of a sexual harassment suit. So it might not be best to bring it up with your wife, your boss, or the coworker. The best advice I've ever read about what to do when that happens is to run like hell. Get out of that person's territory. If you have a crush on a coworker, get some help. If you have a crush on your wife's best friend, move or don't see her. These things do die off in time, and if you put up a firewall, you can extinguish it.

At what point in a relationship is such a challenge most likely to present itself?

> **BARASH:** Any number of things can make the romantic glow of an early relationship a little less intense. That's when I think the issue of not taking one's partner for granted and the issue of being aware of the biological risks of being attracted to others become especially important.
> **LIPTON:** The times when couples predictably turn away from each other and end up becoming icy cold or uninvolved, or doing mean things, are either early in the relationship, when people just aren't suited for each other, or later on, when they've toughed it out for many years to get the kids raised and finally, with great relief, call it quits. "Enough of that already," they say.

Is jealousy an inevitable byproduct of the war between the sexes?

> **BARASH:** My guess is that the inclination for sexual jealousy is every bit as hard-wired as is the inclination to be interested in multiple sexual partners. Again, that's one of the interesting paradoxes: that individuals are inclined biologically to want multiple partners for themselves but equally disinclined biologically for their partners to do the same thing.

How much mate guarding, as you call it, is permissible before you cross the line into obsessive jealousy?

> **BARASH:** Some mate guarding is normal, although my inclination is that there shouldn't be any more of it than one feels absolutely necessary. The most effective way to avoid the need for mate guarding is to work toward the strength of the relationship itself.
> **LIPTON:** I agree. I think some mate guarding is normal. But if either spouse perceives that that the other person's mate guarding is be-

coming obsessive or restricting their personal freedom or not respecting their autonomy, then the guarder has a problem.

OTHER WOMEN, WE HOPE

Percentage of men who occasionally fantasize about others while being intimate with their partners:
67

Is there any way out of this dilemma?

BARASH: What so often is the case is people think if they are aroused or even just mildly interested in someone else, that it's somehow an indication of a failing in their relationship. The idea is to get out in front and recognize our own biological inclinations so we're not blindsided by them. One way to survive the war of the sexes and make it as unhurtful as possible is to say, "Okay, there's this potential for conflict. It's likely to rear its head one way or another. Let's work out a treaty."

Is this the "mutual disarmament pact" you've written about?

LIPTON: Exactly. People should sit down and draft an agreement. The fundamental one we're talking about is "I won't sleep around and make you crazy if you don't sleep around and make me crazy." Monogamy. Each partner will exhibit sexual restraint, not because they're not interested in other people but out of courtesy to the other.

What else can a man do to ensure his mate's fidelity?

BARASH: There are three different biological factors that a mate is concerned with in the other: good genes, good behaviors, and good resources. Good genes are attractiveness in a variety of ways, including physical health. Good behavior is cooperativeness and sense of humor, being each other's best friend. Good resources are literally money, or at least being adequate at bringing home the bacon. If a guy can act in a way that's consistent with good genes, good health, good behavior, and adequate resources, that in itself would help to achieve a higher level of fidelity.

If a man is looking for a keeper, what qualities should he look for?

> **LIPTON:** Choose someone with whom you could be best friends. That's more important than whether or not she has long legs or beautiful breasts or a small waist-hip ratio. People like people because they're friendly, pay attention, and give us quid pro quo: "You scratch my back, I'll scratch yours. You wash the dishes, I'll sweep the floor." The ideal partner for either sex would be a good cooperator.

That would seem to argue in favor of getting to know a woman better before jumping in the sack.

> **LIPTON:** If you're mate shopping, I think it's good idea to delay sexual intercourse for awhile and make sure the person is good friendship material, that they're healthy and honest, and that you get along really well. The problem is, you rush into bed and feelings get involved and you don't have time to become friends before suddenly you're lovers or possibly parents. And then, who knows what kind of person you've agreed to rear offspring with, spend your life with, and pay taxes with?

Do you see think the war between the sexes is getting any better?

> **LIPTON:** The war between the sexes has changed enormously because of technology. So now women can be promiscuous, but if they reproduce, they can get caught. So men can have virtual 100 percent confidence that the baby is their own. So what's going to happen with all this, I don't know. But my hope is that men and women would both start to separate out parenting from recreational sex. You might have people you enjoy sleeping with for all sorts of reasons. But before you actually get married, before you go to all that bother and trouble and paperwork, it would pay to make sure it's somebody you're friendly with. To me, marriage is a commitment to child rearing and estate planning.

Do you see signs that this is already starting to happen?

> **LIPTON:** I do. The average age of marriage is rising and the average number of children is dropping. Even in countries like India that don't

have access to high technology, reproductive rates are dropping. Demographers were wrong about the population explosion. Given half a chance, women have fewer babies than demographers predicted. Women and men delay marriage and baby making until they're in their thirties. It's like they unconsciously know that it's better to be somewhat mature, have resources, and be in a really stable relationship. That's when you should start raising babies, not when you're teenagers.

Might future generations enjoy more harmonious relationships than we do?

LIPTON: In the years ahead, there's going to be a nice balance in the war between the sexes. Because of good birth control, women are free to have sex either for fun or courtship. Because of DNA fingerprinting, no longer can a man be tricked into raising somebody else's baby.

Inquiring minds need to know: Are there any animals that are completely monogamous?

BARASH: Only one that I know of: A tapeworm that lives inside fish. The males and females can't be unfaithful because, once they mate, they stay fused together for life.

QUICKIES

SLICK LICKS

Other than for bachelor-party gags, there's only one good reason to buy fruity-flavored sex goop: It's a way to lure her shy tongue to your body. But if you mistakenly buy the kind that tastes like a fluoride treatment, she'll swear off oral sex forever. That's why our editorial staffers and their partners tested 50 different brands. These are our picks.

● Best Finger Paint: Naked & Naughty Chocolate Finger Paint
She said: "Tastes great. It's not slippery at all, though, so you need a lot of saliva for oral sex."

● Best Balm: Kama Sutra Pleasure Balm
He said: "The menthol's numbing effect is incredible. When she blows on it, it feels as if it goes through your skin."

● Best Lubricant: Xandria's Lube-a-Licious Strawberry and Watermelon Lubricants
She said: "Not too sweet and a little gloopy, which made the whole flesh-on-flesh experience easier."

SECOND-QUARTER LOSSES

We all feel the sap rising right about April or May, right? Winter fading, spring coming, women wearing less. But statistics show that the lowest birth rates in America are in November, December, and January. If you count back 9 months to baby-making time, it appears that February, March, and April are a time of headaches and fat days. Why? It could be a lack of energy caused by sunlight deprivation in winter. Los Angeles clinical psychologist Ana Nogales, Ph.D., theorizes that we're busy tackling new projects in the new year, not to mention spring cleaning, "and sex takes a backseat." (Plus the backseat is probably still chilly.) One more thing: The procreation peak is in autumn. Always our favorite season.

DIVORCE IS CONTAGIOUS

Just like the flu, divorce is something you can catch on the job. Researchers in Sweden have found that the risk of divorce is higher among men when they see colleagues move on to new partners. Yvonne Aberg, a sociologist who surveyed 37,000 people at 1,500 workplaces, says that for men, seeing a colleague become suddenly single could "give them the courage to take the same step." Women react differently: Seeing recent divorces makes them work harder at their marriages.

There can be a chain reaction, too, Aberg notes: A wave of divorces lets loose newly single people who then find new partners—at work.

ANCIENT CHINESE SECRET

Before sex, our hands are usually busy (click, scroll, click). But Chinese acupressure tradition says that massaging a woman in the right places will directly affect her ability to reach orgasm. Use your thumbs, then palms, to make firm circles in these hot spots.

❍ The center of her chest, around her breastbone
Theory: Induces calm by "opening the heart," says Talena DeBaun, a licensed acupuncturist at the Arizona School of Acupuncture and Oriental Medicine.

❍ Down both sides of her spine, to her lower back
Theory: Brings warm energy to the pelvis.

❍ Her belly, from her navel down to her pubic bone
Theory: It's the physical center of the body, and ultimately critical to a person's sexual satisfaction.

❍ Inner legs, working from the ankle up
Theory: Arouses the energy line that begins at the big toe and moves up her leg to the all-important groin area.

THE FUNNY PAGE

"What the hell was <u>that</u>? Something just swept over me—
like contentment or something."

SURPRISE HER

 Almost half of American adults say they've lost interest in sex. Maybe that's because we wallow in so much abundance—including an abundance of sexual imagery—that we think there's nothing new or exciting under the sun. Since we're all creatures of habit, it's awfully easy to stick with the same-old, same-old. But you know something? Boring people tend to have boring sex lives. We're here to tell you how to crank it up a notch without getting burned out. She'll be grateful. And so will you.

10 Tricks of Domestic Bliss

The average suburban house comes with a dining room, bathroom, rec room, family room, and mud room. But no sex room. There's not even a sex nook to be found.

So it's up to you to create one. You can use any room you want for really good, innovative, wake-up-the-neighbors sex. For instance, there's . . .

❶ The study. Swivel chairs are perfect for oral sex. Sit her down and take your place on the floor in front of her. Then get to work with your tongue while you move her—chair and all—side to side. She'll feel almost as if she's floating, says *Oral Caress* author Robert Birch, Ph.D.

❷ The kitchen. "Use a sturdy wooden table, which is more comfortable than the floor and at a better height than the kitchen counter," says Louanne Cole Weston, Ph.D., a sex therapist in Fair Oaks, California. Have your partner lie back on the table with her pelvis near the edge. Then reach for some food—anything that can be licked off is fair game. Giving your tongue something tasty to aim for can help you dwell in one spot longer—and she'll love that.

❸ The laundry room. Your washing machine produces more vibration than any other appliance in your home. Problem is, most people don't use it right. You should be the one with your butt on the lid. "The motion will be transmitted through your pelvis, essentially turning your member into a life-size vibrator," says Perry. Run a warm-water load so the top won't be cold.

❹ The closet. Closet sex works best for a quickie. "It's not the kind of place you want to linger in," says Weston. Pick your timing: When you're both too horny even to find your way upstairs, take her in here, pull down her pants, and have standing rear-entry sex. It's the surest route to orgasm when there's not enough space to lie down.

❺ The bathroom. "Standing up works better than sitting down, unless you have a really big bathtub," says Weston. Your partner should brace herself with her hands on the shower walls. You enter from behind. Stand out of the stream if you're wearing a condom, since water could cause it to slip off. And don't use water-based lubricants in the tub—they can turn the floor into a slip-and-slide.

6 **The window**. It's so much more fun looking down than staring at the ceiling during sex, says Michael Perry, Ph.D., a marriage and sex therapist in Encino, California. Have your partner lean against a window frame (make sure the window is closed) and enter her from behind. If she's wearing a short skirt or dress and you keep your pants most of the way on, people below won't have to know what you're doing.

7 **The family room**. Got a beanbag chair? "You can contour it to any shape you want, and it's almost like being in water—it'll support you in ways you're not normally supported," says Perry. Doggie-style sex works great when she's on her belly, draped over the amorphous blob (the beanbag, not you). So does the missionary position. "Stick a couple of thick books under the bag to keep her from sinking in too far," suggests Perry.

8 **The bedroom**. Two words: *satin sheets*. "Not only do they feel sexy against the skin but they encourage more active sex because you can really move easily," says Perry. Start on top on her side of the bed, then roll to your side after 2 to 3 minutes and let her take the top. Then repeat several times. Then several more. And watch the lamp.

9 **The pool**. Sex here is tricky because water washes away natural lubrication, making thrusting as much fun as putting on rubber gloves lined with sandpaper. The solution: "Non-water-based lubricant," says Perry. He suggests Wet: Classic Platinum, which is silicone based and latex condom compatible. Once you're slippery, move to chest-deep water and have sex standing up. "You're almost weightless in water, so it's easy to do things you wouldn't normally be able to do."

10 **The backyard**. You'll need one of those armless, three-panel reclining lawn chairs. You take the bottom position, then let her straddle you and the chair. Her legs will do all the real work—you can just sit back and watch. Now that's a house party!

ASK THE GIRL NEXT DOOR

The honest truth about women from our lovely neighbor

Q: *I'd like to give lingerie as a gift, but I'm aware that my*
wife may think that's more of a present for me than for her.
Is there a right way and a wrong way to give it?
—T. R., TUCSON

A: Wrong way: buying something that doesn't fit her body or her taste. Right way: giving her a $100 gift certificate from Victoria's Secret or someplace similar. Women love lingerie, but most prefer to pick it out themselves. You have no idea how humiliating it is to go into the bathroom to slip into a slinky new panty set, only to have to come back out and explain to the man lying in your bed that you couldn't get your thighs through the leg holes. Worse, buy something too big and she'll accuse you of thinking she's fat. And if your choice clashes with her personality, she'll feel as if she's wearing a Halloween costume. How psyched would you be for sex if you felt trussed up like the Great Pumpkin? Go with a gift certificate and a card that says how much you enjoy undressing her. The right lingerie makes us feel extra-sexy, and that's as much a treat for us as it is for you.

Q: *What's the real story—do women actually*
enjoy oral sex (giving and receiving)?
—A. G., MODESTO, CALIFORNIA

A: Yes. Most of my friends have nothing but good or great things to say about going down—it's hot and wet, and it feels extra-naughty and therefore extra-sexy. But understand potential hang-ups: One college friend of mine had a bad experience (read: head coerced into some jerk's lap), and another was once told that she tasted "funny." I also know of at least one woman with an overactive gag reflex. So it's better to let your girlfriend initiate going south on you. Then pay attention when you do likewise: If she clamps her legs together or moves your head away, she may be cunnilingus shy.

Q: *My girlfriend and I occasionally watch a porno together. She told me*
the girl-on-girl scenes turn her on the most. Is this normal? Should I

be worried that she's a lesbian? Or should I start dropping hints that she
should get one of her gal pals to join us?
    —B. L., PORTLAND, MAINE

A: Do *not* drop hints that you're gung-ho for a threesome unless you want to get slapped straight back to singledom. Your girl-friend's affinity for the girl-on-girl stuff doesn't mean she wants same-sex action in reality. It's simply a matter of call and response. Let me explain: Growing up, we watched the same TV shows that you and your guy friends did. We peeked at the same dirty magazines and caught a few sleazy flicks. And in all of those, it was—and still is—the female body that's presented as the sexually charged one. Just like you, we learned to associate images of women flashing their breasts and bending over with what's supposed to be a turn-on. And, as you already know, two naked female bodies are twice as nice. But porn has little to do with real life. When it comes to flesh and blood, all the brainwashing goes by the wayside, and our natural sexual desire for a hairy chest, rough hands, and, um, male anatomy reigns supreme.

Q: *Are thongs actually comfortable?*
    —K. H., MYRTLE BEACH, SOUTH CAROLINA

A: Yes. (Like contact lenses, once they're in, you forget they're there.)

Q: *What are women thinking after a random hookup? I recently visited*
an old college friend for the weekend, and we ended up having sex.
I'm not sure how to act.
    —M. K., CHEYENNE, WYOMING

A: If she (or you) has romantic feelings, your friendship is offi-cially changed—for better or for worse, depending on whether or not you can deal with this new development. And sometimes that's just what happens when you bang a buddy. Most likely, though, she's hoping the recent fluid exchange won't affect your relationship. Here's the thing: Because she's your friend, you have to call her—no ex-cuses—within 3 days, whether you want to start a romance or simply maintain the preromp status quo. She expects more from you than from the average man—and she'll be twice as hurt if you dis her.

Pick up the phone! If you're both thinking it was a one-time, purely sexual incident, you may be able to skip the big should-this-have-happened-or-should-it-not-have/what-does-this-mean/blah-blah-ugh conversation. Tell her you had a good time, then shift into usual conversation. If she wants to talk about it further, she'll bring it up. If you do get into an emotional chat, just don't use the words *mistake* or *bad idea*, which she may construe as you thinking she's bad in bed.

Q: *My girlfriend and I recently got engaged. Before me, her sex life was limited. While I'm no Don Juan, I've been around. How can I get her to try new things without freaking her out?*
—R. Y., CHARLOTTE, NORTH CAROLINA

A: Hmm . . . you don't mention what, exactly, it is you'd like to try, but I have a hunch the answer is everything. And why shouldn't it be? You're about to enter a lifelong relationship with this woman, so it's natural to want all the excitement and variety possible (short of anything that lands you in the ER or the backseat of a squad car). There's a very good chance that your bride-to-be wants the same thing.

That said, getting her to engage in a sex act that's more risqué than anything she's ever read in *Cosmo* is going to take some sensitivity and patience. Make it clear that you love everything about making love to her—all the sights, sounds, smells, and tastes—so that she realizes there's nothing she should be shy or nervous about. I know it's sappy, but saying things like "I love everything about your body" and "I want us to make each other feel good in as many ways as possible" is a good way to start. When a woman feels safe and loved in a relationship, as your fiancée probably does with you, she's more willing to experiment.

Instead of having a clinical conversation about it in advance, which may come off sounding skeevy and freak her out, slowly introduce the idea physically. And I mean *slowly!* You want to give her a hint about what it is you'd like to try and then back off to see how she responds. When each small, nonthreatening step feels good and is fun for her, she'll eventually want it to go all the way—whatever "it" is. Just start with the tame stuff, and work up to all things kinky.

For more honest answers about women, look for
Ask the *Men's Health* Girl Next Door
wherever books are sold.

MUST READS

Shameless Sex

Still making love with the lights off? Let writer Logan Davis tell you how to shed your inhibitions and get what you want in bed.

Who among us didn't once have a crumpled copy of *Playboy* hidden beneath his G.I. Joe sheets? Who can swear to never, ever glancing over his shoulder in an X-rated video store or strip joint for fear of being seen by someone he knows? And who can honestly say he hasn't felt a twinge of guilt from fantasizing too graphically or masturbating too regularly?

No doubt a small dose of inhibition is healthy. It keeps us in our clothes most of the time and prevents us from making embarrassing passes at the boss's wife—or the boss, for that matter. But too much inhibition can lead to frustration, inner torment, relationship-threatening problems or, to put it another way, bad sex.

"Inhibitions are leftovers from old messages transmitted to us as children that sex is disgusting, sinful, and harmful," says Ira L. Reiss, Ph.D., author of *An End to Shame: Shaping Our Next Sexual Revolution.* He says that as adults, we still adhere to some of these beliefs infused by well-intentioned parents and teachers. And the result is often unnecessary repression and shame—an inability to fully enjoy one of life's great gifts.

While it's important to get over these inhibitions, we're not going to put you on the couch and revisit the time your father caught you trying to erase underwear from models in the Sears catalog. Rather, we're simply out to help you conquer some common roadblocks to better sex. Read on—go ahead, no one's looking—for advice on everything from testing the far side of kinky to just getting the courage to talk freely with your partner about what turns you on.

Say What You're Afraid to Say

Few men have trouble telling dirty jokes or bragging to a buddy about their Saturday-night conquests. But when it comes to talking openly, honestly, and explicitly about sex, especially with a partner, inhibitions often choke the words. It's true for women, too.

We know we promised not to do this, but think about your childhood for a moment. If you're like most people, just saying the word *sex* at home or in class was enough to get you chastised. Hell, remember how uneasy your family got during tampon commercials? Sex was the dirty deed. No wonder we're embarrassed talking about it.

"Even intimate partners often have difficulty opening up," says New York City sex therapist Shirley Zussman, Ed.D. "They're afraid they'll become too vulnerable, they're afraid of what their partner might think. Often, you'll hear men and women make the excuse 'My ideal lover doesn't need to be told what I like.'"

If such an inhibition shackles you, or if you dream of getting your partner to talk about sex in the same casual, comfortable way you discuss the evening news, here are a few speech lessons.

● **Watch a movie.**

Explicit videos can be excellent conversation starters. Once you experience other adults talking maturely and candidly about sex, you'll become more inclined to do the same. "After watching a sex-education video for the first time, my patients will usually say, 'It looked so natural, so beautiful,'" says Zussman. "Well, that's because it is beautiful. It's just that most people have never seen that kind of image."

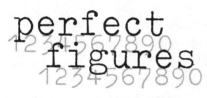

perfect figures

YOU GIVE YOURSELF AWAY

Percentage of cheating men who get caught: 80

Most common way he slips up: Cell-phone bill

Most common way she's found out: Her lover's e-mails

• • • • • • • •

Mind you, the sex-education videos she's talking about are a far cry from hardcore porn films with titles like *An Officer and His Genitals*. Frankly, a lot of X-rated films are cheesy, inane, and, worst of all, not very erotic. For advice on selecting tasteful adult videos suitable for watching with a partner, we turned to Cathy Winks and Anne Semans, who help run Good Vibrations, a kind of inhibition-free zone where you can purchase a wide range of erotic books, videos, games, toys, and sexual aids. Some of Good Vibrations's most popular educational videos are *10 Secrets to Great Sex, The Joy of Erotic Massage,* and *The Guide to Advanced Sexual Positions.* A sleeper, and one that "tons of men buy," according to Winks and Semans, is *How to Female Ejaculate,* which defines the G-spot and concludes with—are you ready for this?—five women having simultaneous orgasms.

● **Read a book.**

If videos are beyond your inhibition threshold, a good instruction book will often do the trick. In fact, it's the underlying ignorance about basic sexual problems that leads to most hang-ups, experts say. The average man, for instance, is unclear about what exactly drives his master cylinder and what to do should the engine sputter, while the average woman is in the dark about her body, fumbling for the G-spot or some other magic switch that will turn on her Harlequin desire.

Among Good Vibrations's best-selling instruction books for men are *The New Male Sexuality*, by Bernie Zilbergeld, and *The Multi-Orgasmic Man* by Mantak Chia and Douglas Abrams Arava. For women, they recommend *For Each Other* and *For Yourself*, both by Lonnie Barbach. In addition, Winks and Semans have authored their own book, a frank sexual primer called *The Good Vibrations Guide to Sex*. For couples, we recommend Miriam Stoppard's *The Magic of Sex*, published by Dorling Kindersley, Inc. It's illustrated with tasteful R-rated photographs of good-looking men and women trying out a variety of sexual positions. Check your local bookstore.

Reverse roles.

This trick is often used by therapists, but you don't need professional supervision to try it. If there's a sexual problem in your relationship and you're having difficulty finding the courage to address it, step into your partner's bedroom slippers for a moment.

"Try to feel what it's like to be that other person," explains Massachusetts sex therapist Gina Ogden, Ph.D., author of *Women Who Love Sex*. "If the woman says, 'You just don't get it,' then the man can say, 'You're right, but it's not because I don't want to or I'm stupid, it's because I haven't grown up as a woman. Why don't we try reversing roles? You be me, and I'll be you.' Then the man starts by saying, as the woman did, 'You just don't get it'. . . . Amazing transformations can take place this way."

Write it down.

If speaking is too difficult, try putting your sentiments on paper. Domeena Renshaw, M.D., has uptight couples in her popular Seven Weeks to Better Sex course in Chicago complete questionnaires in order to uncover their desires and get to know each other better. A sampling includes:

- What is your partner's favorite position for intercourse? Do you like it, or do you just cooperate?
- What is your concept of the proper role of a woman in bed?
- Did anything sexually upsetting ever happen to you?

As an icebreaker, try writing an explicit letter to your partner. But, whatever you do, don't wait. Discussing sex is a lot like eating raw oysters. Once you muster enough gumption to swallow the first one, the rest slide down easy. So say "the word," give voice to your pleasure quest, and help your partner do the same.

Such openness is vital not only for good sex but also for safe sex. "In this day and age, you have to overcome your reluctance to talk about sex," says Isadora Alman, a syndicated sex columnist and certified sexologist in San Francisco. "It's stupid to jump into bed together and then check to see who's got the condom. Those with severe inhibitions just have to practice until they get over being uncomfortable discussing safe sex."

Stop Trying to Be Perfect

Every man wants to be the ultimate stud, but let's be honest, no man is. Still, we make love as if we're on stage, constantly judging and questioning ourselves.

Performance anxiety is probably the most common sexual inhibition among men. It prevents the relaxation that is a prerequisite for great sex, and it fosters feelings of inadequacy that can eventually build on themselves and lead to some real performance problems.

Take the pressure off. Instead of critiquing your moves, just let it happen and enjoy sex for the sloppy, imperfect wonder that it is. Chances are your partner already is.

Although it's tough to get them to admit it, many men are ashamed of their bodies and feel self-conscious about getting naked with the lights on. The secret to getting over these feelings, says Alman, is to face them. Start by looking in the mirror and admitting to yourself that you're no Fabio. (Hey, neither is he.) It won't compromise your manhood. Rather, it will free you to become the best, most distinctive lover you can possibly be, which ironically makes you a stud after all.

"We all need to accept that how we are is how we are," says Alman, who's known as the "Ann Landers of Lust" from her 10 years of counseling readers in alternative newspapers such as the *Village Voice*. "There are no rules. There is no script. Every sexual encounter is what two people make of it. You can have intercourse first and kiss last. There's nobody else involved. It's your negotiated arrangement."

Once again, honesty and openness are the keys to making this happen. If you or your partner is self-conscious about getting naked, or if you're uncomfortable with the thunderhead of impending intercourse hanging over a fledgling relationship, don't rush ahead in silence.

For instance, to get over a body anxiety, Alman recommends going to a beach, slipping into a hot tub, exchanging massages, or doing anything that allows you to display yourself in a nonsexual setting. "You'll find that the other person won't scream and run away," she says. "Then the worst is over, and you can enjoy sex."

Likewise, to ease any performance pressure, don't be timid about voicing apprehension. For example, explain that you're not ready for intercourse, but that you'd love to spend the night anyway. Or, for a variation on the Fabio disclaimer, say, "Look, I want you to know the first time isn't always the best for me." "Most partners will appreciate this," says Alman, "and it'll help you get over any terrible fear."

To put some additional perspective on all this, think about how fickle society's norms can be. What's unacceptable in one age is often permitted in the next, or vice versa. Consider how this era's emphasis on female sexual satisfaction has made premature ejaculation into a dreaded "dysfunc-

It'sBeenSaid…

"Is sex dirty? Only if it's done right."

—Woody Allen

tion." Those afflicted now agonize over their excitability and seek remedies through therapy, squeeze techniques, and numbing creams. But as Reiss points out, quick ejaculation is still a sign of virility in competitive boyhood circles, and women with the same hair trigger are praised as sexually responsive. The point is to "treat it, not demean it," he states, because "most dysfunctions are societal, not physical."

Realize Your Fantasies

Oral sex. Making it with a famous person. Multiple partners. Sex with someone of another race. Using sexual devices. Sex in a public place.

Do you dream about any of these? We know you do, because they're the six most popular sexual fantasies of American men, according to the book *The Day America Told the Truth*. However, with the exception of oral sex, the vast majority of men never realize any of these.

Now, we have no idea where to meet Kim Basinger, nor do we have the time to mold you into a swinger (although we do have a mauve leisure suit we'd be happy to unload). But our experts can offer some advice on overcoming lesser inhibitions using such techniques as experimenting with sex toys, fantasizing guiltlessly, and making love more spontaneously.

● Play with toys.

If you're intrigued by the various gizmos in adult bookstores and catalogs but are too embarrassed, confused, or fearful of what a partner might think, don't worry. "I felt the same way when I first visited Good Vibrations," recalls Semans. "In fact, I left without buying anything."

Catalog shopping is probably the least intimidating place to start. Good Vibrations (800-289-8423), Adam and Eve, (800-274-0333), Eve's Garden, (800-848-3837), and the Xandria Collection (800-242-2823) are all reputable businesses that ship discreetly and won't sell your name to other companies.

For inhibited first-timers, Semans and Winks recommend the $45 Hitachi Magic Wand, which is also sold in some drug and department stores. (There's a lot of back pain out there.) This venerable brand is to electric vibrators what

How Inhibited Are You?

Gauge your comfort level with this pop quiz created with the help of Houston sex therapist and psychiatrist Harvey A. Rosenstock, M.D.

1 If you caught the eye of an attractive person across a crowded room, would you smile, wink, or nod?
- Yes
- No

2 If someone did the same to you, would you walk over and start a conversation?
- Yes
- No

3 Are you comfortable initiating physical contact, be it a handshake, a touch on the arm, asking for a dance, or giving a kiss or hug?
- Yes
- No

4 When taking someone special to dinner for the first time, where do you tend to go?
- A quiet, out-of-the-way place
- Some busy restaurant downtown or near a shopping mall

5 How do you usually dress for such an evening?
- Extra attractive
- Deliberately modest

6 When the time comes, would you start a discussion about the future of this relationship?
- Yes
- No

7 Likewise, would you initiate a discussion about sex?
- Yes
- No

8 Would you ever suggest watching an erotic film together?
- Yes
- No

9 Would you initiate a discussion about safer sex?
- Yes
- No

the Louisville Slugger is to baseball bats: solid, well-made, and, when handled deftly, capable of a grand slam. A vibrator isn't just for your lady, either. "It's a good place for men to start, too," says Winks. "Men are often surprised at how good one feels. And when a woman uses it on herself during intercourse, it'll also indirectly stimulate the man."

If you're buying a toy for an inhibited partner, don't just whip it out during sex, says Semans. Talk about the possibilities first, maybe leaf through a catalog together, then purchase it jointly. You might want to experiment alone beforehand, or start by giving each other back and body massages if it's a vibrator. "Approach it as an experiment," says Winks, "a new avenue of pleasure that you're trying together."

❶❶❶ If your date expressed her desire to have you for dessert in the restaurant bathroom, would you agree?

● Yes

● No

Give yourself one point for every time you chose the first answer, and add up your total.

If your total is 7 to 10 points, you're very comfortable with your sexuality. Please stay away from our wives and girlfriends.

A score of 4 to 6 points means that you have an average comfort level, but keep working on it.

Zero to 3 points indicates that you're pretty modest. And if you're comfortable with that, congratulations. By the way, didn't you have Sister Hildegard for sophomore biology?

● **Be more creative.**

While we're encouraged to fantasize graphically about all other aspects of life, be they business, wealth, sports, or science, when it comes to daydreaming about sex, we've been conditioned to feel guilty. The majority of American men do it (54 percent fantasize about sex at least once a day, according to the Sex in America survey), but it's generally a clandestine operation.

To get over this inhibition, first appreciate the tremendous, untapped pleasure power that your mind possesses. Some women can actually think themselves to orgasm. (And don't forget wet dreams.) Second, understand that just because you enjoy musing about Roman orgies doesn't mean you'll ever organize one on your deck. (In fact, keeping it at the musing stage is bound to be a lot less hassle.) Finally, realize that most people's fantasies don't involve their current partners. This doesn't mean that they're disloyal or that they no longer find their mates desirable. Rather, it's just a case of the mind doing what comes naturally. What's unnatural is trying to stop it. "Without fantasies, we wouldn't accomplish much of anything," says Zussman.

To trigger your fantasy lobe or inspire a partner to reveal a hidden desire, Zussman recommends books such as Nancy Friday's *My Secret Garden*. It's a collection of female sexual fantasies. Friday's *Men in Love* is 542 pages of the same from a male perspective. Board games are also popular ways to stimulate new thinking. (See "Two Can Play These Games" on page 224 for suggestions.)

● **Plan a sexual adventure.**

Spontaneous, rip-it-off-knock-it-over-right-now sex is one of the most popular male fantasies, but as Zussman points out, making it a reality is a challenge. Inhibitions about getting caught or making a partner uncomfortable are usually the cause. Still, we long for this type of passion and relive those precious moments when it did occur. Rather than hope for a chance encounter in your office after hours, Zussman suggests, make a date with your partner or, even though it sounds contradictory, set aside time to be spontaneous. Given a change of venue, a disruption in the rules, and some lustful expectation, you may shatter a few lamps (and inhibitions) after all.

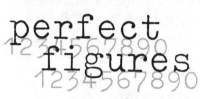

perfect figures

YOU DON'T WANT TO KNOW

Percentage of women who'd forgive their cheating spouses if they confessed:
78

Percentage of men who'd forgive:
23

The Art of the Quickie

Women insist they want lots of foreplay. Joe Kita tells you why it's practical, therapeutic, and just plain fun not to give it to them . . . sometimes.

Who would have guessed Clint would double-cross us? But there he was slow-dancing with Meryl Streep in *The Bridges of Madison County*, looking deep into her eyes, even sharing a bubble bath. Now every woman believes that if tough-guy Eastwood can make a lady's day with endless foreplay, then maybe her Dirty Harry can, too.

For proof, take a peek at women's magazines. "It was the most romantic, careful, drawn-out sex I'd ever had," reads a highlighted confession in one.

And in another, there's this recipe for the perfect romantic weekend: "Fill the house with flowers, dance together in front of a fire, kiss and cuddle—but don't have sex until the end of the weekend."

Gentlemen, we're in trouble. There's a plot afoot, a growing conviction among women that great sex must be preceded by a timeless tease. While we're all for a good session of footsie, there's another style of sex that's being forgotten, one that's just as important to men as storybook seductions are to women. It's fast, furious, mindless sex. Sex without music by Kenny G or flowers from FTD.

We speak, with reverence, of the quickie, the ultimate guy sex act.

It's not that we're advocating degrading sex. In fact, with only a few enhancements, it can be just as fulfilling for women as it is for men. And in these busy days, when the alternative to perfect sex often is no sex, it can be a relationship saver.

Sex Lite

Think for a minute about all the prerequisites you place on sex. For example, you and your partner probably like to shower beforehand, brush your teeth, slip into something more comfortable, dim the lights, make sure the kids are asleep, lock the door, pull the shades, and ready the birth control. It's like some NASA countdown, where any one of a hundred preliminary checks can signal trouble and postpone the mission. Then, if all systems are finally go, comes the act itself: the kissing, the touching, the positioning, and all the other sequenced bedroom behavior leading to blast-off.

Despite all the expert advice and attention given to mood-setting and sensitivity, this is all contrary to nature. Evolution designed humans for fast sex because the more time we spent preoccupied with procreation, the more likely we were to be taken by surprise by salivating, sharp-fanged predators.

A slow sexual waltz may be detrimental to the species in other ways as well. While big hungry carnivores are generally no longer a threat, more men than ever are seeking professional help for performance anxieties and premature ejaculation problems. It seems we know how to have sex, but we aren't so sure about how to make love. And it's tearing many men apart.

"Performance anxiety runs rampant among the men I see," says Chicago sex therapist Michael Seiler, Ph.D. "Men are struggling with issues of sexual desire. They're often confused about their own right to assert themselves sexually."

Given all this, quickies can be therapeutic, in addition to just plain fun. They can not only help men (and women) find time for the relaxing, rejuvenating flush of sex during a hectic day but also take the pressure off men to always be the Clint Eastwood of her dreams.

"Every act of sex doesn't have to be a relationship seminar," says Tara Roth Madden, author of *Romance on the Run*. "Think of quickies as 'sex lite': more satisfying, but less time-filling. They can be surprisingly thrilling, and they may lessen performance anxieties. When you know you'll be having sex more often, you'll be more relaxed about it."

It doesn't take much to convince men of the merits of quickies. The tricky part is making the case to their partners, largely because women have been culturally conditioned not to let themselves be cheapened by speedy sex.

Women also have a physical hurdle to overcome, in that while the penis is directly stimulated during intercourse, the clitoris is only indirectly aroused. However, this doesn't mean that women are incapable of quickly reaching orgasm. In fact, according to sexual-medicine professor Judith Seifer, Ph.D., R.N., of the Institute for the Advanced Study of Human Sexuality in San Francisco, both men and women can usually masturbate themselves to climax in 1 to 2 minutes.

Thus, if you encounter any hesitation, the challenge is first making your partner comfortable with the idea of a quickie and then helping her do whatever is necessary to guarantee complete satisfaction.

Six Steps to Great 5-Minute Sex

❶ Propose the idea.

For quickies to work, you can't just spring out of the closet and ravish her—at least not initially. Such behavior would produce screams and result in severe facial lacerations. Instead, at an appropriate moment outside the bedroom, tell her how desirable she is and how you'd like to have sex with her more often. Be playful but sincere, explaining that you really need to be with her, if only for a few additional minutes a week. Then broach the subject of quickies, even showing her this article if needed.

"It works best when expectations are clear beforehand," explains Seiler. "It should be understood that this isn't lovemaking. 'I'm not going to stare into your eyes for 15 minutes or bring you roses. This is a base, primitive expression of lust. We're just going to get off.' There's something terribly exciting and arousing about that."

❷ Promise that it won't replace romance.

That weekend in the Berkshires, those Saturday nights in the hot tub—reassure her that these won't become snapshot memories in your bedding album. Quickies are simply about variety, which is really the secret to keeping sex as exciting as when you first shared it.

"If you let quickies become your only way of being sexual, you'll create problems," says Seiler. "The key is to make them a part of your sexual relationship. It's like food. Sometimes you just want to use the drive-thru at Mc-Donald's to get a double cheeseburger, but you don't eat that way every day."

❸ Let the mood set itself.

Once you agree to experiment with quickies, let the thought simmer for a while. Think about the possibilities while you're at work, and encourage your partner to do the same. Then when the kids are momentarily preoccupied or when you spot an open broom closet while visiting Uncle Ernie in the hospital, you'll both have already engaged in some stimulating mental foreplay.

"Getting ready is never really a problem," says Roth Madden. "In fact, forget about setting a mood or waiting for sexual inspiration. Just get started, and the mood will follow."

❹ Respond to your urges.

Part of enjoying a quickie is recognizing and indulging your sexual desires when they strike. Our libido rides a roller coaster all day, but most of the time we make it sit in the last car with its hands on the bar. A quickie, though, gives it permission to ride up front, raise its arms, and scream. Quickies are the same kind of spontaneous, I-want-you-now sex that motivates the young and the adulterous.

Start with an intense embrace, then move the clothing out of the way as quickly as possible. Hit the most convenient stable surface, whether it's a bed, a floor, a kitchen counter, a car, or a wall. Pull her pelvis as close to you as possible so your penis is fully inside her. Then thrust and ejaculate. Women we polled said they like this; they become aroused.

❺ Be selfish.

Although it may sound callous, there's no time to think of anyone but yourself during a quickie. It's every man and woman for himself and herself in a mad thrash for ecstasy. If you're thinking about pleasing her or she's thinking about

perfect figures

COED NAKED MARCO POLO

Percentage of men who have skinny-dipped in mixed company: 26

Percentage of women who have: 12

satisfying you, you're both missing the point. Don't think about anything except giving yourself pleasure. (For the woman, this may involve manually stimulating the clitoris during intercourse to reach orgasm faster.)

❻ Be creative.

Quickies don't necessarily have to involve intercourse.

Seifer suggests mutual masturbation or a quick bit of oral sex. "You've
heard of a 69?" asks Seifer. "Well, a 68 is 'You do me and I'll catch you later.'
Women enjoy oral sex as foreplay, but they usually stop short of orgasm. Why
not elevate it to an art form and make it the entire act instead of just the pre-
amble? Man or woman, it's still one of the best ways to ensure orgasm."

"Couples have this natural power to make their relationship stronger," adds
Roth Madden. They're underemploying a great tool in marital relations. "Three
quickies a week is only 15 minutes. Anyone has time for that."

Two Can Play These Games

*Put away the Stratego. As writer Chris McDougall can attest, with these sex board
games, you win every time.*

We love the game Risk because of its simple, provocative goal: Penetrate your
opponent's defenses. Adult board games are built around the same principle.
You try to sneak past your lover's inhibitions. But here, no one loses. After all,
when she invades your territory, what's to complain about? And there's something special about handling game pieces shaped like buttocks.

But the real reason we like these games is the way they break the ice. Rather
than risk humiliation by asking your mate to cover herself with strawberry
whipped cream, you can get the game cards to do it for you.

We checked out seven games (one for every night of the week!) and rated
them on their laughs/lust quotients. Pick one up before next year's Valentine's
Day party. It beats cheap whiskey.

Enrichments Massage Kit and Game

❍ Equipment

One wheel-of-fortune-type spinner and three kinds of goo: cinnamon, peach
brandy, and kiwi spice.

How you play

You spin the wheel and rub goo on whatever part of her body the arrow points to—applying it with whatever part of your body the wheel commands. Spin, rub; spin, rub. It's better than the lottery. You must rub for a minimum of 5 minutes and allow 10 minutes of "glow time" when switching from rubber to rubbee.

Is it messy?

Yes. But so is a monster-truck show. Both are worth the cleanup time.

Verdict

Squirting oil on your partner is fun from the get-go, and time limits are erotic pressure cookers. We failed on three separate attempts to stick to the 5-minute guidelines, so we chucked the game. That proves its usefulness.

To order

Purchase it through the Sinclair Intimacy Institute at www.intimacyinstitute.com.

Rating

3 Volcanoes

Romantic Rendezvous

Equipment

A heart-shaped die, a game board, cards, and game pieces.

How you play

Roll the die, move the pieces, and when you land, follow the instructions, which may require you to sing, strip, or tell jokes in the nude.

When Good Games Go Terribly Wrong

It's Saturday night. You're snowed in with nothing but old board games and two warm bodies. That's all you need to score.

Monopoly

Make up your own Community Chest and Chance cards. Use sex to pay the rent (just like real life). And think what might happen in jail!

Risk

Substitute various body parts for countries. Your goal: a major thrust into Kamchatka.

Chess

Take a piece, get a piece. And there's a horse involved! (But watch the bishop.)

Battle Strip

Draw your clothes, and hers, on two paper grids. You say E5, she loses her bra. She says F7, you launch the torpedo.

Twister

You've already thrown down the plastic tarp. Now make it slippery.

Candy Land or Uncle Wiggily

You figure it out.

○ Verdict

The sleeper hit of the testing lab. The rose-covered box fooled us into expecting a game that was heavy on feelings and light on frolics, but we frolicked plenty.

○ To order

Buy Romantic Rendezvous online at www.lovegames.com.

○ Rating

3 Volcanoes

Sexsational

○ Equipment

Question-and-answer cards and blank "fantasy desire" cards.

○ How you play

Modeled loosely on *The Newlywed Game*. One player picks a question card with four possible answers. For instance: "No matter what the weather, I get hot when you (a) say naughty things, (b) give me 'your look,' (c) touch me—you know where and when, (d) serve me salsa." If you predict your partner's answer, you get a point. More important (much more important), you act out the winning scenario. The player with the fewest points at game's end has to act out a fantasy that the players have agreed on beforehand. Sounds like a no-lose situation, unless the fantasy involves painting the living room.

○ Verdict

One good answer can lead to an excellent delay of game.

○ To order

Check www.xandria.com.

○ Rating

2½ Volcanoes

Foreplaying Cards

○ Equipment

Candles and a deck of cards. You provide the accessories: booze, snack foods, a scarf, ice cubes—and a Polaroid camera, if your partner agrees. Think of the possibilities for your Web site!

○ How you play

Light the candles and play a card game, such as blackjack or poker. The twist is that the playing cards have instructions printed on them: "Have partner lick and suck body part you choose."

◐ Verdict

Anything that involves scarves, vodka, and a camera has promise. You do have to go grocery shopping before you play, but cruising the salad-dressing aisle never felt this good. Green Goddess or Ranch: You make the call.

◐ To order

Click on www.xandria.com.

◐ Rating

3 Volcanoes

Fantasy and Romance

◐ Equipment

A game board, dice, and seven articles of clothing on each player.

◐ How you play

It's strip poker for people who don't know how to play poker. The dice determine whether you shuck a garment or perform an act. ("You must play doctor for 2 minutes!") It's a trip back to the late '60s, with tiny Hefners dotting the game board and ample references to "tushies."

◐ Verdict

The time limits keep sexual tension percolating without boiling over.

◐ To order

Go to Adam and Eve at www.adameve.com.

◐ Rating

2½ Volcanoes

The First Fantasy Collection

◐ Equipment

A tube full of fun: fake-fur-lined wrist or ankle restraints, a big feather, a blindfold, and a tiny leather butt swatter.

◐ How you play

You make up the rules as you go, so it's a nonscary intro to light bondage, tickling, and spanking. It's cool as long as neither of you is allergic to leather. You

perfect figures

YOU MEAN IT'S NOT THE PLOT?

Percentage of men who say physically attractive contestants are the main reason they watch reality TV shows:
31

get to experiment without the embarrassment of admitting that you really sorta like this stuff.

● Verdict

Two highly independent testers verified that the best sex toy you can buy is pulled off a duck's ass.

● To order

Go to www.stormyleather.com.

● Rating

4 Volcanoes

The Erotic Way

● Equipment

Tucked inside an ornate faux book are a silk cord, a velvet blindfold, a candle, a feather, a bottle of oil, and an anthology of erotic stories. Wow—it's educational!

● How you play

Choose a story and read it aloud as your partner acts out one of the roles. In Private Business, she's the "wildly successful head of a major multinational corporation" who's pissed off at your performance. And you know those corporate suits: Blow one assignment and they're ordering you to stroke their stockings and rub massage oil on their thighs.

● Verdict

The best bedtime stories we've ever heard, although they didn't make us at all sleepy.

● To order

Go to Good Vibrations at www.goodvibes.com.

● Rating

4 Volcanoes

The Best Sex in the World

Think you're experienced? You can always learn something, says writer Brian Good. Knowing what other cultures do behind closed doors will put you back on top.

Some of man's favorite things come from other countries. Off the top of our heads, there's the Porsche, Anna Kournikova, the Swiss Army knife, Vendela, a pint of Guinness, and Heidi Klum. That got us thinking. Mostly about Heidi Klum, but also about what we can learn about pleasure from the other 192 countries in the world. So we dusted off our passports and dug up some statistics on what it's like to have sex in other lands. Consider this our United Nations of Great Sex, where representatives have gathered in one place with one common goal in mind: making you the world's best lover.

Lesson from France

KEEP HER HOT TO KEEP HER INTERESTED.

● Percentage of French people who claim to have no interest in sex: 20
● Percentage of American people who claim to have no interest in sex: 48

The French may have an infinite supply of wine, but you don't need alcohol to keep your partner's interest as high as yours. Here's your three-step recipe for making her as hot as a fresh croissant.

Which Foreigners Have the Most Sex?

Country	Nookie Sessions Per Year
Russia	122
France	121
Greece	115
Brazil	113
Hungary	110
Great Britain	109

SOURCE: Durex Global Sex Survey

● **Simmer.**
The more you tease her during the day, the more willing she'll be at night, says Rachel Carlton Abrams, M.D., coauthor of *The Multi-Orgasmic Couple*. Make erotic calls to her at work. "The dirtier the better," she says. Doctor's orders.

Which Country Has the Best Sex?

As rated by sexual satisfaction of partners

1 Canada

2 Mexico

3 England

4 Italy

5 France

6 Australia

7 Russia

SOURCE: Durex Global Sex Survey

○ Increase heat.
Touch the underside of her breast, too. "It's more sensitive than the top of the breast, and it's an area that most men tend to ignore," says Dr. Abrams.

○ Bring her to a roaring boil.
Lie down on your back, with your partner on her knees, straddling you. After you introduce her to your Eiffel Tower, have her arch her back and lean backward at a 45-degree angle so that she can support her weight on her palms. Use shallow upward thrusts to stimulate the upper wall of her vagina. This position allows you to hit the clitoris easily as well as give her control over the speed and depth. "That significantly improves her chances of reaching orgasm," says sexual-medicine professor Judith Seifer, Ph.D., R.N., of the Institute for the Advanced Study of Human Sexuality in San Francisco. More orgasms for her equal more sack time for both of you.

Lesson from Italy

HAVE SEX WITH A STRANGER.

- ○ Percentage of Italian men who have paid for sex at least once in the past year: 32
- ○ Percentage of American men who have paid for sex at least once in the past year: 0.5

While we wholeheartedly endorse Italian women, we can't endorse paying for sex. That doesn't mean you can't turn your familiar partner into an unfamiliar face. Start simple, by asking her to pull back her hair or wear a hat. If she enjoys that, try something more adventurous. A wig is the easiest way for her to change her appearance drastically without feeling uncomfortable, says Hollywood makeup artist R. J. McCasland. McCasland suggests a jet-black wig with shoulder-length straight hair and short bangs. "The bangs will change the shape of her face, while the black hair will alter her skin tone and coloring," McCasland says. Look for one at www.wigs.com.

Lesson from Germany

YOUR NOSE IS A SEX TOY.

- Percentage of German men who are aroused by women's underarm odor: 23
- Percentage of American men who would probably refuse to take part in such a silly study: 99.87

German men are attracted to body odor because underarm hair sends out scent-gland odors intended to attract a potential mate. We prefer our women to shave as well as exude a less natural scent. Try misting her with Sexual Arousal, a perfume that combines the scents of cucumber, lavender, and pumpkin. Research conducted at Chicago's Smell and Taste Research Center found that men who smelled the scent experienced a 40 percent increase in penile bloodflow, which, according to at least one study, is a very good thing. The fragrance is $20 a bottle and available at www.esexualarousal.net or (800) 951-0939.

Lesson from England

APPRECIATE HER BREASTS EVEN MORE THAN YOU ALREADY DO.

- Percentage of English men who consider breasts to be the sexiest part of a woman's body: 27

- Percentage of American men who consider breasts to be the sexiest part of a woman's body: 21

Some chaps might pick up a British tabloid for a daily glimpse of buxom page-three girls, but we suggest wrapping your mitts around something else. Here's what to do with . . .

perfect figures

OR, WHAT ALEX RODRIGUEZ MAKES EVERY HALF-INNING

Amount of money the largest brothel in Melbourne, Australia, makes each year: $1.4 million (U.S.)

• • • • • • • • • •

• A woman who has small breasts

If you're with a woman who has a B cup or smaller (B cups sell more than any other bra size), try this position. Lie on your back with your head near the headboard, your knees up, and your feet flat on the bed. Lift your pelvis until your body is in a straight line between your shoulders and your knees (stick a couple of pillows under your butt if you need help maintaining the angle). Have her straddle you and then lean forward. She can brace herself by putting her hands on top of the headboard (or against the wall). Gravity will draw her breasts away from her chest, turning her Bs into Cs right before your eyes. Fondle as needed.

● A woman who has big breasts

The best position is standing rear entry because it prevents her breasts from rolling and hiding under her armpits, says sex educator Lou Paget, author of *The Big O.* Plus, it puts your hands in a natural position to cup her breasts. Move to the bathroom, and stand directly in front of the mirror. She can lean on the sink for support as you enter her, and the mirror will provide an unobstructed view of her body, face, and double-decker bust.

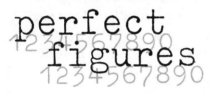

perfect figures

IT MAY BE TIME TO DISTRIBUTE A PAMPHLET

Percentage of married Malaysians who've enrolled in family-planning clinics, only to find out that the reason they hadn't conceived yet was because they hadn't had sex yet:

2

Lesson from Brazil

DON'T LET HER FAKE IT.

- Percentage of Brazilian women who at least occasionally fake orgasms: 44
- Percentage of American women who at least occasionally fake orgasms: 70

Get soapy. Have her stand facing the showerhead (for direct clitoral stimulation), and enter her from behind. In this position, your hands are free to do the handiwork that the showerhead can't handle. If you suspect she has more fake-out moves than Allen Iverson, try this technique to stimulate her: With your palm up, penetrate her with your index and middle fingers. Move your fingers up, down, and to the sides as you slide them in and out. Paget suggests using the same motions with your fingers that your legs would make if you were doing the breaststroke. Your fingers should be near her perineum—which is behind her vagina. If you feel contractions there, that's an honest-to-goodness orgasm, because women can't control those contractions the way they can control ones near their vaginal wall.

Lesson #2 from Brazil

DOUBLE YOUR STAMINA.

- Number of minutes the average Brazilian man lasts during sex: 30
- Number of minutes the average American man lasts during sex: 14

You can increase your stamina by reducing your muscle tension, says Marc Goldstein, M.D., a professor of reproductive medicine and urology at Cornell University. Here's one way: Think of a top-less beach in Rio. Another way: Have her mount you (prefer-ably on a topless beach in Rio). Your muscle tension is greatest when you're supporting your own body weight, so any position in which your back is flat on the bed (or car hood) will work. Also, alternate between shallow and deep thrusting, instead of using one steady rhythm. "You want to increase stimulation gradually, and the best way to do that is by making slow, deliberate thrusting motions rather than fast, uncontrolled movements," says Dr. Goldstein.

"Oui, Oui, Oui, Oui, Oui!"

How do you know whether she's having a good time? Listen for the ultimate affirmation: a string of a couple of hundred yeses in a row. Here's the approval rating in several, um, tongues.

Language	"Yes!"
Cherokee	"V!"
Danish	"Ja!"
Finnish	"Kylla!"
Hungarian	"Igen!"
Polish	"Tak!"
Portuguese	"Sim!"
Serbian	"Da!"
Swahili	"Naam!"

Lesson from Russia

CATCH A TRAITOR.

- Percentage of Russian women who admit to having cheated on their partners: 60
- Percentage of American women who admit to having cheated on their partners: 50

Now we know why Russian men lost interest in the Cold War: They were so preoccupied with their wives' hunger for stuffed blini—and their own desire to plant warheads in neighboring territories—that they just couldn't be bothered with superpower politics. Their keen interest in domestic affairs is something you

Where Are You Going on Your Next Vacation?

Country	% Who Think Premarital Sex Is "Not Wrong At All"
Sweden	90
Germany	87
Slovenia	82
Netherlands	77
Norway	77
England	70
Austria	69

may want to consider as well, if you suspect your mate of improper alliances. As in any espionage case, it all comes down to how you pose the question. Don't ask her outright. "In person, men have a much harder time detecting lies because they don't generally pick up slight inconsistencies in verbal language or tone," says Rutgers University anthropologist Helen E. Fisher, Ph.D. In person, your partner may say *nyet*, but you can tell whether she's lying by asking your question on the phone. You'll have a better chance of picking up unusual voice inflections or stuttering—either of which may suggest she's trying to cover up something.

Lesson from Australia

USE IT OR LOSE IT.

- Percentage of Australian men who have mild erectile dysfunction: 19
- Percentage of U.S. men who have mild erectile dysfunction: 31

Nobody has ever questioned the testosterone Down Under: They play football without pads and wrestle crocodiles. Why don't they seem to need to spend any time enticing their own amphibious creature to the surface? Maybe it's the testosterone. Deficiencies in the hormone are a main contributor to erectile problems, and studies show that your testosterone levels can drop by 1.2 percent each year of your life. So get pumped. "Even thinking about sex more frequently can help to boost testosterone levels," says Dr. Abrams. So will eating meat, having more sex, and playing General Maximus in *Gladiator*.

Lesson from Japan

SATISFY THE SAME WOMAN, OVER AND OVER.

- Percentage of Japanese whose marriages ended in divorce: 2.6
- Percentage of Americans whose marriages ended in divorce: 12

It's a myth that 50 percent of U.S. marriages end in divorce. Sure, 1.2 million marriages go south every year. But 2.4 million new knots are tied annually, and they join 54 million married couples, a full 88 percent of whom will remain hitched till death do them part. If you hope to be in that number, just keep your spouse happy. Try this oral-sex position: Have your wife straddle you at the top of the bed and arch her back against the wall. You can give her oral sex and stimulate her breasts.

Lesson from China

ENLIST A THIRD PARTY.

- Percentage of Chinese married couples introduced to each other by a third party: 80
- Percentage of American married couples introduced to each other by a third party: 23

The Chinese have it easy: A matchmaker or a parent arranges the marriage. That's it. It's a heck of a lot harder (yet more fun) for us to find the right partner, so we asked 1,800 married *Men's Health* readers where they met their wives or current girlfriends. The most popular choice: at school. Already have your GED? About 20 percent of our readers found their current significant others through a friend. Lost your friend when you left high school? Some of our survey respondents hooked up with their mates in these unusual situations: after a car accident, while playing ultimate Frisbee, during a hockey game, after being deployed to a foreign country, through the mail, and while shopping at Kmart.

Lesson from Gambia

TAKE YOUR SPERM FOR A WALK.

- Average number of births per woman in Gambia: 7
- Average number of births per woman in the United States: 1.3

Only 7 percent of women in Gambia use modern methods of birth control,

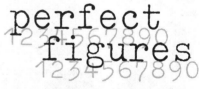

perfect figures

THINK THERE'S A CONNECTION?

Percentage of English psychologists who admit to having had sex with one or more of their patients: 4

Percentage of English women who say they enjoy sex more since starting therapy: 84

which we assume has something to do with the numbers. But if you're having trouble passing on your DNA, maybe your lesson comes from the sunny Gambian climate, in which rainfall has dropped 30 percent over the past 30 years. Your wife should spend more clear, sunny days in the countryside. Studies show that being out in the sunlight naturally aids her fertility. In addition, a recent EPA study found that clean air builds healthier sperm.

Lesson from South Africa

MAKE THE MOST OF WHAT YOU'VE GOT.

- Length of the most popular condom in South Africa: 8.07 inches
- Length of the most popular condom in the United States: 7 inches

South African men came up with a good excuse for not wearing condoms: They said their rubbers didn't fit. Durex now makes the Comfort condom, which has 10 millimeters more cargo space. The South Africans are happy. What if your masculinity is more like Liechtenstein than Russia? Remember, supersizes really count only in weapons, offensive lines, and drive-thrus. So during sex, push against her pubic bone when you thrust; you'll be more likely to hit her clitoris—making your penis seem to do the work of one twice its size.

Our Favorite International Exports

Nation of Origin	Export
Canada	Shania Twain
Cuba	Daisy Fuentes
Czech Republic	Daniela Pestova
England	Elizabeth Hurley
France	Laetitia Casta
Germany	Heidi Klum
Italy	Sophia Loren
Malaysia	Bond girl Michelle Yeoh
Mexico	Salma Hayek
Netherlands	Frederique van der Wal
New Zealand	Rachel Hunter
Russia	Anna Kournikova
Somalia	Iman
South Africa	Charlize Theron
Spain	Penelope Cruz
Sweden	Vendela
Wales	Catherine Zeta-Jones
Zambia	Thandie Newton

Lesson from Niger

LAND A YOUNGER WOMAN.

- Average age difference between spouses in Niger: 6 years

● Average age difference between spouses in the United States: 3 years

You know the best way to attract younger women—but you'd look silly carrying that Backstreet Boys lunch box. Instead, convince her that marrying an old fart like you is her best chance at long-term happiness. A 1994 study of 134,000 couples found that the greater the age gap between older husbands and younger wives, the lower the chance they'd split up. Remind her how happy Anna Nicole Smith and J. Howard Marshall were!

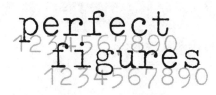

perfect figures

HONEY, PARIS SOUNDS BETTER AND BETTER

Percentage of French women who admit either they're more attracted to other women or they've had sex with other women: 18.5

● ● ● ● ● ● ● ● ●

Fly the Really Friendly Skies

An Interview with Elliott Hester

The novelty, the muted lights, the risk of getting caught . . . and the oxygen depriva-tion from the stale, recycled air. All these things can combine to provide the ideal sce-nario for a thrilling sexual encounter. Too bad high-altitude antics are such a logistical challenge. We asked Elliott Hester, a veteran flight attendant and author of Plane In-sanity: A Flight Attendant's Tales of Sex, Rage and Queasiness at 30,000 Feet, *for his tips on creating your own onboard turbulence.*

Now that the airlines are more security-conscious, are we going to see more or less in-flight sex?

> I don't think it'll ever stop. People have sex during bad times and they have sex during good times. When people are the most afraid and the most vulnerable, I think there may be even more sex.

From what you've observed, how much in-flight sex is between established couples and how much is between people who have just met on the plane?

> I think the majority of it is between established couples. But there are people who get a rush out of meeting somebody on an airplane. I met a girl once on an airplane and started kissing her. That's all that hap-pened. But had we been different people, and if we'd had a couple of drinks, maybe something else would have happened.

Having sex in an airplane lavatory or coach seat is a little riskier than having sex at home. Do flight crews tolerate such public displays of affection?

> Flight attendants have been taught to be more alert and to watch for suspicious behavior. So if you're doing something suspicious, you're probably going to get caught faster than you were before because flight attendants have their eyes peeled. When it comes to sex, some attendants are extremely conservative and uptight, and others are middle of the road. They don't care what happens as long as nobody gets hurt. Personally, I think two people enjoying each other, as long

as nobody's offended by it, is one of the most pleasant things in the world.

Suppose you get an extremely conservative flight attendant. Can you end up getting busted?

The moment your genitals are exposed, that's lewd and lascivious behavior. That's why George Michael was busted in that bathroom a few years ago when the cops followed him in and he was jerking off. If someone under age 16 happens to witness such an event, it becomes a felony. But if you don't see people exposed, it's not a problem. The weird thing about sex in a public place is if you see two people having sex beneath a blanket, technically you don't know what they're doing. She may be moaning and screaming, but if you don't see anything naked, you can only infer. In a court of law, they can just say they were rubbing each other. So, technically, there's no law broken.

Have you witnessed a beneath-the-blanket boinking?

Yeah, and it was amazing. After we finished the meal service and dimmed the lights, the woman threw one leg over her boyfriend and straddled him so she was facing him. Then she grabbed the blanket and draped it over their heads in an inexplicable attempt at camouflage. It's like 5-year-olds who cover their eyes and think everybody's disappeared because they can't see them. I guess they thought if they couldn't see anybody, nobody would see them. Wrong. I watched this blanket going up and down, up and down. Then she had an orgasm and let loose a shriek.

Did the other passengers realize what was going on?

Fortunately, it was a very sparsely populated flight. I saw several heads pop up and look around. By then, she had fallen into his arms and there was nothing to look at. So the situation sort of defused itself.

Are such people just incorrigible exhibitionists?

There are exhibitionistic types. But you also have people who are shy, conservative, and away from home and the people they know. They're in an environment where they think they can get away with something without ruining their reputations, because nobody knows who they are. That happens with traveling anywhere. People tend to get crazy when they go on vacation. They'll do things on vacation that they would never do back home in Des Moines.

It's BeenSaid...

" You can do it on cruise ships, you can do it at home, so why shouldn't you be able to have relations on planes? "

—Richard Branson

Do some flight attendants actually encourage sexual activity between passengers?

One attendant I know was stationed in first class. The only passengers up there were a couple on their honeymoon. He told them, "Look, if you guys want to go at it, I'll post myself in front of the curtain between first class and coach so you can have a little privacy." He covered every base. He even told the pilot so he wouldn't come out of the cockpit. Then he gave them a bottle of champagne and stood guard while they went at it full throttle.

Wow, that's service.

The kind of service everybody would like to have.

Do a lot of flight attendants get off on this?

I don't know if they get off. The guy who helped the honeymooners was probably peeking through the curtains. Some of us do get a kick out of watching funny things happen. You know, we need in-flight entertainment as well. We can't sit down and watch the movie, but we can certainly watch passengers who are going at it.

What can happen to passengers who go at it a little too publicly?

One couple, both married to other people, started screwing right there in business class. They were charged with outraging public decency and being drunk aboard an aircraft, among other things. It was the biggest story in all of England for 2 or 3 months. Both of them ended up losing their jobs and jeopardizing their marriages.

**We've heard about porno movies in which the pilot gets it
on with a flight attendant. Does this ever happen in real life?**

It's happened on the ground. One of the flight attendants I've interviewed has been flying for 30 years, which is twice as long as I've been flying. She's seen pilots and flight attendants having sex in the cockpit.

**Aside from the obvious fact that they're horny,
why do so many people have sex in airplanes?**

A lot of people have fantasies about having sexual encounters with strangers in strange places. Most of the encounters I've seen or heard about have taken place on long-haul trips. That's when you've got a chance to sit down and have a few drinks, and either meet somebody or get frisky with somebody you already know. You're bored. It's dark. Maybe there aren't that many people on the airplane. There's this allure of doing something bad, doing something that's not supposed to be done, especially on an airplane.

**People who do this jokingly say they've joined the Mile-High Club.
Who was the club's first member?**

Lawrence Sperry, of the Sperry Rand family, who had sex in a biplane while flying over New York in 1916.

**You report that this adventure ended with a nonfatal crash landing.
Did his paramour bump the throttle?**

I tried to find more information about this, but I couldn't. One could surmise that during the moment of ecstasy, he hit the wrong button or something.

**Are there any great pickup lines for guys
who want to join the Mile-High Club?**

I don't believe in pickup lines because I think they're cliché. Because I work on an airplane, I'm really close to a lot of women as friends. I hear their complaints, how they laugh at guys' pickup lines, and how stupid they think some guys are. So I've gotten a pretty good idea of what doesn't work.

So what does work?

It's much smarter to just go with the flow. Just talk to her, be natural, and be honest.

How does a guy convince a woman he's just met on a plane to have sex with him right then and there?

It's not necessarily the guy trying to convince the woman. We live in a very open society these days. When I was working, a woman came on to me at the beginning of the flight and asked me to meet her in the lavatory. She said, "I'm horny. I need to get laid."

What happened next?

This was one of those fantasies that I thought would never come true. Then, when the possibility presented itself, I choked. Since I was in uniform, I could have lost my job.

But you made up for it later, right?

Yeah, in the lower galley of a DC-10 while the plane was parked on the tarmac. So I'm not an official member of the Mile-High Club. Maybe that makes me a member of the Twenty-Foot Club.

Does a guy need movie star looks to make out on a plane?

I don't think so. It all has to do with the chemistry between two people. Sometimes the hum of the engines puts you to sleep. Sometimes it has an erotic feel to it. You're sitting there, and you hear this buzzing engine, and you're talking to someone, and she's looking into your eyes, and you're looking into hers. Boom, anything can happen.

Even in a cramped lavatory?

You know what they say: Where there's a will, there's a way. As long as you have enough space for two people, you have enough space for sex.

Now that some airlines have introduced semi-private "sky beds" in first class, it would seem that almost anyone could safely and comfortably join the Mile-High Club.

It's possible that this has unleashed a whole new form of behavior in first class, especially on Virgin Airlines, which is kind of ironic. On some airlines, you're even allowed to bring up a friend from coach to join you. I don't know if they realize what plebian possibilities they've unleashed, but it's definitely gotten a lot more interesting.

This would seem to argue in favor of an ever-increasing amount of in-flight sex. Is this good or bad?

I don't know about the whole sleeping around and screwing on airplanes bit. But if the world's leaders were getting laid on a regular basis, I don't think there would be any more war. If people would be a little bit kinder to the person next to them, and if they get involved with someone—it's very difficult to be angry and nasty when romance is in the air.

Do you have any words of advice for passengers who just want to enjoy a show like the one you saw with the couple beneath the blanket?

That would depend on the logistics. I had freedom of movement because I was a flight attendant. I walked past them several times, and so did the other flight attendants, because it was obvious they didn't care whether anyone was watching. So we camped out a few rows behind and were pointing and laughing while they were going at it. If you want to get a peek, you could stand up and pretend to stretch, or you could use your own cunning and walk down the aisle.

Hey, everyone's gotta go to the restroom once in awhile, right?

Absolutely.

QUICKIES

MY BALONEY HAS A FIRST NAME

In a decidedly unscientific survey, we asked whether you or your partner had a pet name for your penis. After sifting through hundreds of replies, many from blushing girlfriends and wives who swore us to secrecy, we can say unequivocally that you are a creative (and decidedly twisted) lot. But before divulging the top vote getters, permit us a few interesting observations.

The most popular nicknames have one thing in common, by far: They denote size, power, and respect. Examples? Thor, Godzilla, The General, and any name preceded by Mr.

Naming your penis is evidently so much fun that you can't stop there. Frequently, the testicles are also christened, as in Big Jim and the Twins, Mr. Bo Dangles, Buddy and the Sidewinders, Spaghetti and the Meatballs, or The Big Hardy Combo (with apologies to Hardee's restaurants).

While women are less likely than men to name their privates, couples often have pet names for each others', such as George and Martha, Walter and Zelda, Hugo and Patricia, and (our favorite) Enos the Penis and Miss Kitty.

The chief reason couples like nicknames is that they allow them to flirt in public. For instance, whenever one guy's wife mentions that she could really go for a Big Burrito, he knows she's not suggesting a trip to Taco Bell. Or when another fellow asks his partner if she'll be eating lobster tonight, it has nothing to do with boiled crustaceans.

A number of sarcastic women remarked that the reason men name their penises is that they don't want total strangers making the majority of their decisions.

And now, the winners:

1. Any name preceded by Mr. (Happy, Wiggly, Belvedere, Peabody, Pink, et cetera)

2. Any name preceded by Big (Daddy, Red, Lube, et cetera)

3. Any name incorporating One-Eye (Cecil the One-Eyed Sex Serpent, Herman the One-Eyed German, et cetera)

4. Willy (free him, please!)

5. Fred

⑥ Herman and Pete (tie)

⑦ Moby, as in whale, and Stanley, as in power tool (tie)

Others: Crotch Snorkel, Russell the Love Muscle, Womb Cannon, Little Elvis, Love Pickle

TAKE A BUSINESS STRIP

Your client wants to visit a gentlemen's club, but you haven't seen that many naked women in one place since your *National Geographic* subscription expired. Here's how to keep your client—and your dignity.

❍ Enlist the waitress.
If your guest goes into a trance when a certain dancer appears, buy him personal attention. The slick way: Slip the waitress 5 bucks to send her over. Then pay the dancer before she starts her routine.

❍ Pick your spot.
To find a club, check www.mensclubguide.com, which lists clubs by location.

❍ Don't talk about her body.
Touching a dancer is the ultimate blunder, but conversation is welcome. She'll linger around your client longer if you compliment her outfit and shoes—she chose them herself and would appreciate your noticing.

❍ Blend in.
If you want to disappear, slip the floor man $20 and ask to be seated in the VIP section. Also, some clubs have black lights, so you'll want to wear dark colors; a white shirt will catch stray rays and make you glow like a Chernobyl survivor.

❍ Give her a good tip.
Fold tip money lengthwise, and hold it out so the dancer can grab it. She may even lift her garter so you can slide it under. "Your hand won't touch her. That's cool," says Don Waitt, publisher of *Exotic Dancer* magazine. Yeah, maybe for her.

❍ Get some play money.
Be prepared to spend about $50 on each person in your party, for drinks and tips. Use your credit card to buy a wad of the club's play money, which you can use for tipping the dancers. That way, you'll have a respectable receipt to hand over to accounting.

HOW LOW WILL SHE GO?

You know that the compu-weasels in your office can read your flirtatious e-mails and check your surfing history. Now even your home may not be safe. The maker of one spying program, SpectorSoft, claims lots of women use its software to spy on their men. This version scares us—it's hard to detect, and the record of computer activity is an actual "snapshot" of every Web page visited, all chat conversations, every keystroke, and all e-mail activity. And your line about the gynecology extension course won't work twice.

SHE'S LOOKING FOR MR. GOODBAR

If you want to give her something really sexy next Valentine's Day, forget lavender lingerie and bejeweled baubles. The following surprising statistics, from a naughty little book called *Chocolate Sex*, by Richard Barber, Nancy Whitin, and Anthoney Loew, leave little doubt as to what melts a woman's heart (and inhibitions).

- Amount spent on chocolate for Valentine's Day 1994: $580 million
- Amount of chocolate sold in the United States in 1994: 5.7 billion pounds
- Percentage of women who think about chocolate while having sex: 86
- Percentage of men who have ever thought about chocolate while having sex: 1
- Percentage of women who think about sex when eating chocolate: 98
- Percentage of women who think that eating chocolate is sex: 78
- Maximum number of orgasms achieved by a woman during sex as documented by Masters and Johnson: 19
- Maximum number of orgasms achieved by a woman eating chocolate: 43
- Number of calories burned during a passionate kiss: 26
- Number of calories in a Hershey's Chocolate Kiss: 25

THE FUNNY PAGE

"Be honest, are you seeing someone else, or did you get that from 'Men's Health'?"

Index